D0557666

Gliding Safety

By the same author
Beginning Gliding: The
    Fundamentals of Soaring Flight
Derek Piggott on Gliding
Gliding: A Handbook on
    Soaring Flight
Going Solo: A Complete Guide
    to Soaring
Understanding Flying Weather
Understanding Gliding: The
    Principles of Soaring Flight

Also available
Meteorology and Flight by
    Tom Bradbury

Gliding SAFETY

Derek Piggott

A & C Black · London

First published 1991 by
A & C Black (Publishers) Ltd
35 Bedford Row, London WC1R 4JH

© 1991 Derek Piggott

ISBN 0 7136 3397 2

A CIP catalogue record for this book
is available from the British Library.

Acknowledgements
Front cover photograph courtesy of
Steve Bicknell.

Printed and bound in Great Britain
by Hollen Street Press Ltd of Slough.

Contents

Acknowledgements

I would like to thank Maria for the idea behind this book, and Peter Disdale and my two editors for their help with correcting the text and making suggestions for improving it.

Like one of my previous books, *Derek Piggott on Gliding*, some of the chapters have been adapted from articles published in magazines which I thought were of lasting interest to beginners, power pilots and instructors.

Derek Piggott

Section 1

Avoiding gliding accidents

Gliding safety depends on good training and on instructors encouraging novices to develop safety-conscious habits. Most accidents occur because the pilot is unaware of, or chooses to ignore, possible hazards.

Safety must be everyone's concern – the majority of accidents could be avoided if every pilot is aware of the common hazards. Reading or hearing of other pilots' experiences emphasises how easy it is for even seasoned pilots to make mistakes.

Instructors and senior pilots have a big responsibility to pass on their expertise and knowledge and to look out for poor airmanship and flying techniques in others which could lead to mishaps in the future.

In Section 1, I have chosen various gliding areas which involve special hazards for the unwary, and have suggested how to prevent accidents by being conscious of potentially difficult situations.

How glider accidents happen

Considering that so many gliders are flown across country on every possible soaring day, the accident rate for gliding is extremely low. However, it must always be remembered that, like the sea, the air is an environment which is potentially dangerous to the unwary. There are, of course, always a number of minor incidents and accidents during training. The result of every accident, however minor, is a rise in the cost of insurance, the loss of the aircraft while it is replaced or repaired and, sometimes, injuries to the pilot and other people involved.

Most glider pilots have never experienced anything more hazardous than a bad landing, so reading and talking about other people's mistakes is almost the only way of becoming aware of the kind of situations which lead to broken gliders. Few pilots realise how much even minor damage can cost to repair. Just slipping and dropping a wing while loading it into the trailer will cause hundreds of pounds' worth of damage, and although most gliders are insured, every accident eventually results in higher premiums and higher costs for gliding enthusiasts.

It is quite rare to have an accident directly caused by some kind of technical failure. The main cause is almost always something to do with the pilot's flying skills or judgements. 99% of all gliding accidents happen when the aircraft hits something. A few pilots manage to stall and spin in; some fly into the ground during their final turn; many make such bad landings that they damage their glider; and, finally, far too many run into other gliders or obstructions during take-offs and landings. This indicates that instruction is failing to get across the vital aspects which could reduce the risk of accidents.

Are you fit to fly?

When an emergency situation arises the pilot needs all his wits about him. A surprising number of accidents and incidents happen because pilots are in some way not 100% fit on the day in question. Obviously, if you have a heavy cold, a headache, are suffering from lack of sleep or are jet lagged, you should not be flying. But the decision about whether or not to fly is left to you, the pilot. You alone have to make that judgement. It is best to make a firm rule not to fly if you are feeling unwell or unenthusiastic. If you have spent a long day on the airfield, it will be difficult to refuse your turn to fly, even if you are tired. However, if you are going to fly solo, refusing is the only sensible thing to do.

Flying demands all your concentration and it is not wise to risk flying if you have business worries or some other mental stress on your mind. Even a violent argument will leave you mentally high and quite unfit to fly.

You can also become unfit in the air through lack of food and drink. Both these factors can cause lack of concentration and apathy. In warm weather,

11

dehydration is a serious problem, and sufficient liquid must be taken during the flight even if this has its disadvantages afterwards!

Keeping in practice

It is probably true to say that the first few solo flights are the safest that a student pilot ever makes. This is because he has recently practised safety procedures for almost every conceivable emergency, and they are therefore fresh in his mind. Also, the pilot will be in very good flying form and his instructor will have made sure that he has not been getting into bad habits. It is important to try and keep in practice in order to reinforce all the things which have been learned during the pre-solo training.

Most gliding clubs have a system of re-checking pilots during the first few hours of solo flying, but then pilots are left very much to their own devices to improve their soaring techniques. They may go several years without a cable break on the winch launching, and so they will scarcely give the possibility any thought. An annual briefing on cable break procedures and other emergencies would be very valuable for everyone who flies gliders, and particularly those who stop flying for long periods over the winter months and so get badly out of practice.

Many pilots select the days on which they fly so that the weather is near ideal and not too windy. It is easy to forget exactly how much allowance should be made for the wind and other factors on a rough day. Pilots who have only flown in light winds will be dangerously incompetent in rough weather, particularly if they are also out of current flying practice. If they do attempt to fly on a windy day, then a check flight should be made to ensure that they remember the hazards and how to avoid them.

When pilots from a big, flat site visit a hill site, they are at risk and often make absolute fools of themselves unless they get a very thorough briefing and listen to what local pilots and instructors have to say. It is always wise to have a dual flight before flying solo at an unfamiliar site. There is always something to be learned from a knowledgeable local instructor, and a flight is far more valuable than just a site briefing.

Being in practice is also important for a first flight in a new and unfamiliar type of aircraft. Always avoid doing too many new things in one flight; i.e. do not fly a new type of aircraft on an unfamiliar airfield. Try and get a dual flight on the airfield so that at least you know something about the airfield and its surrounds.

Wire launches

A large proportion of gliding accidents and incidents result from launch failures. Too many pilots seem to believe that they can cope with these failures and then are proved wrong. Most accidents happen when a cable break occurs close to the ground. Here a failure calls for immediate action if you are to level out into normal flight and so prevent a stall. Always ensure that the initial climbing angles on a winch or car launch will allow time for a safe recovery into the glide if the cable breaks. Too many pilots allow their glider to zoom up too steeply as they leave the ground. This is always dangerous because at that moment the glider has insufficient speed to allow for safe recovery and landing. If pilots continue to do this, sooner or later they will get hurt.

Far too often with a low cable break, the pilot goes for the airbrakes when there is a mile of field ahead and no hurry whatsoever. The actual speed at the time is usually far too slow to allow for any use of the airbrakes, but there is plenty of room ahead for a safe landing.

If the failure occurs higher on the launch, again a snap decision can be fatal. Lower the nose and check the actual airspeed before doing anything else. The most common cause of serious accidents on wire launches is making a snap decision to turn off for a 360° turn without ensuring that there is enough speed. Even though the nose has been lowered well below the horizon, a glider takes time to regain speed, and any attempt to turn off immediately results in a potential stall and spin accident. The first question you ask yourself is 'can I get down straight ahead?' If the answer is no, then check the speed before starting to turn.

Reacting too slowly and taking too long to make a decision can also be hazardous. If you obviously cannot get down ahead or if you have doubts about it, then you have no alternative but to turn off, but check your speed first!

How to avoid problems with wire launches

1 Go over the launch failure procedures after any long lay-off from flying.

2 Try and think systematically about your actions in the event of a launch failure.

3 Always assess the special considerations and conditions for the day (e.g cross winds, turbulence etc.).

4 At an unfamiliar site, talk to the locals and discuss the best course of action for launch failures.

5 Before you take off, ask yourself the following questions. Is the glider ready? What about the weather conditions? Are you ready for a launch failure? Is it safe to go now?

6 Always expect and be ready for a launch failure in the first 500 feet on every launch.

Soaring

Inexperienced pilots get into difficulties when they are soaring. They often get lost because they have not kept the airfield in sight and within easy gliding range. It is important for these pilots to develop the habit of checking the position of the gliding site immediately after releasing the tow and to re-check it regularly every few circles. It is also important to be aware of the wind direction and the amount of drift, and to avoid drifting down wind whenever possible. Beginners often continue to struggle with weak lift without realising that they are, in fact, losing height and drifting further away. If the variometer is fluctuating and reading up on one side of the circle and down a little on the other, the probability is that the glider is not climbing at all but is just drifting further down wind.

If the glider is down wind of the site, the decision to return must be taken before the glider gets to less than an angle of about 20° to the field in light winds, and 30–40° in windy weather.

Allowance must always be made for wind strength and the possibility of strong sink, since it can never be known beforehand whether there will be lift or sink on the way back. A common mistake is to try to use lift on the way back instead of gliding on through it at a sensible speed. This nearly always results in drifting further back without much gain of height and ending up in a worse situation than before.

If it begins to look doubtful that the site can be reached and the glider is down to 1,000 feet, it is time to select the best possible field within easy reach and to make a safe landing in it. If you glide back any lower, the choice of landing area becomes very limited, until finally there is no choice at all. Be decisive. If you are uncertain about whether or not you can get back with a reasonable margin of safety, make a safe landing while you can; a planned approach into a poor field is better than an out-of-wind crash into a good field!

For inexperienced pilots flying in light winds, a good general rule is to allow a maximum of 3 miles' glide per 1,000 feet with nothing for the last 1,000 feet. However, an extra allowance must be made for any head wind, and in poor visibility inexperienced pilots should make sure that they are close enough to keep the field in sight all the time.

Almost all accidents start with a simple error on the part of the pilot that leads to a chain of events, each of which makes the situation worse and an accident more and more difficult to avoid. The art of safe piloting is to learn to avoid the initial error whenever possible. But, if an error of judgement or a bad decision has been made, the vital thing is to recognise that, admit it and take immediate action to break the chain of events while a safe course of action is still possible. Forget the error or the cause of the problem and get on with correcting it and avoiding a worse situation. A similar situation occurs when soaring cross-country. Although you may get ridiculously low because of pressing on too hard, when, a few minutes later, you are back in the good conditions several thousand feet up, you must forget the wasted time and concentrate on flying normally.

Ground handling damage

Nothing is more heartbreaking than to see a beautiful glider damaged by incompetent handling on the ground. For every incident which causes damage to a glider while it is being flown, there must be many more that happen because of careless or thoughtless ground handling. Sometimes these accidents are caused by laziness, but more often they are the result of someone not realising the significance of doing things the right way. All of them are avoidable and cost time and money.

Student pilots need very thorough briefing about the hazards of ground handling in a strong wind and, since most flying is restricted to light winds, this must be reinforced whenever the conditions make extra care necessary.

Towing

The danger involved when towing the glider into a strong wind cannot be stressed too much. This is when there is the greatest risk of the glider being lifted off the ground by the first strong gust. With no one in the cockpit and the tail on the ground, most gliders will develop enough lift to leave the ground at well under 30 knots. To prevent this happening, the nose of the glider should be held down (or the tail held up) to reduce the wing incidence, as this in turn reduces the lift significantly. Usually, the weight of a person on the extreme nose will prevent the glider lifting off the ground, but to be safe it is best to put a person in the cockpit.

Anyone sitting in a glider must always be properly strapped in. If a glider was blown over with someone sitting inside it unstrapped, that person could be killed. The airbrakes should always be opened (tying them open with a harness strap, if necessary) as this reduces the lift and increases the 'lift-off' speed by several knots.

A student at Lashan Gliding Centre was badly hurt once when the glider lifted off the ground and came down on top of him as he walked by the nose. This was caused by a combination of a very strong gust and the fact that no one was keeping the nose down while the glider was being towed into wind. The wind that day had been increasing with the approach of bad weather and the instructor, who had decided that it was time to stop, was towing the glider to the hangar. In such situations, it is always worth considering whether it is safer to have another launch and fly the glider to the hangar. Flying is often safer than towing into a really strong and gusty wind. Obviously, the slower the tow is into wind, the less airflow there is over the wings, and thus the safer it is.

On a windy day, more care is usually taken, but even then a few moments' inattention, or the wrong drill, can result in the glider being blown over and written off.

When a glider is being moved around the airfield, one person should take charge of the whole operation and be responsible for the safety of the aircraft. This is normally either the pilot or the instructor. This person must brief the helpers if they are inexperienced. He should insist that the correct wing is held, and direct the car or tractor driver so that they take a safe route which is clear of any hazard from dropping winch cables. It is his responsibility to decide whether the glider should be manned at the nose or tail, and whether someone is needed in the cockpit. In a strong wind he must refuse to move until sufficient additional crew arrive to handle the glider safely. Many accidents happen through impatience. If you cannot be sure of handling the glider safely, turn it out of the wind, hold the wing down and wait for help.

Ground handling

Wing-tips

It is generally agreed that only one wing-tip should be held while the glider is being moved about. This is because if there is a person on both wing-tips, neither may have a good grip. Furthermore, it is all too easy for both people to decide to let go at the same moment, so that no one is left holding a wing-tip.

Traditionally, it was usual to take the upwind wing-tip and to hold it slightly below the horizontal. This was because with the older gliders like the T21 or T31, the wings were very high and they could not be held securely except by keeping one wing low. However, when towing in a cross wind, the glider will tend to weathercock into wind, and the person on the upwind wing will have difficulty in pushing forward enough to prevent this happening. With a modern glider which has a lower wing and the wheel well ahead of the c.g., this weathercocking will be even more pronounced, so it is better to hold the down wind tip. (Just as with the cross wind take-off, the down wind wing should be held so that any slight pull will not help the weathercocking into wind.)

Groundhandling an ASK13

Light winds

It is a great temptation to tow a single-seater back with only the pilot on the wing-tip. This may be reasonably safe with a very long tow rope, but if there is only a shorter length of rope available the glider may overrun and smash into the back of the car, causing hundreds of pounds' worth of damage to the glider.

If towing is permitted with only a wing-tip man, it is vital that the pilots all recognise that this is only safe if the ground is more or less level and the wind is very light.

Strong wind conditions

In windy weather every effort should be made to avoid having to move the glider upwind; it is far safer and easier to land well into the field and then to move the glider back down wind. It is safe to push backwards, moving down wind with the nose into wind, provided that the airbrakes are open and weight is applied down on the nose. The effective wind-speed is reduced by the movement down wind and, as long as the tail is not held down, this is safer and easier than turning the glider right round. (Always put a knowledgeable and reliable person at the tail, and remind them only to hold the tail down if that is necessary to move the glider easily.) Towing forwards going down wind means that there is no possibility of being blown over, but the controls must be held or locked otherwise the control hinges may be damaged by the surfaces slamming across against the stops.

In very strong winds the critical place for ground handling is at the tail. Always make sure that the person on the tail is briefed to hold it up until someone has their weight on the nose. After coming to a stop with the glider facing into wind, holding the tail down is the worst possible thing, and even leaving the nose unattended for a few moments is dangerous. It is always safer to transfer the person on the tail to the nose, where his extra weight can be more effective. Many modern machines do not have hand holds at the tail and are very tail-heavy on the ground. Weight on the nose or in the cockpit will be sufficient to prevent the glider lifting.

There is always a tendency for pilots to relax as the launch point is reached. Unless the glider is going to be launched without delay, it should be turned out of wind and held with the into-wind wing down until it is needed.

Tail and wing-tip trolleys

Britain must be one of the only countries in the world where the club members manhandle the two-seater gliders all the way out to the launch point. Most private owners discovered the use of a tail and wing-tip dolly a long time ago, making it possible to tow out with a car single-handedly on most days. It is a harsh punishment to have to walk the glider all the way back, particularly after a cable break where the glider lands in the middle of the airfield. I am always surprised that clubs will happily buy an expensive tractor to pull gliders back, but will not provide aids to make it all less strenuous and time-consuming. The proper equipment makes the whole operation far easier and safer, and encourages instructors to practise those exercises which can so often result in a long walk back to the launch point. However, it is essential to recognise that towing aids are only really safe for use in normal flying conditions, and caution is needed if they are used in windy weather.

Parking

If the wind can be trusted to stay in much the same direction, safe parking is an easy matter. With the lighter machines, the into-wind wing should be picketed or weighted with tyres or weights, and the tail-skid or wheel should be blocked to prevent the glider moving round into wind. The front skid or main wheel will also need to be chocked, and an easy, effective way of doing this is to run the main wheel into a rut in the ground. Parking with the airbrakes open is very little trouble and is helpful if the wind does swing. The canopy should always be locked down.

Gliders are often left for short periods with tyres on the wing-tip only. If this is done, the tyres should be right on the tip and not half on the ground, otherwise if the glider does move, the tip will slide out from under the tyre and be freed. This can be disastrous and may easily occur if there is no wind in the early morning when the gliders are parked outside the hangar with a single tyre on the wing-tip. Later, when the wind has picked up, the gliders weathercock round and can be free to tip over so that the into-wind wing is upwards. Another hazard is the wind swinging and increasing during the day so that the glider ends up parked facing directly into the wind.

If the glider is facing across the wind with the into-wind wing held down, the wind will be blowing on to its top surface, producing an extra down-load. However, in a strong wind several tyres are required to stop the into-wind wing lifting up. The upper tip will be high in the air where the wind is stronger, while the lower wing will be close to the ground where the wind is much lighter. The glider is not secure with only one light tyre on the wing-tip.

Blow-overs

If the glider is facing more or less directly into the wind, and there is a pilot in the cockpit, it is just as safe as it would be after a normal landing. Some people think that holding the wing down or putting a tyre on the wing will stop the glider blowing over. However, facing into the wind while waiting for a launch, a tyre on the wing-tip is just a convenient way of preventing the wing from lifting off the ground.

When conditions are very squally it is better to have the wings held level, with as much weight on the nose as possible. Having one wing down may result in a light glider being blown over if the wind changes direction and gets underneath the raised wing. Then, all the weight in the world on the wing-tip would not stop it going over.

When a blow-over does occur, you will always hear the people concerned state, quite truthfully: 'Up to that time the wind had been quite acceptable and then there was this bad gust . . .'. Of course, had the wind been very gusty before, they would already have stopped flying, or they would have taken extra precautions to make sure that there were enough people to prevent an incident. The moral is clear: when gustiness is getting near to the limit for safe flying, assume that at any time it could suddenly increase. Stop flying before it becomes too windy to move or fly the glider.

Blow-overs were a common occurence in the early days with lighter gliders and they sometimes even happened on almost windless summer days. Although the gliders were left facing at right angles to the wind and were weighted down with tyres in the approved manner, when the first strong thermal went off nearby the wind would become gusty and change direction completely. This meant that the gliders were then parked the wrong way and, being light, they often blew over.

This kind of blow-over can only be avoided by manning the glider all the time or by tying it down with pickets, preferably with the wings level and all its control surfaces locked to prevent them flapping against their stops. This is standard practice in more tropical countries where there are 'dust devils' or 'willy willies' which can produce a 40-knot wind in almost any direction with little or no warning. Even the towplanes are taxied to a nearby picketing point and tied down properly between each flight.

Now that modern gliders are so much heavier and have their wings closer to the ground, it is fairly usual for private owners to park 90° out of wind with the into-wind wing up. Although perhaps vulnerable to strong winds in this position, in lighter winds it is stable enough to ensure that no tyres are needed. The result is that many glider pilots are becoming complacent about parking and on a really windy day it is not unusual to see gliders at risk, just waiting for the first really big gust of wind to blow them over.

The whys and wherefores of these procedures need to be explained to students, otherwise they might conclude that proper parking is not really important and that it is all right to leave a glider with either wing down.

Line squalls and thunderstorms

The worst situation for accidents is a good soaring day with a risk of thundery showers. This means that a large number of gliders will be rigged and brought out on the airfield. Then, when the first big shower starts, rather than stand under the wings in the rain everyone will desert the launch point for a cup of tea, leaving the gliders apparently well parked and weighted with tyres but, in fact, vulnerable to a change in the wind direction. Often, even after insisting that everyone goes back to the launch point, there will be barely enough people to hold all the gliders down, turn them around and re-park them if the wind changes. This is an easy way to have a number of gliders wrecked by the wind, but luckily it does not occur very often. The only safe solution is to get the gliders into the hangar before the squalls arrive, or to make sure that there are at least two people close to each glider all the time, ready to swing them round when necessary. Everyone gets very wet but it is worth while getting soaked if it saves even one glider from serious damage.

Finally, remember that if a cold front is due in the summer-time, it may be preceded by some hours by a line of unpredicted severe squalls and storms.

Overnight or long-term parking

In dry and settled weather conditions it is quite safe to leave gliders out overnight. However, permanent parking outside in all weathers has been shown to cause rapid deterioration to the finish of all non-metal gliders. Never risk parking out overnight without checking the weather forecast for a strong wind warning or the approach of a cold front.

Provided that all the controls can be locked to prevent them getting damaged by slamming against the stops, parking the aircraft facing down wind will be safest, because then the wing is meeting the airflow at a negative angle. In lighter winds they can be picketed out, facing into wind with the wings level.

For long-term picketing out, the main wheel can be run into a hollow or trench in the ground to reduce the wing incidence and to lower the wings still further. Wing covers will also help to reduce the lifting qualities, but they can damage the finish if they are allowed to thrash about in the wind.

Protecting the instruments

It is always worth while covering both the pitot and static vents to prevent rain entering the systems. However, it is unwise to seal them off completely with tape as a large change in atmospheric pressure may cause damage to some instruments. I usually make a tape hood over the static vents to allow them to breathe without letting water droplets get into the tubes. If this does happen, the only solution seems to be to disconnect the instruments and to pump air through the system to blow out the water and dry the tubing. Never blow down the vents or the total energy and pitot heads because this can destroy the instruments. The venturi-tube type of total energy system can be dried out by venting it to cockpit static to allow the venturi to suck out the water in flight. This leaves you with a working variometer but without total energy.

Always take precautions against rain. You never find out about the water in the instrument systems until you are airborne and it will ruin that flight, if not the entire flying for that day. It takes at least an hour to get the system clear and dry again, and is a very frustrating problem, particularly if it occurs in a competition.

Rigging and de-rigging

With the help of good rigging aids such as trestles and a stand for the fuselage, it is often just possible to rig with two people. However, it is always a little risky, especially if the ground is slippery or uneven. One slip may mean that the wing-tip is dropped, causing some very expensive damage to the wing or the fuselage structure and fittings. It is rarely an impossibility to find a third person, and in gusty weather this must make sense. Think how often you see two people struggling to rig or de-rig because they are too embarassed or independent to ask someone to help.

In the early days of gliding, trestles were not considered essential as an aid to rigging; I remember the very first ASW17 to arrive in the UK being rigged without them. Like most new machines, everything was a tight fit and by the time we had the glider rigged, we had worn out several people with the sheer weight of the wings. Trestles make it all so much easier and safer, and it is worth while having a second one so that everyone can relax for a few minutes if it is proving difficult to align both wings to get the main pins in place. Trestles are also very useful for holding the wings level if the glider is being picketed overnight.

The routine for rigging and de-rigging is usually passed on by word of mouth, or is self-taught. As a result it is not unusual to see people doing things which increase the risk of serious damage if things go wrong. I have often seen pilots fitting the tailplane on before the wings. This ensures some very expensive damage in the event of the fuselage falling over, whereas without the tailplane very little or no damage is likely. If you put your tailplane on first, you might say, quite rightly, that this will not happen with your equipment. However, someone seeing you may do the same thing using a crude 'dead man' to hold the fuselage upright. If it falls over it will certainly be weeks before he flies again.

Make sure that the fuselage is secure and is not liable to move. In windy weather there will be a definite tendency for the fuselage to weathercock round into wind unless the tail-wheel or skid is chocked. Anything which makes rigging and de-rigging more difficult increases the risk of someone getting tired of holding up a wing-tip and so letting it droop or even drop.

The most common cause of damage when getting the glider out of the trailer and putting it back at the end of the day's flying is impatience, and the only answer is never to rig without an adequate number of people. If in doubt, get help, and don't rig until enough help is available.

Hangar rash

It is often said that more damage is done inside the hangar than out! This is often the result of inexperienced people trying to give a helping hand to get the gliders out. Usually the problem is that no one is really taking charge and telling the others exactly what to do. A quick but careful briefing would, in most cases, prevent incidents such as someone lifting a wing without first checking that the other wing will not come down on to another glider's canopy.

Moving through a confined space, for example if the glider is too large to go through the door, it is always wise to go nose first, swinging the glider right round and out with its nose close to one door. (Leading edges are much stronger than trailing edges or tailplanes and rudders.) Don't try to go out backwards unless there is ample space for the glider to go straight through.

Some hangars have doors at each end and these make a good wind tunnel if both ends are opened at the same time. Even in light winds there can be a venturi effect sufficient to blow the gliders about. Unless the wing-tips are weighted down with a tyre, one wing lifting off the ground means that the other will come down on to another glider with expensive results. Always close the doors at one end before opening them at the other, unless the wind is very light, and never leave both ends open in case a wind springs up later in the day.

Trailer towing

Unfortunately, most people learn about towing trailers by trial and error, which can prove to be a very expensive way of doing things. Every year a number of trailers are rolled over on our roads and trailer accidents account for a great deal of glider repairs.

Snaking

Glider trailers can be stable or unstable, depending on the car and the trailer combination. If a trailer begins to 'snake', the swinging often develops so quickly that within seconds there is no way of stopping it and avoiding going right off the road. Even a fairly stable trailer will start to swing if it overtakes or is overtaken by a large truck. The pressure wave from an overtaking truck strikes the rear of the trailer first, setting up a swing. In addition, the venturi effect between the two vehicles assists this swing and tends to suck the two vehicles together. This is particularly common on motorways where trucks are overtaking at quite high speeds. It is vital to have good side mirrors on the car in order to be aware of traffic which is behind or overtaking. Judging by the number of trailer accidents on the motorways, it may be wiser to keep off them whenever possible.

Factors which influence the stability of the combination include the softness of the car and the trailer's suspension, plus the balance of the trailer. It is a good idea to add an extra 5 or 10 p.s.i. to the pressure in the car tyres and to keep the trailer tyres at a higher pressure than might at first seem necessary. If you are building a trailer, fit a suspension rated for a trailer heavier than the actual weight.

The balance and dynamic stability of the trailer, loaded or unloaded, is affected by heavy items like spare wheels, which should be up front when possible. The ideal seems to be to have a down load on the tow bar of 10–15 kg (20–30 1b). Anti-snake devices have been proved to be worth while. They work by stiffening the coupling between the trailer and car.

Many swinging and jack-knife accidents seem to start on slight downhill gradients, and particularly if the road surface changes or is uneven. Once the swinging has started, there is very little even a skilled driver can do. Slowing down does not help, and generally the driver is not brave enough or quick enough to try accelerating.

I learned about trailer driving the hard way during a competition retrieve, when an enthusiastic crew member took us off the road with an Eagle two-seater in the trailer. Both the car and the trailer were badly damaged, but because the glider was securely held in by the fittings, it survived the trailer going over on to its side without damage. As a result of this incident, I am very cautious and rarely drive above 80 k.p.h. (50 m.p.h.) with a loaded trailer. It is a frightening experience, and I have never heard of anyone doing it a second time.

With a trailer that you have not towed before, your first priority should be to explore its stability carefully. You can do this by driving on a quiet, wide road with no traffic about, gradually increasing your speed and moving the steering slightly to produce a very slight weave. As the speed is increased, the damping becomes less and you will be able to decide on a reasonable limit to keep to for the first half hour. By then you will have become tuned in to the driving and will be better able to judge if it is safe to go a little faster. Remember to reduce speed on downhill stretches and to watch in the mirror for traffic which may be about to overtake, and which could therefore set up a swing.

Gears must be used more frequently with the extra weight of the loaded trailer, and it is important to change down in plenty of time to prevent having to brake fiercely. The major effects of this will be poor acceleration and a reduction in effective braking. Allow for greater braking distances with a loaded trailer and always use the lower gears going down steep hills.

Many trailers are dangerous much above 80 k.p.h. (50 m.p.h.) and it is just not worth taking any chances going much faster. A flat or burst tyre can mean no flying for months!

Parking the trailer

Simply parking the trailer with the stands firmly down will not prevent really strong winds from doing irreparable damage. Trailers are usually safer if they are parked close together so that they protect each other. However, never park your trailer near one which has poor stands and is liable to swing in a wind. Ideally, every trailer should be anchored by the ball hitch on to a ball mounted in the ground. Alternatively, they need tying down securely at both ends. This should prevent incidents where trailers are blown for hundreds of yards and wrecked.

It is worth while designing trailer fittings so that the glider is held firmly in place even if the trailer rolls over. Often, the only cause of damage to the glider is if the wings or fuselage break loose. It is also a good idea to make covers of some kind for the trailer tyres. These tend to rot in the sun and though the treads might be as good as new, they will have to be changed because of the cracks in the walls.

Conclusion

The main thing to realise with trailer driving is that it only takes one mistake to wreck the trailer and a nice glider, as well as possibly writing off a new car. Clearly, it is important to consider each of the ways in which you can safeguard your equipment because it is no use avoiding all the flying hazards if you are going to write off your glider on the ground. Repairs take time and money to carry out, and if they can be avoided gliding will be less expensive in the future.

Cockpit checks

There was a time when many gliding instructors scorned the use of a rigid drill, and taught their students instead to check everything logically by going round the cockpit from left to right. The disadvantage of this method is easily demonstrated by asking the students as they finish if they are sure that they have not forgotton something. They will then start all over again and go round the cockpit a second or even a third time.

This can easily be avoided if a simple, systematic check is followed. Thus if you go through a drill of vital actions, or check-list each time, you will ensure that you do not forget any item. You can then take off with complete confidence, knowing that you have checked all the really vital things for the flight. However, this confidence is only justified when the check is done systematically and correctly. For example, checking the items in the wrong order is totally unacceptable because it can so easily lead to missing something out altogether. A re-check should never be necessary, since this only implies the acceptance of a half-hearted check in the first place.

The idea of having the person attaching the cable ask if the airbrakes are closed and locked has been introduced in some clubs to try and prevent incidents where pilots take off with their airbrakes unlocked. However, if you are going to re-check the airbrakes, it would seem logical to check all the items in the check-list as well.

Many instructors are not careful, or thoughtful enough about either their initial teaching or their subsequent monitoring of their students as they do their own cockpit checks.

In the UK the pre-take off checks are standardised and remembered by the mnemonic CBSIFTCB. Each letter represents a vital item to be checked, i.e.

C – Controls	F – Flaps
B – Ballast	T – Trim
S – Straps	C – Canopy
I – Instruments	B – Brakes.

Long before going solo the student should have learned the mnemonic by heart. It is a good idea to say the key words aloud every time as you check each item so that it becomes a habit. If you do this when you are solo, you will be less likely to skip an item or become careless about the checks when you are more experienced.

It is important for every student to understand the philosophy behind having a rigid drill and the reasons for precise actions such as checking and locking the airbrakes. Without a convincing explanation and an insistence that the checks must be done properly, many students will become careless and slap dash when they are on their own and away from close supervision. All aspects of flying require this combination of understanding and self-discipline, and the vital actions make a good starting point.

It is also important to differentiate here between the first flight of the day and subsequent flights. A careless daily inspection after rigging may easily leave the glider with one aileron or the elevator disconnected. The control check is often better done initially *before* the vital actions, perhaps even before getting into the cockpit, when the control surfaces can be seen more easily. On the other hand, the check for full and free movement must be done *after* strapping in, because it is possible in some aircraft to jam the controls by tightening the straps round a cable or control rod.

The importance of the vital actions drill may even be undermined in the eyes of the student if the instructor insists on a complete check of each control movement for every flight (stick to the left, left aileron up, right aileron down, stick to the right, etc.), since it is clear that things like this cannot change between flights, and the majority of experienced pilots only do that check on the first flight of the day. I think that the instructor should treat the first flight on a particular glider as if it was the first flight of the day, and on subsequent flights he should just check for full and free movement and that the surfaces are moving fully. At the same time he should check that he can reach the full rudder and stick movements without undue stretching, and that cushions or other objects are not limiting the movements of the controls.

The canopy

An incomplete or sloppy check carried out on the canopy can be lethal, because if it comes off it is a matter of luck whether it hits or misses the tail. In addition to checking the canopy lock for security, it is essential to push up on the perspex itself to confirm that the hinges or pins are secure. It has been known for the hinges on a canopy to fail or for poorly designed and faulty catches to fail in flight, resulting in a lost canopy. Most of these expensive incidents might have been avoided by this drill.

The airbrakes

The method of checking that the airbrakes are correctly locked is all-important. Since the majority of modern machines have airbrakes which are held closed by a geometric lock, it is essential that the method of checking them must be foolproof for this kind of system.

First open the brakes or spoilers fully, checking them visually whenever this is possible. Then close them with a firm push on the lever in order to establish the habit. The pilot should be able to feel the geometric lock operating just after the airbrakes are flush with the wing surface. In some cases there is a gate for the lever to go into once the brakes are correctly locked.

This operation needs to be explained and demonstrated to every student. It must be understood that unless the geometric lock is felt, either the brakes are not locked, in which case a harder push is needed on the lever, or the locks themselves need adjusting. If it is the latter, the aircraft is unserviceable and must not be flown until the brakes have been re-adjusted.

If the basic training is being done on a Falke, or on any other type of glider fitted with simple spoilers or airbrakes which do not have a lock, the differences must be explained. However, the method of checking should be just the same in order to establish the right habit.

The cause of almost every incident where the airbrakes open during the launch is that the pilot has failed to lock them correctly. The amount of force needed to lock them will vary considerably from aircraft to aircraft and even perhaps from day to day. Merely pushing the lever forwards as far as it will go is not enough because the lock may be very stiff. Modern gliders usually have spring-loaded caps which are pulled down firmly to prevent air leaking into or out of the wing. This makes the lock much stiffer to operate than on the earlier types of glider.

A geometric lock which requires no force to lock is seriously out of adjustment. It may allow the airbrakes to open during a launch if the lever is knocked or if one side is unlocking a little before the other.

However, despite careful instruction, there will still be incidents in which the airbrakes open during a launch. On a wire launch the best hope is for the car or winch driver to build up extra speed to get the glider as high as possible. This gives the glider pilot more time to find out why his glider is semi-stalled and is sinking like a brick. With an aerotow, if the towplane pilot realises that the airbrakes are open, he can signal to the glider pilot by rapid rudder-waggling. In both cases this is a real emergency, because in the event of a cable break the pilot does not have time to realise what is wrong, and he may well stall and spin if he flies by attitude and tries to turn without checking the actual speed.

Taking your time

Pilots sometimes complain about being rushed through their cockpit drills. Ideally, you need a few minutes to settle comfortably before setting off, but if you have to rush you can usually blame yourself for not getting in before the cable or towplane arrives. Whatever happens, don't rush those vital actions. They take less than 30 seconds to do and they should be left until the last moment before the cable or rope is attached.

Swinging and ground looping accidents

The pilot's responsibility

During the last few years there has been an increase in swinging and ground looping accidents and these must be analysed to see if there are new lessons to be learned.

In one instance, a young pilot started a launch with another glider standing only a few yards to the side and just ahead of the take-off point. With a normal take-off the glider would have cleared the obstruction. However, it should have been obvious to the pilot, and to everyone at the launch point, that with either a swing or a wing-drop there would almost certainly be a collision. Unfortunately, the glider did start to take-off, it did drop a wing and swing, and there was a collision.

Where there is a slight risk in the event of a swing, a pilot may be said to have made a simple error of judgement or taken an unnecessary risk. However, in the aforementioned case I think we must look further for the factors influencing the pilot.

When students are learning to glide, the instructor is not only teaching them the technique of flying a glider, but also how to make decisions and judgements in the air. The final stages of training amount to the handing over of all the responsibility for safety to the student. Ideally, the student should be making all the decisions and choosing actions in the interests of safety and efficiency.

By setting the student problems during the final flights before going solo, the instructor can test his ability to think logically and to deal with situations as they arise. An experienced instructor will stop helping the student at this stage and will refuse to comment until after each flight. In this way, the student can gain confidence by knowing that he made the decisions and that they were sensible ones. As he reaches the first solo stage, therefore, the pupil must either achieve a standard of flying which does not leave room for criticism, or he must learn to accept the particular instructor's comments as fair and helpful.

In the air, decisions are relatively easy and concern only the student and the instructor. On the ground, however, the situation is not so simple. Even with ground handling someone must take charge, but it may not be the pilot. A young and inexperienced pilot may not feel able to take command of the situation and so prevent a stupid accident or an unnecessary risk being taken. Nevertheless, he should try and take control and tell the other handlers what to do.

Inhibiting situations

Whereas in the air pilots may make good decisions and behave responsibly, on the ground they may feel that each move is being watched and criticised by the other members. This will make them less decisive and may inhibit them from giving orders or taking charge of the situation. Since it is quite unusual to need to stop a launch, a shy person would certainly hesitate about shouting out.

Many incident and accidents of this nature would be prevented by expert supervision on every flight. However, 100% supervision, even of early solo flying, is impractical for 365 days in the year as there are bound to be moments when the instructor's attention is diverted.

The real solution is to train pilots to accept responsibility, whether they are sitting in the aircraft or are merely bystanders at the launch point. The more timid personalities must be encouraged to take charge and to give orders. When there is an opportunity during training for the pilot to decide whether or not a situation is safe, they must be taught to assume that the worst will happen, and then to assess whether there is a risk or not. The rather shy students must be encouraged to shout the launching orders clearly and loudly, so that if they need to shout 'stop', they do not hesitate because they are reluctant to raise their voice.

Normally, the instructor is inclined to emphasise the 'All clear above and behind', without making the student think consciously about the area ahead. Too often the instructor may allow a take-off when there is an object to one side. This would certainly be hazard in a cross wind and, to an inexperienced pilot, in any wind direction. In these cases the student probably relies on the instructor to make the decision and knows that he is there and can save the situation if things go wrong.

It is important to make the student aware of the subtle difference between being safe at all times and being safe in particular conditions. Above all it is vital for every pilot to have the old adage 'safety first' indelibly imprinted on their mind. In other words, if in doubt, don't take a chance. The mature glider pilot would never hesitate to make a fool of himself in the interests of safety.

However, it is not just beginners who make mistakes and get caught out. On one occasion a very experienced pilot in a Nimbus 2 was starting on a car launch when it swung off the runway into a K8 which was some distance ahead. There was a very light cross wind from the right which caused a swing in that direction, and as the Nimbus has only a tail-skid, it swung as it started its take-off run. The pilot released the cable but could not keep the glider straight, or stop in time to prevent the collision. The Nimbus was undamaged but the K8 had one wing severed at about half-span as well as other serious damage.

Realising that the take-off would involve an element of risk, the Nimbus pilot had, in fact, refused to go at first, and had asked for the K8 to be moved. After it had been moved a short distance away, the pilot was persuaded that the situation was all right and he accepted this, rather than face being unpopular for causing further delay.

The accident caused considerable consternation and it became clear, talking to the members present at the launch point, that many pilots did not really understand all the factors which caused the accident. Obviously, the Nimbus pilot was at fault for allowing the other people at the launch point to influence his judgement. Perhaps the most important point is that, regardless of who may be at the launch point, the pilot alone bears the responsibility for accepting or rejecting the launch in the light of the situation as he sees it from the cockpit. If he has the slightest doubt about his ability to launch safely, bearing in mind such hazards as swinging to one side or a cable break at any stage, then he must refuse the launch. Moreover, if a pilot decides not to launch in a situation like this, he must never be overruled or criticised for playing it safe.

Accidents due to swinging on take-off and landing are so common that it is worth studying the causes in detail. The behaviour of some modern gliders during take-offs and landings is very different to most of the training gliders, and it is vital to understand why they are more prone to swinging.

Cross wind effects

The two main effects of a cross wind on the ground run are well known. The first is that the wind tends to lift the upwind wing-tip and the second is that the glider tends to weathercock into the wind. This applies to every type of aircraft and not just to gliders.

Light cross winds, and in particular those with a slight down wind component, create by far the most treacherous conditions for both take-offs and landings. If there is a cross wind, there will be a tendency for the glider to start to swing, while if there is a down wind component on take-off, it will take the glider longer to gain enough speed for the controls to become effective.

Prevention is always better than cure. The person holding the wing-tip should always run the down wind wing-tip so that any pull that he may exert is against the weathercocking swing into the wind. He should hold the down wind wing-tip a little above the horizontal and be prepared to run with it, not just balance it and let go. Once again it is up to the pilot to insist that this wing is held and not to accept someone on the upwind wing-tip.

The pilot himself can help anticipate the swing into wind by applying full out-of-wind rudder before he starts to roll. As the controls become effective, the amount of rudder will have to be reduced long before full flying speed is reached.

A bad swing can easily lead to a serious ground loop or even to cart-wheeling and a broken glider. This can only be avoided by releasing the tow promptly before the situation develops. Always keep your left hand close to the release toggle until you are sure that the glider is stabilised, i.e. in a modern machine until the tail has come up.

Strong cross winds

Unless the wind is more than about 45 ° to the direction of take-off, a strong cross wind seldom creates problems. This is because good control is reached at a much lower ground speed. Provided that there is normal acceleration on take-off, the pilot should have good aileron control and be able to stop any swing into the wind by means of the rudder.

Of course, there is a definite limit to the strength of cross wind that can be accepted by some machines, particularly those fitted with tail-skids rather than tail-wheels. The main precaution is always to leave plenty of room on both sides of the take-off path to allow for a possible swing. Room must be left on the upwind side in case there is a cable break or premature release, and on the down wind side in case the wing touches and causes a swing that way. If the wing-tip touches long grass or rough ground, there will certainly be a bad swing and the launch will have to be abandoned.

The most serious swings and cart-wheels usually occur when the wind gets under the wing-tip so that the down wind tip scrapes along the ground. A few seconds later, as the glider gains speed, the full aileron suddenly takes effect. If this happens at the same time as the inevitable swing into wind, it can result in a very rapid rolling over on to the into-wind wing-tip. By then the glider may be airborne nad a cart-wheel will be unavoidable. This situation can be prevented by being prepared to release immediately if things start to go wrong, or by being ready to stop the wing coming up suddenly.

Tow-rope loads

On a car or winch launch, the pull of the rope or launching cable exerts very little stabilising effect, but the rapid acceleration usually ensures that enough speed is gained to have good control.

A nose hook provides more stability for aerotowing, and it is a slight advantage to start the take-off a little on the upwind side of the towplane. This ensures that there is a sideways pull on the nose, helping to prevent both the glider and the towplane from weathercocking into wind. The poor acceleration of an aerotow makes a swing or a wing-drop more likely.

Directional stability

In flight

In flight, the directional or weathercock stability is maintained by the fin and rudder, which provide extra side area behind the c.g. Thus with the aileron and rudder held in a central position, a glider will always weathercock into line with the relative airflow, just as the wind vane on a church steeple will always swing into the wind. When rudder is applied, the nose of the glider yaws to the side until the force produced by the rudder is balanced by the tendency for the aircraft to swing back into line with the airflow. (In the air this is nothing to do with the actual wind. The aircraft is flying in a mass of air which may be stationary or moving.)

If an aircraft is very directionally stable because of a large fin, then the rudder will be less able to produce a large angle of yaw before this balance of forces occurs. With a smaller fin, the directional stability will be weaker, the rudder will be more effective and the angle of yaw will be far greater.

On the ground

This particular accident, like so many others, would never have happened if just one of the dozen or so people at the launch point had recognised the danger and shouted 'stop'. To say that it was not their business to stop the launch is not good enough. Safety is everybody's business.

When a glider is on the ground it does not pivot around its c.g. as it does in flight. Instead it pivots around the main wheel. If the main wheel is further forward, the glider will have a stronger tendency to weathercock than in the air, and the rudder will be even less effective at preventing this. Conversely, if the main wheel is behind the c.g., the directional stability will be less and the rudder more effective.

Most modern gliders have their main wheel well ahead of the c.g. and sit with their tail-skid or tail-wheel firmly on the ground. This wheel position affects the behaviour of the glider once a swing has started. Any swing will be increased by the inertia of the glider because the mass is behind the wheel, trying to move on in a steady direction. In light winds, when the ground speed is much higher, this inertia effect is stronger, and therefore control is relatively poor, making ground looping more likely. This is why the worst risk of swinging and ground looping is always in calm or light wind conditions. In a strong cross wind, the glider will tend to swing into wind, but will then be directionally stable and stop swinging. In lighter winds it will be far easier for the glider to continue the swing, accentuated by the inertia effects.

Swings often start by touching down with drift in a cross wind and it is worth remembering that, from the point of view of avoiding a bad swing into wind, it is better to overdo the drift correction. This tends to induce a slight swing out of wind on touchdown, which is useful.

Tail-wheels and tail-skids

Glider designers sometimes choose to fit a tail-skid rather than a wheel for simplicity and cheapness, saying quite rightly that they offer a little less drag. In addition, they can be made to break off under a large side load and in so doing, perhaps prevent further damage being done to the fuselage. However, a tail-wheel is more convenient for ground handling, particularly as with these types of glider the tail is extremely heavy and awkward to lift when the glider needs turning around on the ground.

A swing can only occur if the tail is sliding sideways over the ground. A tail-wheel with a rubber tyre will resist skidding sideways over tarmac, but it will not grip quite so well when it is bouncing over rough grass. On the other hand, a tail-skid will not grip at all on tarmac, but is better on the grass or earth, particularly if it is soft. Any extra load on the tail will help to increase its resistance to moving sideways and so help prevent a serious swing. Some people think that it is useful to hold the stick back during the early part of the ground run, until sufficient speed has been reached to ensure good rudder control. However, it is doubtful whether this really has much effect, because in the tail-down position at such low speeds, the tail cannot develop much, if any, down-load. It may be better just to concentrate on keeping straight, holding the wings level and getting the tail up as soon as possible, to reduce the wing's angle of attack and so improve the aileron power. (See use of flap on take-off on pages 93 and 94.)

After landing, the stick should be moved slowly right back to increase the tail load, unless there is good reason to deliberately steer the glider to one side. This helps to prevent the glider from bouncing on any rough ground.

With strong winds, the tendency to swing into the wind is far more pronounced, and after landing the swing cannot always be controlled by full rudder. In very high winds it is usually better to deliberately let the glider swing into wind so that it comes to a stop facing directly into wind. Otherwise, if the wind is squally it may end up with the wrong wing down in a fierce cross wind.

Steering on the ground

It is vital for every pilot to learn to steer on the ground because it is a completely different technique to turning in the air. Students should be given experience of steering the glider off to one side so that they learn how to use the controls independently instead of co-ordinating them. Otherwise, they will try to stop a swing with the stick and rudder together thus putting the wing-tip onto the ground. Sooner or later students will need to swing, or stop a swing, to avoid a collision on the ground. However, as a matter of principle and good airmanship, at least one full wing-span of clearance should always be left to allow for inadvertent drifting or swinging during landings. This is the absolute minimum, and whenever possible much more room should be left, or an alternative landing area should be chosen.

Winch and car launching

With winch or car launches, it is essential to consider whether a cable break could result in a part of the cable falling on or near to a glider or anything else in mid-field. Whereas a glider on the upwind side of the launch line may be out of danger, it is not safe to launch until any glider on the down wind side of the cable run has been moved. If such a risk is accepted, sooner or later the cable will break at the wrong moment and an accident will occur. The pilot who takes a chance is always to blame if he creates an unnecessary hazard.

Use of the wheel brake

Many violent swings and ground loops occur because of heavy braking after landing. If the wheel brake is powerful, the effect of any rapid deceleration increases the inertia effect of the mass being behind the main wheel, and so accentuates any swinging tendency. It also reduces the load on the tail-skid or wheel and makes it slip sideways more easily. Thus hard braking should be avoided, particulary if the glider has started to swing.

If the glider is running straight, the wheel brake can be applied safely. However, it is best to avoid continuous harsh braking which may just result in locking the wheel and skidding. Intermittent braking is often more effective because it allows the wheel to re-grip between skids. As the glider slows down the braking should be reduced to avoid lifting the tail.

Inexperienced pilots sometimes find it difficult to remember, or to work out quickly, the control movements needed to keep straight. But once the wind direction is known, it is easy. The into-wind wing must always be kept down by moving the stick across a little into wind, and it is always necessary to rudder out of the wind. This applies during any cross wind take-off. It also applies during the landing itself and the ground run, whether the wing-down or crabbing method is being used. As with all flying, anticipation prevents difficulties arising.

At the start of the cross wind take-off apply full rudder in anticipation of the swing into wind, and then reduce it as soon as it becomes effective. Get the wing-tip holder to keep the down wind wing-tip high and apply a little aileron to prevent it falling during the first part of the take-off run. Always leave ample room on both sides for swinging or ground looping.

Do not land behind or close to another glider or obstruction. If the glider is tipped by a gust it may be difficult, or even impossible, to stop it drifting to one side. Make sure that you correct the drift before touch down and then be prepared to prevent the swing into wind. Remember that if the glider is drifting towards an obstruction this can only be stopped by banking away from it and not by just applying the rudder.

Inspections

It is almost impossible to judge what loads have gone into the structure during a bad landing, swing or ground loop. Never assume that the glider is undamaged. Get an expert to inspect the whole glider carefully, paying particular attention to the wing-root and fuselage fittings, and the tail and rear fuselage. It is wise to remove the wings and tailplane to inspect the attachment points carefully, and to pay particular attention to the rear fuselage and base of the fin. In a ground loop there are very high inertia forces on the fin and it takes expert knowledge to detect quite serious damage in these areas, particularly with T-tailed types.

Winch and car launches

Provided that the pilot keeps to the correct procedures, winch and car launches can be very safe. However, they mean that the pilot has to be prepared for a possible launch failure or cable break on every flight. Launch failures account for a very high proportion of gliding accidents, making cable break practice a very important aspect of glider training.

Most students have very little difficulty in learning how to make satisfactory launches. However, the critical few moments at the start of the launch are not always fully understood, and often there is an element of luck in getting it right. Instructors can be mistaken about their students' ability to control the initial part properly if one or two launches go well.

The critical phase is from the time the glider leaves the ground until it reaches a height of about 400 feet. If there is a problem up to that height, failing to lower the nose and abandon the launch promptly can leave the aircraft in a critical position, semi-stalled and with very little time or height to make a full recovery and a safe landing. Above that height an abreviated circuit should always be possible, although it may not be necessay or desirable in very windy and turbulent conditions.

Pilots will tend to try to blame the winch or car driver, or the state of the cable if they have an accident following a cable break. This is quite unreasonable as the pilot should always be in a position to recover and make a normal landing.

Cable breaks are a nuisance because they almost always result in having to retrieve the glider from mid-field. However they should not be a worry for a pilot who is well trained, and who keeps in practice and thinks about the conditions before each flight.

Cables and wires

Single-strand, steel piano wire is often used for car and winch launching. Multi-strand, flexible, steel cable is particularly suited to winching because it does not kink so easily. It is normal practice to use a drogue or parachute to keep the cable under tension after it has been released from the glider.

One problem with normal car launching in light winds is that any poor steering on the part of the pilot results in the parachute dropping outside the normal dropping zone. This is largely eliminated with reverse-pulley car launching and winching, where the parachute is pulled in as it drops.

Although ropes and 'parafil' (a sheathed form of nylon line) can be used for car launching, they are not generally suitable for winching. The advantage of rope and parafil for car launching is that a drogue or parachute are not absolutely necessary. Whereas the parachute keeps the cable under tension as it drops, if there is a cross wind it tends to drift much more than a rope with no chute. The disadvantage of rope or parafil is that it cannot be retrieved at high speed without the friction overheating and burning the material.

Piano wire is less expensive than cable but requires careful handling. If a break does occur the wire tends to coil up, and it is easy to make the mistake of just tying the broken ends together and towing it straight back to the launch point for the next launch. If a loop in the cable is overlooked, it becomes a small kink and it will fail on the very next launch. Moreover, the strength of the kink is so low that it will often fail when the glider is only just off the ground. With the low acceleration of a car launch, unless the pilot recognises that the cable has broken and lowers the nose very quickly, the glider will stall and land heavily. Special care must always be taken during the climb away if single-strand wire is being used, because there is no sudden jerk or noise if a kink breaks early on the launch. (Stranded cable is expensive and wears quickly when dragged over runways or any other abrasive surface, making it uneconomical to use for car launching.)

Weak links

Cable which has a large reserve of strength is mostly used so that a weak-link device of some kind safeguards the structure on a fast launch in gusty conditions. It is now common practice to use a series of different strength weak links, and to select one suited to the strength and weight of the glider. For many years all British clubs used 1,000 lb weak links which failed on any two-seater launch where the pilot tried to get the maximum height. Breaking the weak link proved a bigger hazard than actual cable breaks or power failures. With the weak-link strength recommended by the glider manufacturer, breaking the weak link is now comparatively rare and the risks of error have been reduced. However, with fewer breaks pilots tend to take it for granted that they will not get a cable break, and this makes them more vulnerable when one does occur.

Launching speeds

To prevent overstressing the glider during a launch, the weak link should break if the climb is made too steeply at speeds above the maximum shown on the placard. Below that speed it is impossible to generate sufficient lift to overload the weak link.

Nevertheless, above the placard speed a severe gust can raise the loads on the wings and cause damage before the weak link has had time to break and relieve the situation. This means that in rough air it is only safe to pull up hard if the speed is below the maximum launch speed. At other times the exact speed is not critical and the pilot can always reduce the load on the glider by relaxing the backward pressure on the stick.

The loads on the structure are lower during the first half of the launch and it is not unusual to exceed the placard speed for a few seconds during the initial steepening of the climb. This is not critical because at this point the winch driver is adjusting the power. Failure to get up into the full climb is the usual cause of serious overspeeding during the first third of the launch.

The 'too fast' signal should not be given until the glider is well up into the climb and putting a load onto the cable. Of course, there is a small increase in speed as the climb gets steeper, both because the glider is starting to ascend the

35

arc of a circle and also because of the effects of the wind gradient. This can be allowed for by the winch or car driver reducing the power slightly. However, this increase in speed must not be relied on if the launch is too slow and the pilot wants more speed, because the cause of a slow launch may be the beginning of a power failure, in which case steepening up in the hope of creating more speed would be dangerous.

During a winch launch the potential load on the glider is at a maximum near the top of the launch, when the pull of the cable adds directly to the weight of the glider. Excessive speed at this time can be dangerous in rough air if the pilot is pulling back hard.

The take-off

If the glider leaves the ground in a very tail-low attitude, with the tail-skid or wheel on the ground, it has the minimum of flying speed. Worse still, if the stick is being held back the aircraft may bounce off the ground into an even more nose-high attitude and at an even lower speed. A loss of power or cable break in these situations leaves the pilot helpless, and a very heavy, stalled landing will be inevitable. In spite of this very real hazard, however, it is not uncommon to see quite experienced pilots leaving the ground with the elevator up, which results in the glider zooming up into a dangerously steep initial climb.

To avoid these situations it is important for pilots to be taught the right technique for the take-off run. This involves getting the aircraft into an attitude with the tail-wheel or skid just off the ground. In this position it will not leave the ground until a little more speed is gained. The control movements needed to achieve this vary according to the configuration of the undercarriage. Thus the pilots who are flying several different types of glider, or a glider which is unfamiliar to them, must ask themselves before each flight, 'Do I need the stick forward to lift the tail, or back a little to lift the nose?'

With gliders which have a front wheel or main skid, a main wheel just behind the c.g. and a tail-wheel or skid like the K13, Grob 103, ASK21, Puchazc, Schweitzer 233 and most of the older single seaters, it may be necessary to ease back a little during the take-off run to raise the front wheel or skid. A few seconds later as the aircraft gains more speed, it will need more forward movement to prevent it from unsticking with the tail-wheel or skid touching the ground, and climbing away too steeply. When the main wheel is ahead of the c.g. so that the glider is sitting tail-down, a forward movement is needed to raise the tail a little for take-off.

The exact movements required will vary depending on the amount of acceleration. A rapid winch launch will tend to pitch the glider back on to the tail, making a larger forward movement necessary to get the tail off the ground and so ensure a margin of speed when the aircraft takes off.

With all types of glider, it is wise to hold the stick right forward for the initial part of the ground run, so that there is no possibility of the glider zooming off the ground and into a steep climb if the winch driver applies full power too quickly. However, as soon as it begins to accelerate smoothly, that movement is no longer necessary, and the control should be moved to get the glider balanced nicely on to the main wheel. Care must be taken not to keep the stick forward for too long, as too much forward movement during the take-off run will prevent the glider from leaving the ground until a much higher speed is reached. It is also undesirable because, if the glider is bounced off by bumpy ground, it will fly back into the ground heavily a few moments later.

In very light cross winds there is always the possibility of dropping a wing on to the ground and swinging badly. In these conditions it is vital for the pilot to have a hand close to the release, ready to pull it if the need arises. If the grass is long, touching a wing-tip may result in a serious ground loop. But worse still, if the pilot is able to pick up the dropped wing after the initial swing, because of the acceleration the controls suddenly become effective, and this often results in the other wing touching just as the aircraft becomes airborne. This can cause a cart-wheel and major damage or even injury. Always be ready to release during the take-off run and if in doubt, abandon the take-off.

Many gliding clubs use multi-drum winches so that several cables are pulled out at the same time. Unless the cables are well spaced, or the truck driver keeps absolutely straight, there is a risk of two or more cables becoming tangled. Thus when the glider is launched it takes a second cable and parachute up with it. This may cause an abnormally slow launch and the winch driver, seeing the other parachute, may cut the power. However, this should not lead to any particular problem, and it can be dealt with as a normal cable break.

Another possibility is the glider swinging and catching the tail-skid under another cable. This is particularly dangerous because the weight and drag of the second cable may make it difficult to get the nose down. Therefore prevention is better than cure. Cables are dangerous, and where there is more than one cable it is important to keep the glider straight and well clear of any other cable. Always be particularly careful to avoid swinging across another cable in a strong cross wind.

The initial climb

The ideal is to leave the ground balanced on the main wheel; and to hold a constant attitude for the first few feet of the launch while the aircraft gains height and speed. The glider should not be steepened up or levelled out immediately after leaving the ground. After a few seconds the attitude should be allowed to steepen up gradually and smoothly until the full climbing angle is reached. The rate at which the angle is changed must depend on the speed at the time, and this has to be judged because there is insufficient time to check the ASI. If the acceleration is healthy, the change into the climb can be made normally; if the acceleration is slower than normal, then of course the climb must be restricted. At all times the angle of climb and the combination of speed and height must be such that a safe recovery can be made if the launch fails.

When the change in angle is made smoothly, the glider will be climbing at a safe angle and will be able to recover if there is a launch failure at any point. Students used to be told that it was dangerous to steepen the climb below 100 feet. This made them hold the glider down and often caused overspeeding or even overrunning of the cable or parachute. Pulling up suddenly at that height puts a sudden, uncontrolled load on the cable and often results in a cable

ASK13 on a winch launch

break. Obviously, it does not suddenly become safe to steepen the climb at a certain height, and it is now recognised that the angle should be progressively steepened.

With a low-powered winch or tow car, the acceleration is far slower and there is plenty of time to get the glider nicely balanced on the wheel so that it leaves the ground with a safe margin of speed. Again, if the acceleration is poor the climb must not be steepened quickly or it will be impossible to recover in time if the launch fails. The climbing angles for winch or car tow can be similar once the initial climb is over.

Controlling the speed

There are two completely different systems of speed control on wire launches. Most operations depend entirely on the winch or car driver judging the speeds from the bow in the cable and the way in which the glider is gaining height. Unless the winch or car is very under-powered, pulling up steeper on a fast launch has little or no effect on launching speed. All the pilot can do is to signal if the launch is too fast or abandon the launch if it is to slow.

The other system requires a device to measure the load in the cable or to control the maximum pull that the vehicle will provide. In this system the speed is largely controlled by the glider pilot. If the launch is too fast the pilot simply pulls up into a steeper climb. When the driver sees that the load is getting too high, he reduces the power slightly. If the speed is too low, the pilot reduces the climbing angle and the driver, seeing the reduction in load, applies more power. Similarly with the power-limiting device the pilot can control the speed once the optimum power for the type of glider has been set.

Obviously, the pilot has to understand which system is being used. Also, there may be confusion if winches and cars fitted with the power-limiting device become common, and launch heights will suffer until both pilots and drivers are familiar with the new system.

Dealing with a launch failure

A failure very close to the ground frequently results in damage. The cause is always one of the following: failing to recognise the loss of power in time; over-reacting and flying into the ground; opening the airbrakes instead of landing ahead with no airbrake.

If a cable break occurs just after the glider has left the ground, care must be taken not to overdo the lowering of the nose and fly into the ground. Instead, you should simply level out and land ahead. On no account use the airbrakes unless there is time and height to check the actual speed: usually, you will be flying very slowly, and a heavy landing will occur if the airbrakes are used. With no airbrake the glider will float some distance even at low speed, and it must still be held off for a proper touchdown. Opening the airbrakes at that moment will prevent the glider leaving the ground again. With a cable break close to the ground there is always plenty of room ahead for the landing.

If it is a slow launch, any wind gradient will make the situation even more critical. The speed will then be dangerously low by the time that the nose has been lowered, and even more speed will be lost during the descent through the wind gradient.

As a pilot becomes more experienced, there is a real danger of the control movements becoming 'programmed'. If this happens he will change the angle of climb automatically as the glider starts to gain height, and he will continue to pull it higher for a few seconds even if a power failure has occurred. The pilot should always be prepared for an unexpected power failure during this critical stage of the launch. The normal reaction to a launch failure or cable break is to lower the nose and regain speed, and then to pull the release twice, hard, to get rid of any remaining cable.

Higher on the launch

Higher up on the launch the drill should be: lower the nose into the approach attitude; release the cable; assess if a landing ahead is practical. If the latter is the case the speed should be checked by the ASI and, provided that it is adequate, the airbrakes can be used for a normal approach and landing.

Unless the failure has occurred below 50 feet or so, once the speed has been regained it is always best to apply full airbrake first to use up any excess height quickly. The airbrake can then be reduced if necessary for the round-out and landing, provided that there is still plenty of room to do so. This is far better than opening a little airbrake, then some more, and then finally having to use full airbrake for the landing in order to avoid overshooting into the far boundary. It is important to realise that if the glider stops just within the boundary, another few feet of height could have meant a serious overshoot and perhaps a damaged aircraft.

Insufficient room to go straight ahead

After the initial reaction of lowering the nose and checking the speed, a quick assessment of the situation is necessary. If it is obvious that there is plenty of room to land ahead, that is always the first and best choice. In light winds the situation is far more critical than in windy weather, when it may be possible to land ahead from 500 feet or more, even on a relatively small site.

Students and instructors often fail to realise that it is not the amount of height that matters but how much room there is ahead. If there is not enough room to get down straight ahead, obviously a turn has to be made regardless of the height; there is no point in flying on into wind and losing valuable height and space ahead. However, it is vital to check that the speed is adequate before making this turn. A snap decision to turn has been the cause of many serious stalling and spinning accidents, often when, in fact, there was ample room for a landing ahead. During the turn-off, there is time for a reassessment of the height remaining relative to trees and buildings, and a decision has to be made either to continue turning to make a low circuit, or to turn back into wind after using up a little more height (this is known as an S-turn). If, by then, it is obvious that there is plenty of room to turn back into wind and land, this is the sensible thing to do.

If the decision is made to continue with a circuit, use a well-banked turn and monitor the airspeed every few seconds. If there is plenty of height, it may be wise to straighten up and fly down wind a little to allow more room for the landing. Do not try to get all the way back to the launch point unless you have ample height. Remember, if the height is marginal it may be safer to land across the field a little out of wind, rather than try and complete the turn with insufficient height.

The direction of the turn

On a small site it is important to think about the conditions and to consider what is the best way of turning to make use of a longer run on the airfield, or to avoid having to dodge obstructions. In a cross wind it almost always pays to turn off to the down wind side first. However, if you are correcting for drift with one wing well down, and then the cable breaks, you may find that you have already turned quite a long way, and that it is easier to keep that turn going if you cannot get down ahead.

It is seldom possible to land down wind or in the opposite direction to the take-off. This would normally result in overshooting and flying out of the field altogether.

Slow launches

The optimum speed for a launch depends on both the type of glider and the wind strength. A minimum safe speed for most gliders is the minimum cruising speed, but this is only safe at height, where there is time for recovery if a stall occurs. In windy conditions, the glider will climb higher if the launching speeds are on the slow side, whereas on a calm day the best speed is closer to the limit shown on the placard. Special care is needed if the wings are wet when extra speed is necessary, because the stalling speed is raised.

Often, on a small field the most critical situation will be a 'stop–go' launch. This is a slow launch which picks up speed and fades several times, and it is usually caused by a shortage of fuel or mechanical trouble on the winch or car. It is tempting to hang on to the launch, thinking that it will pick up speed, but if you do you may arrive almost over the end of the field with very little height or speed – an awkward situation. It is best to abandon any really slow launch while there is still plenty of room for a landing ahead.

If the glider stalls on the launch it will probably drop a wing and may spin. If the launch seems slow, check the speed every few seconds. Reducing the climbing angle slightly will help the driver to recognise the need for more speed. However, levelling out too much will cause a large amount of slack in the cable and a further loss of speed, often leaving the aircraft in a dangerously nose-high attitude with no pull from the cable to maintain the speed.

With a slow launch the pilot must decide if the speed is sufficient to continue climbing. If it is, he should hold the present attitude and stand by to lower the nose if the speed drops any further. If the launch is much too slow, the nose must be lowered and the launch abandoned immediately. Whereas it is obvious that the launch must be abandoned anywhere near the ground, half-way up the launch it is reasonable to hold on for a few seconds to see if the speed picks up again. A further complication may be that any sideslipping to correct for drift may cause the ASI to under-read so that the speed may have to be judged. If the ASI is reading 20 knots there is an obvious slip error, because that is well below the stalling speed of the glider. Any symptoms of the beginning of a stall, such as buffeting or poor control response, must be dealt with by immediately releasing and lowering the nose.

Fast launches

Most modern machines have maximum launching speeds of 70 knots or so, making it relatively difficult and unusual for the launch to overspeed. The 'too fast' signal is made by yawing from side to side. If the glider is in a very steep climb this should be reduced slightly before yawing. A common fault is to level out too much, which results in a completely slack cable and makes the winch driver's job of judging the correction quite impossible.

In turbulent air the launch should be abandoned if the launching speed becomes really excessive. (Usually this is the pilot's fault for holding the glider down too much during the initial climb, or failing to get right up into the normal angle of climb.) If a decision is made to abandon the launch at height, it is safer to release first and then to lower the nose, as this prevents the risk of the cable parachute opening and flying up over the aircraft. Should the latter ever happen, it is best to land ahead regardless rather than attempt a circuit. The drag of the cable over one wing can make the aircraft uncontrollable in a turn, making a serious crash almost inevitable.

Hang-ups

Situations where the cable or tow rope cannot be released are now very rare. They are most likely to occur because of a jerk in the cable causing an overrun, with the rope becoming tangled in the main wheel of the glider. The launch should always be stopped if an overrun occurs, and if the launch continues in spite of pulling the release the pilot should make every effort to prevent the glider from leaving the ground by keeping the stick right forward. Because of the automatic override system used on all the winch tow release hooks, this is now an extremely rare cause of accidents. Suggestions on how to deal with a hang-up are covered in my other book *Derek Piggott on Gliding* (A & C Black).

Pilots are most vulnerable to all of these problems when they are out of practice or when they become blasé and do not think about the procedures regularly. If pilots are apprehensive about cable breaks it probabiy means that they are uncertain about what they should do in all situations, and whether they can manage. This is a sure sign that they need more practice.

Many pilots quite unwittingly take off with the stick right back, not realising that if the launch fails when they have just left the ground, an accident will be inevitable. Good supervision can prevent pilots developing careless habits, and students can learn by watching and listening to the instructor's comments about good and bad launches.

Gliders lining up for a competition launch

Stall and spin-related accidents

Although the majority of gliders have extremely docile stalling characteristics and are very reluctant to enter a full spin, most of the more serious accidents in the sport are caused initially by stalling. If the stall occurs above about 500 feet, the accident can be put down to lack of awareness and poor stall and spin recovery training. Where it occurs much lower down a recovery is unlikely, and the accident should be put down either to the failure to maintain a safe airspeed at low altitudes, or to bad planning leading to a situation from which a crash is almost unavoidable.

Stalling at low altitudes

If the glider is very low and there is not a clear area immediately ahead and below, a stalling type of crash will be inevitable. Even if the pilot is fully aware of being close to the stall, he will instinctively hold off until the glider stalls down the last few feet rather than fly into obstructions at speed. It is easy to realise that in gusty conditions, if the glider is being flown slowly, the stall may occur high enough for a wing to drop and for an incipient spin to develop with even more serious results.

Obviously it is very important to train every pilot to recognise when his planning is leading to a disastrous situation, and to take action in time to avoid it. Usually these situations arise from running out of height on the circuit, but they can also arise from arriving back far too high and by badly planned manoeuvring in an attempt to correct that kind of position.

Student pilots need plenty of practice at dealing with both these kinds of situation during their basic training if they are to learn to be able to spot them developing. If they can do this, a change of plan at an early stage can usually prevent the situation from developing and leading to an accident.

Very often during training, a student will be rather short of height but will just have sufficient for a normal approach. The instructor may have been wondering if the height was going to be sufficient for a normal approach even though the student had already cut out the base leg to make a 180° turn on to finals. The question in this situation is, would the pilot have recognised that this would not have been possible if the aircraft had been 50 feet lower? Would he, in fact, have turned in earlier, or would it have been another near miss or accident in the making?

In many training organisations all over the world, student pilots get no training at all with this kind of problem. It is therefore not surprising that incidents and accidents happen when this kind of situation occurs, especially if it is during an early off-field landing when the pilot is under pressure.

Undershoots

Most undershoot accidents occur because the pilot has not recognised that the glider is critically short of height until it is desperately low. In very open country, the judgement of heights, even down below 200 or 300 feet, is surprisingly difficult. Where there are trees or buildings nearby a direct comparison can be made, and this is a good way of eliminating serious misjudgements. This is an important lesson for every student. Most pilots do not instinctively look across and compare their height with the trees unless they have been taught to do so, and more often than not a pilot will try to judge by angles and positioning alone.

Often, the pilot does not even consider what he will do if the glider hits some sink and loses some extra height. This possibility should always be in the mind of the pilot and some reserve of height must be carried all the time. However, too much height often leads to situations where even full airbrake cannot prevent a drastic overshoot.

When the glider is desperately low the pilot's handling often goes to pieces, and he may over-rudder in an effort to get round a final turn without touching a wing-tip or turning any steeper. Over-ruddering causes extra drag and an extra loss of height or speed, and it often leads to stalling in the turn.

Anticipation

The solution to these problems is anticipation, that is preventing them from developing by thinking ahead and taking action early. Many situations where the glider is very low and flying slowly are insoluble quite a time before the accident actually happens. More stalling and spin training will not help to stop this type of accident.

Such incidents can only be avoided if the pilot has a more open mind about where he is going to land. For example, if the glider is too low to land conventionally in the normal landing area directly into the wind, it may well be possible to land across wind and behind the normal launching point, so that the low turn can be completed safely. All too often the pilot has a plan in his mind and sticks to it even when it should have become obvious that the situation has changed and his plan is no longer feasible. It is sometimes quite hard for a person to do the unconventional, but that may be the only safe option. However, if the pilot is thinking ahead, that option could have already been considered and he could have had the plan ready for use if more height was lost.

Trying to do the normal thing can be the cause of accidents with cable breaks and winch failures on smaller gliding sites. Sometimes the only safe thing to do is to land out of the site altogether in a nearby field. By not considering this as a possibility, the pilot gives himself little or no hope of a safe landing, especially if the alternative is a very low 360° turn and he is already flying rather slowly.

Stalling on the actual approach is usually caused by failing to monitor the airspeed regularly, or by failing to react to its indications. There is no point in reading the ASI and knowing that you are too slow unless you lower the nose to correct it. Stalling can also be due to trying to stretch the glide instead of closing the airbrakes, or stretching the glide after getting into a desperate undershoot position. This is more easily done when landing in an unfamiliar place, particularly if it is in a hilly area and means landing on an uphill slope.

If a bad undershoot seems inevitable, again prompt action is needed rather than waiting to see what happens and how far you get. If there is a possible area for a safe landing, use the brakes and get down into it. Remember that it is far better to get down and then to run into obstruction than to stall on to it at flying speed. In a case like this it is often a matter of assessing quickly 'Am I sure that I can reach the field, or if I get more sink will I fail to get there?' If there is any doubt about getting there in the worst circumstances, it is better to get down short in any open space ahead and risk rolling into the hedge. On a windy day with a strong wind gradient, you are quite likely to lose some extra height and speed and low approaches are always very risky.

Unintentional stalls at height

It is obviously very important for the student pilot to learn to recognise all the symptoms of the stall and to become familiar with them. If they are recognised, there is almost always plenty of time to prevent a stall occurring. However, many inexperienced pilots get so thoroughly engrossed in the thermalling or what is going on elsewhere that they are temporarily 'switched off' to how they are flying. Perhaps the work-load is high at the time, looking at the map and the ground for possible clues as to where they are, looking for signs of possible lift to climb in, together with all the other little worries involved in a field landing. It is often at these times that the glider becomes stalled without the pilot noticing, and then his instincts are bound to be automatic as the nose and wing drops.

If you stall accidentally it is almost always because you are not aware of the low speed, etc. and therefore all the training in the world will not prevent you from responding instinctively because you are not at that moment aware that you are stalled. (If you were aware, you would have prevented the stall!) In this situation you are bound to pull back and apply the aileron and rudder to stop the nose and wing from dropping. Hopefully, a few seconds later you will have recognised the situation, taken heed of your training and moved forwards on the stick.

Occasionally the stall is recognised by the pilot so that a preventative movement can be made before any serious wing-drop has had time to develop. Accidental stalls seldom happen when the glider is being flown straight, and most result in one wing stalling before the other, causing a wing-drop.

Incipient spins

Any time that a wing begins to drop at a stall it is the beginning of a possible spin, but the spin can only develop if the wing is kept stalled and the glider is allowed to continue to yaw.

In the UK there has been much discussion about teaching stall recoveries with a view to making it all easier for the beginner to understand and remember. It has been suggested that 'incipient' is an unfamiliar word, that associating the stall with a spin might get the student worried, and that to simplify things we should only talk about stalls and spins. Although it is obviously accurate to call an incipient spin a stall with a wing-drop, I think that this is trying to avoid the issue, which is that it is really the beginning of a spin and at least a potential spin.

Recommended recovery

The recovery action now being recommended for any stall is to move forwards on the stick to unstall the wings by reducing the angle of attack. A few seconds later the glider is unstalled and can be brought level and back to normal flight with the normal use of the controls. This has the advantage that it does not require the pilot to remember any special movement of the controls other than the movement forward to unstall.

Perhaps in an effort to justify this simplification, some instructors have been warning against the use of the rudder to stop the yaw if a wing drops at the stall. They have been inferring that applying the opposite rudder has been the cause of reversing the spin, whereas the real cause of this happening must be the failure to unstall the wings.

Use of the rudder

Additional yawing caused by the excess use of the rudder in a turn will make the wing-drop much sharper. At the instant of applying the excess rudder, it speeds up the outer wing-tip, creating more lift there, and gives the inner wing 'sweep back' in relation to the airflow, thus increasing the tendency to tip stall on that wing while reducing it on the other. Additional yaw will also occur if the ailerons are used to try to stop the dropping wing because of the extra aileron drag. However, the aileron may well still be effective, and in most gliders applying the aileron to stop the wing dropping at the stall, while not recommended, does not have any noticeable tendency to cause further stalling at the tip.

How far the glider rolls over into the beginning of the spin depends to a large extent on the amount of yaw present. Applying the opposite rudder will tend to reduce the yaw and so help even out the stalling of the wings. In fact, the rudder power of most gliders is very poor in relation to the huge inertia of the heavy, long-span wings, and there may not be any visible effect when opposite rudder is applied in an incipient spin. However, it is not true to say that it is dangerous to apply the opposite rudder in an incipient spin.

Applying the opposite rudder cannot possibly cause the spin to reverse as is sometimes stated, unless the pilot is keeping the stick right back. The only reason for an incipient or full spin changing direction is if the stick is held right back so that the glider is either kept stalled, or is re-stalled as the rotation stops. If the incipient spin has progressed for more than about half a turn because the pilot has kept the stick back, applying the full opposite rudder must be a good thing because it helps to stop the rotation and to even up the stalling of the wings. Probably the most effective way of dealing with an incipient spin in practice is to move forwards on the stick, apply the opposite rudder to check the yaw and then to use all the controls normally to bring the aircraft level. This method has been taught for many years and I do not think that pilots who have learned to do it this way need bother to change. New pilots will be taught just to unstall the wings and then to get the wings level using the normal co-ordination.

Of course, unless the pilot is aware that the glider is stalled, he is bound to respond instinctively at first, applying full aileron and rudder to try to stop the rapid wing-drop and pulling right back to try to stop the nose dropping.

If the pilot is aware that the glider is stalled, applying the opposite rudder at the same time as moving forwards on the stick should result in some reduction in the yawing movement towards the dropping wing, and therefore must be a good thing. In my experience, the only occasions when I have stalled unexpectedly and known what was happening at the time, have been in very fierce stubble fires and dust devils. In these violent thermals it is possible to be flying with a good margin of speed at one moment and to be falling with virtually no speed the next. In such cases it is easy to make a correct recovery because it is so obvious that the glider is stalled.

Unexpected stalls

Most unintentional stalls occur, by definition, unexpectedly and usually the first obvious sign of what has happened is that the pilot is banging the stick on the rear stop with the nose still dropping – a frightening feeling. However, provided that a movement forwards is made to unstall, the possibility of a full spin will have been avoided. The order of movements is relatively unimportant compared to the necessity of making an immediate forward movement to reduce the angle of attack of the wing so that it unstalls.

If you imagine suddenly and unexpectedly finding yourself in an almost vertical dive facing the ground, it is easy to understand why so many pilots fail to make a movement forward on the stick to help the glider unstall itself. Below a certain height it may be a hopeless situation, but even where there is enough height for a recovery, you can imagine how hard it is to make that movement forward unless you have practised stalls and incipient spins until the movements are well drilled.

Most types of glider are reluctant to enter a full spin unless they are being flown with the c.g. on or very close to the aft limit, that is by light pilots. However, whether it is a full spin or just an incipient one is academic if the glider stalls a few hundred feet up.

Problems arise because many pilots do not understand much about spinning. They are often told that gross over-ruddering is needed to spin, but this is not the case. It is possible to spin with the rudder centralised if the glider is one which will spin fully. For example in a 232, Puchacz, or the older Bocian and Eagle, it is usual to be able to get a full spin of several turns without using any rudder. In this case the necessary yawing movement is caused by the high drag of the badly stalled wing. Usually after one or two turns these gliders will unstall themselves and build up speed rapidly in a spiralling dive. Recovery is simply a matter of relaxing the backward pressure on the stick and using the controls quite normally to bring the wings level and to ease out of the dive.

With any recovery from a steep dive, 'ease' is the operative word. If the glider is trimmed for a normal cruising speed, because of the longitudinal stability it will require a forward movement and pressure on the stick to keep it diving at a higher speed. This means that in most cases it is more likely to be a matter of relaxing the forward pressure to allow the aircraft to level out rather than pulling it out with a positive backward pressure on the stick.

The stick position

The position of the stick in steady flight is a very clear indication of the angle of attack, and having the stick back near the rearmost stop should warn the pilot that he is close to the stalling angle for the wing. If the nose is dropping in spite of pulling back and hitting the back stop, this is a clear indication that the glider is stalled, and a forward movement is needed for a few seconds to let the wing unstall. In most unintentional stalls, the stick position on the back stop will be the first symptom to be recognised. However, although the stick position and the total lack of response to the elevator are by far the most important symptoms of the actual stall, many instructors hardly mention it.

By this stage of a stall, very often the noise of the airflow will have increased because of the yawing movement, and most of the other symptoms will either be absent or will go unnoticed in the moments of panic. The fact that the glider is not responding normally must cause alarm to any pilot until the cause is identified.

If the glider is stalled and enters a spin at height, the inability to recover must be due a lack of spin recovery training. With insufficient experience, the pilot is likely to be slow to recognise the spin and slow to react. Moreover, because it occurs unexpectedly it may well cause a temporary panic. Clearly while we do have gliders that spin, it is vital to give pilots enough experience to recognise what is happening and to make the right moves instead of panicking and doing nothing.

The effects of rain on the stall

Many pilots are unaware of the significance of dirty wing surfaces and of rain or drizzle on both the performance and the stalling characteristics of gliders. Tests show that on most high performance machines, a spread of splattered flies on the leading edges can account for up to a quarter of the glider's performance, reducing a glide ratio of 40:1 to less than 35:1 and making a mockery of glide calculations. This is so serious that for world championship flying, many gliders are now fitted with a means of cleaning off the leading edges of the wings in flight.

In light rain I have measured an increase of about 8 knots in the speed for the pre-stall buffet and stall of a K13, although the stall itself did not seem to have changed in character. However, some gliders do have a definite change in both speed and characteristics. For example, with wet wings the Falke motor gliders, the Bergfalke and the Spatz all become viscous at the stall and will flick over if they are stalled during turns.

A pilot taking off in rain on a winch or car launch is at risk with any type of glider unless the launch is faster than normal. It is not unknown for gliders to stall and drop a wing badly on a slow launch, and the behaviour of most gliders in the rain may be far worse than in normal flight. The combination of the poor visibility, together with the misting up of the canopy and the effects of the rain on the stall, make launching in rain foolhardy and almost always pointless from the point of view of achieving a soaring flight.

However, it is not unusual to see pilots take off towards a heavy rain shower on a good soaring day instead of waiting until it has passed. Usually this is because they got ready before the rain started falling and are unable to see that they are not going to stay up unless they wait until the shower has passed. Inevitably they come straight down in a few minutes looking rather sheepish! It is as though they are unable to change their minds and this is a very dangerous trait in a glider pilot.

Really heavy rain can be disastrous. Even in a car the wipers do not clear the windscreen in torrential rain. Snow looks less innoccuous but is even worse than rain because it blots out visibility more. Flying in even light snow is like being in a fog, and unless you are up high and can manage to fly clear on instruments, you are liable to have real trouble.

More about spin recovery

The standard method of recovery must be taught because it has been proven to be effective during testing. It involves applying full opposite rudder and then, with the ailerons central, moving the stick steadily or progressively forwards until the spin stops. Finally, the pilot centralises the rudder and eases out of the dive. (To reduce the risk of over-speeding with modern machines, the airbrakes can be opened fully at any time during the spin or the recovery.)

If every type of glider required a different recovery there would be the risk of a pilot using the wrong method for the type of aircraft. All gliders and light aircraft have to recover satisfactorily with the standard method. This is not to say that other methods would not work, but it is unwise to use non-standard methods for recovery from a fully developed spin, even if they appear to work better.

In the standard recovery, the full opposite rudder is always applied first, and if it does slow down the rotation, the nose of the glider will automatically drop, helping to unstall the wings. In this way the rudder is a very powerful influence on the spin recovery because it helps the pitching movement and also slows the rotation. (The full opposite rudder must never be taken off if the aircraft is reluctant to recover, because any additional yaw would further flatten the spin.)

Blanketing

Before the days of T-tails, there was a possibility of the downward movement of the elevator causing some blanketing of the rudder and reducing its effectiveness. This is another reason for standardising the rudder movement first, but it is not relevant to gliders with T-tails where no rudder blanketing can occur.

Modes of spinning

A more important reason not to experiment is to avoid the possibility of getting the glider into an untested mode of spin from which it might be difficult or impossible to recover. It is possible for an aircraft to have several different modes of spinning, and all of them may not have been discovered during the testing. Using the ailerons during the recovery, for example, may be the means of entering one of these other modes of spin.

It is not always realised how little spinning is carried out during the test flying of a new type of glider. Entries are made with every different kind of control input: full in-spin aileron, full out-spin aileron, airbrakes in and out, c.g. forward and c.g. aft, etc., using the standard method of recovery to stop the spin. Finally, to check the recovery from the stabilised spin, the glider is held in the spin for a full five turns if that is possible. The authorities do not require other methods of recovery to be tested, and it is therefore not always possible to be sure whether using the aileron, for instance, will flatten the spin and make it more difficult to stop.

In the past there have been a number of problems with spin recoveries with light aircraft. Some have been due to the aircraft getting into a new mode of spin, but others have been due to poor recovery techniques. Often the instructor or pilot knows the correct recovery and thinks that he is using it, but because of the unusual forces on the controls, he is failing to apply the full recovery action. This used to happen on both the Chipmunk and the Tomahawk where the elevator control loads become much heavier during the spin and where a half-hearted movement forward on the stick may be insufficient to stop the spin.

The position of the c.g.

With any type of aircraft the characteristics of a spin vary according to the loading, so that the spin becomes flatter as the c.g. is moved back. This will also affect how far the stick has to be moved forwards to effect a recovery. This depends mainly on how deeply the wing is stalled. It is therefore important to teach and always to think of the stick movement as being a progressive forward movement made until the spin stops.

The effect of the rudder

In many gliders the spin may stop as soon as the full opposite rudder is applied. In others the stick will have to move quite a long way forwards before the wing unstalls and the spin stops. Where this is the case, the full opposite rudder may not even appear to change the spin, and the spin will continue until the movement forward is sufficient. Because each spin may be slightly different, it is important not to try to guess how far to move forwards. Always make a progressive, steady movement forwards until the spin stops.

If the spin is unexpected, it may even be difficult to tell in which direction it is going. If you have spun out of cloud, the turn needle always shows the direction of the spin. Usually, but not always, the ball of the slip indicator is out the other way.

Control loads

In most gliders the rudder will have overbalanced and moved hard over in the direction of the spin. So if you are in doubt about the direction of the spin, push against the overbalancing load and reverse the rudder.

One very deceptive thing about the control loads is the effect of the airflow at very large angles of attack and with the yawing and rolling movements during a spin. The rudder will certainly be overbalanced and it will require far more force to apply the full opposite rudder than at any other time in flight. The airflow over the ailerons often tends to move the stick towards the direction of the spin and they should be centralised for the recovery. In addition, the elevator may overbalance so that the force needed to move forwards on the stick is abnormally high. Do not mistake stick pressures for stick movement. The stick must be moved forwards to make the recovery.

Training problems

In many training gliders it is difficult to demonstrate spinning and the spin may stop when the full opposite rudder is applied. If this happens, it is important to move the stick forwards sufficiently to ensure that the glider does not re-stall. When a glider recovers so easily, a rapid movement forward on the stick often results in a very steep recovery and a high speed dive.

After doing this several times in a two-seater during training, the student may find both that applying full opposite rudder will stop the spin and that the glider does not in fact re-stall again even if the stick is kept back. (Sometimes a little of the pre-stall buffet can be felt but the glider levels out all right.) If this is allowed to go unnoticed because the glider stops spinning each time, it will encourage the habit of keeping the stick back. This will, in turn, guarantee a delayed recovery, or no recovery at all, on a glider which requires a more positive recovery action.

If the spin stops when the full opposite rudder is applied, the stick *must* be moved forwards to allow normal flight. Failure to do this is the only reason for a reversal of the spin from one direction to another.

Incidentally, if an aircraft is very difficult to get into a spin, it also may be very difficult to recover. It is not unknown for so-called 'unspinnable' aircraft to come to grief by getting into a stable spin.

Light stick forces

It is very important to watch for any tendency to use a jerky forward movement on the stick during the full recovery. This is often a sign of nervousness and usually means that more spin training is needed. The following incident with an experienced pilot on a K6E drew attention to the importance of making smooth stick movements.

This particular pilot was an instructor who was in good practice in a K13 two-seater but out of practice in his K6E. The E-model, unlike the K6CR, has an all-moving stabiliser with no tabs to provide feel. Without the spring trimming there would be no pressure required to change speeds or to pull out of dives, and the controls would be very light indeed. Since the force exerted by the spring is the same at both low and high speeds, this makes it feel rather twitchy, and it is not difficult to overstress the aircraft at high speeds.

In this case the spin itself was quite normal, and after a few turns the pilot initiated the recovery by applying the full opposite rudder and then moving the stick forwards. However, with the negligible stick forces of the K6E, he must have rather overdone forward movement. He stopped the spin but pitched the nose down rather violently. At this point, his head hit the canopy and dislodged his glasses.

What occurred next is somewhat uncertain. He was unaware of any high 'g' or, indeed, of anything at all, until he found himself regaining consciousness in a near vertical climb, about to tail slide.

After landing, the aircraft was found to have split fabric and extensive minor damage to the wings, which could only be attributed to overstressing at high speed. He was lucky not to lose the wings altogether!

Avoid abrupt movements

Subsequent checks with this K6E pilot showed that during spin recoveries in the K13 his elevator movements were rather abrupt and uncontrolled. In fact he found it very difficult not to jerk the stick forwards for recoveries. Since most of these control movements are semi-automatic and largely pre-programmed, it is almost certain that this was the initial cause of his reaching such a high speed.

Instructors should therefore insist that the movements of the stick must be a controlled, progressive movement rather than a rapid, uncontrolled push or jerk. They should also use the term 'ease' the glider out of the dive rather than 'pull' it out. There have been several cases of two-seaters being overstressed by pilots pulling back hard to recover from steep dives after spin recoveries.

Piecing together the evidence from the incident with the K6E pilot, it seems almost certain that the pilot blacked out during the recovery. Susceptibility to high 'g' is greatly affected by the duration of the loading, and whereas most people can cope with 3 to 4 g for a few seconds, a sustained loading of that amount may cause loss of vision. In this case the pilot had possibly pulled about 5 g for 4 or 5 seconds. Much also depends on the seating positions and whether the pilot is expecting the extra 'g' and prepares for it by tensing himself up. For example, when sitting relaxed in a T21b, I have been nearly blacked out by a student during a tight loop.

The details are unimportant but the lessons are clear. Extreme care is always needed when flying at high speeds with gliders fitted with an all-moving stabiliser and spring trimming, particularly when recovering from extreme attitudes. The elevator loads remain almost constant at all speeds and are so low that any jerky movement may result in very high 'g' loadings. Fortunately, glider designers seem to have given up all-moving stabilisers in favour of a fixed tailplane and normal elevator. As a result, most of the new breed of gliders are more pleasant and safer to fly.

Interesting demonstrations to try

The following are several interesting demonstrations and experiments to try out on your own gliders, or to show to students.

The effects of slight slip or skid on stalls in turns

If a student has a habit of over-ruddering in turns, it is often worth showing him the effect on the stall of using even a slight amount of extra rudder in a gentle turn. Most pilots have been shown the effect of gross over-ruddering during their basic training. The following demonstration compares a stall with a little too much rudder to a stall in a slightly slipping turn, and shows how even slightly too much rudder has a significant effect at the stall.

Start to circle in a normal turn with about 20° of bank, keeping the yaw string *exactly* in the middle while you reduce speed very gradually. (On most types of training glider it will be possible to get down to the pre-stall buffet and continue with either a slight rocking of the wings or a very gentle inner wing-drop.) Keep the rudder where it is and allow the speed to increase a few knots so that both you and the student can observe the exact position of the rudder pedals. Most types of glider should be showing a very small amount of rudder being held on into the turn.

Next, watching the rudder pedals, increase the amount of rudder by a movement of about one inch forward on the rudder pedal and try again to reduce the speed. Note how this time the glider has a very pronounced inner wing-drop at the stall and tries to spin. After getting back into the accurate turn as before, apply a very small amount of opposite rudder to create a slightly slipping turn and try the stall again. This time the glider will be totally innocuous.

This demonstration shows how even very small amounts of extra rudder in a turn cause a bad wing drop, whereas using too little is a safer fault because it inhibits the stalling characteristics. The ideal, of course, is the accurate turn with the yaw string central or, as some pilots say, showing a very slight slipping movement (because the cockpit is ahead of the c.g.).

To emphasise the stick forward movement

This demonstration is intended to counteract the tendency for pilots trained on very docile gliders to remember the full opposite rudder but to forget the stick movement.

In this case the instructor brings the aircraft to a stall and applies full rudder as if he is going to spin. As the wing drops and the spin starts, he move forwards on the stick, leaving the rudder applied. The wing unstalls immediately and prevents the spin from developing. (After a few seconds the rudder must be recentralised to avoid getting to high speeds with full rudder applied.) This shows conclusively that any movement forward will prevent a spin developing even if the rudder is forgotten altogether.

The stall is approached once again but this time in a very slight turn and, if necessary, with a very small amount of extra rudder – just enough to make the wing drop. Keeping the rudder still and pulling right back on the stick sharply as the stall occurs, should make the wing drop. This time the stick is held firmly back with the aileron central, and the wing will (usually) continue dropping so that the glider spins for a turn or so. A normal recovery is then made.

If height permits, I then like to make a series of stalls using large amounts of rudder and handing over control for a quick recovery, moving the stick forward and using normal stick and rudder together to bring the wings level.

The point about these last two demonstrations is that they emphasise that spinning depends on stalling and keeping the aircraft stalled. Any forward movement will prevent a spin from developing, whereas failure to move forwards can result either in the spin continuing or, if the opposite rudder has been applied, in the direction of the spin suddenly reversing.

These demonstrations serve to emphasise the importance of moving forwards every time the glider is stalled. But although they work well in the older types of glider, they are not practical with the modern machines which have a very docile stall and which will not drop a wing at the stall without gross over-ruddering.

Most of the other simulations of accidental stalling involve almost unrealistic handling of the aircraft, and are therefore not very convincing, although they may result in a rather more violent wing-drop.

Conclusion

There is no doubt that many of the serious stall/spin accidents are caused by poor planning which leads to situations involving difficult manoeuvring near the ground, putting the pilots under stress so that they make mistakes or fly badly enough to stall and spin in. Careful instruction and constant practice is needed if the stall and spin accidents are to be prevented altogether. It is important to be able to recognise all the symptoms of the approach of a stall in order to be able to prevent it.

It must be emphasised that to prevent or to stop a spin the wings must be unstalled by means of a forward movement. Unstalling the wings takes away the cause of the autorotation and then the wings can be brought level using the stick and rudder normally. In most cases with either incipient or full spins, any movement forward, or even just relaxing the backward movement of the stick, would prevent or stop the spin immediately.

The most important thing to emphasise is that, regardless of the attitude of the glider, if it is not responding to moving back on the stick or if the stick is hitting the back stop, a forward movement must be made to allow the glider to unstall.

Advice on making field landings

Flying cross-country

With all the airspace restrictions in operation it is most important to keep track of your location so that the glider does not inadvertently stray into controlled airspace or other restricted areas. This is particularly true for early attemps at flying cross-country, where it is vital to use a priority system for concentrating on the important aspects of the flying.

Flying above 1,500 or 2,000 feet on a reasonable day, you should concentrate mainly on climbing efficiently, selecting the next good clouds, and checking and confirming your position and progress on the map between themals. Below 1,500 feet, the maps should be ignored and priority should be given to checking for suitable fields below while also searching for lift, re-checking on the local wind direction and moving towards a better area of fields if necessary.

At about 1,000 feet you should put away the maps, select a good field and check it for slopes and surface etc. Use any area of lift but do not drift away from the chosen field. Keep re-checking the field and reselect if a better one becomes apparent. Move away to avoid flying directly over the field, but keep it within easy reach all the time.

At about 800 feet AGL, re-check your position to the side of the field, re-check for obstructions, choose the 'turn in' position and prepare for landing. Consider the effects of the wind. Will there be bad turbulence from obstructions upwind of the field? Is it an uphill slope and how much extra speed is necessary? At this point it is a good idea to say out loud to yourself, 'Now I am going to land', and from then on not to change your mind.

Many field landing accidents occur because the initial decision to choose a field is left far too late. Often the pilot is lost and has been worrying for the past half an hour about where he is. Then he gets low and is already in a state of anxiety which tends to make him make poor judgements. If you are getting low, you should forget all your other problems and concentrate on selecting a good field first. Then try to use any lift nearby, keeping within easy reach of the field and in a position from which it is easy to drop on to the circuit.

The lower the choice of field is made, the fewer fields are within reach and the less time there is to decide which one is best. By the time that the glider is down to 500 feet or so, an inexperienced pilot often will have forgotton the wind direction, and if he realises this it will increase his anxiety. Finally, below a few hundred feet, if no definite field has been chosen there can be little or no choice, and an accident is almost certain to happen. Often the pilot is in such a state of panic that the flying becomes dangerously inaccurate.

This kind of accident is relatively common with inexperienced pilots, especially when they are flying in competitions. The final glide back to the base airfield at the end of the day is a particularly stressful time. Usually it is at the end of a long day's racing, with a number of stressful periods all adding to the

Bergfalke 11 landing at Ein Shemer, Israel

pilot's fatigue. Perhaps the glider is theoretically just within range for a straight glide home, but has very little extra height in hand and not much prospect of getting another climb. At 1,000 feet the pilot may be some distance from his base when some extra height is lost because of strong sink. He badly wants to complete the task and continues hoping to pick up more lift on the way. More sink puts him well below the intended glide path, but instead of making the decision to choose a field and look around near it for more lift, he glides on. Eventually he finds himself at 500 feet, unable to see a good field ahead, unable to remember the wind direction, and trying to select a field with very little choice.

Even worse off is the pilot who still believes he will make it and takes no action until he arrives on the ground or in a hedge. When you are tired out and upset with yourself for not having taken that extra piece of lift some miles back, there can be a tendency to become apathetic and not even try to prevent an accident. It is as though you are drugged and have ceased to care. This is one of the effects of lack of oxygen, but also of dehydration at the end of a long day's excitement. It can be overcome if you recognise that you are tired and getting complacent, but the onset is very gradual and often you do not recognise that anything is wrong. If you give yourself a shake, change your seating position slightly, open the clear vision panel for some fresh air, change hands on the stick for a few moments and have a sweet or drink, you can snap out of it and start to work normally again.

Think about the problems

A surprising number of inexperienced pilots haven't really thought about how they would tackle having to land in a field. Since they don't have problems landing on their gliding site, they don't see why there should be any particular problem landing elsewhere.

They can be the quiet, but unthinking types who are simply unaware of their lack of knowledge. They probably have never even considered that they could have an accident and damage the glider. So, the idea that they need some training to do it safely just doesn't occur to them.

With many aspects of flying, we need to have reached a certain stage or standard to be able to appreciate the problems, or to understand and take in the facts. There is often a tendency for pilots to think that, because they are solo and have managed a few soaring flights and their Bronze C, they should be allowed to go cross-country. What is seldom realised, until a first cross-country, is the vast increase in mental workload involved when soaring, map reading, field landings and flying have to be thought of, instead of just how to stay up.

Many incidents and accidents are caused by lack of experience and the pilot unwittingly putting himself into situations beyond his capabilities. For example, it is important for an inexperienced solo pilot to avoid a field landing until he has had some training in how to tackle one.

Hundreds of landings on one particular airfield or gliding site do not provide good training for landing in fields. Unfortunately, being familiar with an approach takes away much of the need for real judgement. Pilots, and even instructors, often believe that they have good judgement and can land accurately anywhere because they can manage on their own site. However, even if it is a small field, all they have really learned is to position themselves by habit, using the local landmarks to help. The really valuable experience comes from landing in many different, unfamiliar places, whether they are fields or large aerodromes.

Unintentional out landings

Throughout the training, landing out is usually treated as such a serious misdemeanor that the inexperienced pilot is often influenced into trying desperately hard to get back if he either inadvertently drifts away from the site or gets lost during a local soaring flight.

On an early solo some pilots do get rather far from the field, which causes their instructors to become apprehensive for their safety. The inexperienced pilots often try to soar in unusable lift, and they concentrate so hard that they don't recognise that they are drifting away and are not going to get back to the field. Then they may fail to make any choice of field or plan of action until it is too late. If the fields below happen to be large, they may get down safely, but a safe landing is often due to luck rather than to good judgement.

After the pilot's personal safety, the safety of the aircraft must be the next most important consideration; it is always safer to land out than to risk trying to get back with marginal height. Forget about embarrassment: a landing out has to be made if there is any doubt about getting back. If an inexperienced pilot finds himself in a situation where a field landing seems necessary, he should make the decision to choose a field and plan the landing properly, while there is height and time to spare. This is not the time to be thinking about what the chief instructor is going to think or say. Worrying about people's comments instead of keeping calm and concentrating on the flying and on getting down safely is often the root cause of a bad landing.

There is really very little excuse for the student wandering out of reach of the field if he has been taught well in the first place. However, during training, decisions such as when to leave the lift and start to get back to the field are too often taken by the instructor. If this happens, the student may not form the habit of checking the situation after every turn and of making his own decision about when to turn back.

Hints on choosing fields

Obviously if you are flying over a bad area, with very few good sized fields, it is necessary to divert towards the best area within range and to start looking seriously for a field at several thousand feet.

Where the countryside is more hospitable, this can be left to a thousand feet or so. Of course, turning downwind will increase the range and the choice of the fields, and it also makes joining a regular circuit very much easier. Choosing a field some distance upwind on the other hand, is not such a good idea. By the time that you have battled against the wind to get there, you may find that it has some hazard that you could not see from a distance, and then there may be no other good field within reach.

Do not waste valuable height trying to fathom out how to get down in an unsuitable field. Discard it if it has awkward wires or some other hazard on the approach, and choose another field. Time spent puzzling how to avoid these problems is time wasted which you could use for looking around more.

If you cannot see a suitable field, don't be afraid to make a well banked circle to look right round the whole area. Looking further out you will probably be able to see dozens of fields and also the lie of the land and the main slopes. Disregard any fields which would entail landing on a downhill slope. Landing down wind is a silly thing to do. Unless you do it every day at your particular gliding site, you are certain to misjudge such a landing, besides having the hazards of the higher touchdown speeds and loss of control during the ground run to contend with. Don't look at the fields immediately below, because the slopes cannot be seen from directly above. You can only see three of four fields and if they all look bad your morale will suffer.

Positioning

Once you have selected a possible field, move towards it, checking its size, slope and colour, and look out for possible wires on the approach. Don't fly over it unless you have more than enough height to allow you to reposition yourself well to the side again. Being directly overhead, the field is one of the worst positions from which to extricate yourself because you have to fly blind, away from the field, for quite a long time to get out to the side for a reasonable base leg. Try putting yourself at five or six hundred feet directly over the landing area of your gliding site and see for yourself how difficult it is to plan and make a spot landing.

Be careful that you do not continue to reject fields at the same time as getting lower and lower until it is too late either to have any selection or to achieve a good approach. If there really are no suitable fields within range, then you have left the choice far too late and you must choose the best you can. It will be a matter of making a good landing directly into wind, if that is possible, and of hoping for a minimum of damage to the glider.

Formal circuits

You do not need a complete conventional circuit with a long downwind leg, although this will obviously give you more time in which to have a better look at the field. But whatever happens, you must get into a good position for the start of the base leg.

Unless you have a great deal of spare height, do not try to fly right round the field. Experience shows that people often run themselves short of height on the way right round. Instead, they could have stayed on the side they were flying and made a right, instead of a left circuit, with height to spare. The positioning is made easier by imagining your field to be the normal landing area on your home site and by using the same angle for the positioning.

Since it is usual in training to make circuit patterns from 800 feet or so, inexperienced pilots are often seriously put out if they find themselves unable to do this on a field landing. Instead of accepting that their normal circuit is not possible and organising an alternative, they may try to make their formal pattern and so run themselves into an even more difficult situation. Alternatively, they may continue to worry about their initial error of judgement instead of making a revised plan of action to get into a good position for the base leg and approach.

Positioning the final turn

It is surprisingly easy to make the circuit and base leg far too close to the field, particularly if the surrounding countryside is rough and unlandable. After you have selected the field, it is a good policy to choose the approximate position to complete the final turn and to start the approach. With average British fields, this needs to be at least one field length back from the boundary. This is slightly more than the distance that most pilots would like for a spot landing at the gliding site because you need a little more time for the approach in a strange place. Obviously, if the fields are small, two lengths might be needed. Then, provided you are not running short of height, the final turn must not be any closer than your chosen point. This system helps to prevent you from getting too close for a normal approach. Only come closer if you are anxious, because the base leg is going to be rather low.

The base leg

The secret is to have sufficient height and to get the angle to the field about right before turning onto the base leg. If the angle is too steep, and you arrive too close, it will mean having a very short base leg and no time for adjustments by moving in or out and using the airbrakes. By the time that you turn onto the base leg you need your chosen speed and the airbrakes unlocked ready for use.

Unless you are in the habit of using the airbrakes on the base leg, you will tend to hesitate about using them and will end up too high. With every approach, try to get into the habit of thinking ahead about the height of the final turn and to become familiar with the idea of using the airbrakes to bring you down so that the final turn is not too high.

Experience shows that even after doing this, pilots tend to overshoot through being rather too high. This is because it is much more difficult to recognise being too high than being a little on the low side. For this reason I always emphasise that if, as you complete the final turn, you are happy that you have got the field 'made', you should always open full airbrake for a few moments to check that you would undershoot with that setting. The airbrakes can then be reduced once it is clear that the glider will not overshoot with full airbrake. If full airbrakes are needed for more than a few seconds, and it looks as though they should be kept on, sideslipping should be used to get rid of the excess height so that for the last part of the approach less than full airbrake approach is required. A full airbrake approach is a potential overshoot if the glider flies through any lift.

S-turns

If it becomes obvious during the base leg or final turn that you are far too high to be able to get down in the chosen field, it is often possible to make an S-turn to use up some of the height. However, effective S-turns are not easy to do, and they need to be practised if they are not to end up in dangerously steep turns or in bringing the final turn too close to the field.

Often they cannot be practised on the home site because they are not acceptable on a busy airfield. However, they can be demonstrated and tried at height to get the idea and to see the problems which can arise if they are not neatly executed. They are a sign of poor planning and of not thinking sufficiently far ahead, but they can be useful as an option, just as sideslipping is an extra skill which can prevent a serious overshoot and a broken glider.

Beware of 'suckers' gaps

Be very cautious about approaching through a gap in a row of trees. If trees are alongside a road they are likely to conceal telephone or power wires, making it dangerous to go between them. Look carefully for single wires leading off the main lines and running across the fields to individual cottages. Unless you can spot all the poles, single wires will be very difficult to see.

In Australia single wires are called SWER (Single Wire, Earth Return) lines.

They comprise a single wire strung across from the main power wires to the farms or homesteads. They are often hung between trees or old posts a long way apart, and they are extremely difficult to see. The only real clue to spotting them is that every homestead has electricity and if you see the buildings, you must find the wires going to them before making an approach.

I was amazed to discover that pilots sometimes forget the large wing-span of their glider and risk touching a wing-tip on one side when flying through a gap. It seems as though the pilot is only worrying about his cockpit getting through and forgets the wings.

Experience in many hundreds of practise field selections and approaches in a motor glider show the most common faults to be: leaving the choice of field far too late, and poor planning and judgement of the circuit and approach.

Practising in a motor glider with a knowledgeable and competent cross-country pilot is the best way to gain experience quickly at both selecting and field landing procedures. There is no substitute for this kind of training.

Summary

The following are some of the most common errors, together with suggestions on how a pilot can avoid them and what an instructor can do to help.

Failure to accept that a field landing is necessary
Be realistic about the chances of finding lift low down. Ask yourself, 'How often can I "get away" from below 800 feet when the soaring conditions have already deteriorated'. Always say to yourself, 'I will select a field just in case I don't find lift.'

Failure to keep wind direction in mind and to orientate
This is largely a matter of forming the habit of noting the wind from smoke or some other indication and of orientating yourself relative to the sun or an obvious feature such as a coast line, i.e. remember something along the lines of 'Into wind is into sun', or say to yourself, 'I must land with the sun over my left shoulder', etc. If you are scratching in weak lift, you may be able to see which way you have drifted after a few circles. Near the coast, watch for large wind changes due to sea breezes. Flying through the sea breeze front without realising it is a common cause of inadvertently landing downwind and ending up in a hedge.

Late choice of field
Don't keep putting off the choice. Few fields are perfect and all you need is a good sized field with a level or uphill gradient and a good surface. You know that it is extremely risky to leave the choice late and that, at the very latest, you must be organised in time to have a good look at the proposed field and to get into a good position for a proper base leg.

Poor selection
Practice is the only solution. During local soaring, select good-looking fields, and then go and have a look at them after the flight to see what they are really

like. Travelling by road or train, try to make a quick choice and evaluation of the nearby fields.

In the air, look right round as you make a quick circle. This way, you will view a large number of fields. Don't look immediately below because you won't be able to see the slopes. If all four of the fields below are poor, it is very demoralising. Discard difficult fields straight away. Think systematically for size, slope, surface, colour and obstructions.

Failure to recognise slopes until committed to landing

Make a point of looking for the lay of the surrounding countryside. River valleys and railway lines are usually fairly level, with the ground sloping down to the rivers. Usually one side of the river will present all uphill into-wind slopes, while the other side can be dismissed as being unsuitable except when landing parallel to the river.

Keep well away so that you can see slopes properly and, when possible, view the field from at least two sides. By choosing an uphill slope, at least you know that it will not be a downhill one! Slopes which are visible from a thousand feet looking straight down from above are far too steep for an easy or safe landing. Flat fields need to be larger as they may turn out to have slight downhill slopes.

Bad planning; failure to plan at all

This is one of the most dangerous faults and requires extra training to combat it. More experience is needed at problem circuits and joining from different unconventional positions, such as starting directly overhead, or just downwind of the site.

Keeping far too close to the field

Re-learn to judge the 20-to-30° angles for circuit planning. Never get within 45° of the field unless you are running out of height. Choose a ground mark for the position of the final turn about an average field length back.

Failure to fly accurately when under pressure

More flying experience, together with more situations training, is needed. Lack of flying experience leads to overloading and panic when under extra pressure. This can result in dangerously inaccurate flying.

Failure to try to recognise if the height is excessive at the start of the base leg

This is caused by poor basic training and not thinking ahead. Many inexperienced pilots do not even consider what the situation is going to be and only think about what is happening at that moment. *Think ahead!* Do more circuit planning flights with the last five hundred feet of the altimeter covered and try to guess ahead of time what the height and position will be (not in feet, but in terms of very high, about right, or rather low).

Failure to use airbrakes or to move back further when necessary during the base leg

Many pilots consider, quite wrongly, that it shows lack or judgement to use airbrakes on the base leg. If you have been thinking this way, practise having height in hand and using the airbrakes on the base leg.

The instructor should encourage the pilot to talk through his thoughts aloud to find out whether not using the airbrakes is caused by failing to realise the glider is too high or by not being quick enough to decide and act.

Serious misjudgement of heights during the circuit

Blank off the last 500 feet on the altimeter and practise guessing heights below 600 feet. Height judgement above that height is not essential and is largely guesswork. Instructors should encourage the use of comparison for judging low heights so that the pilot is more confident about recognising when he is low. Lack of confidence often results in the pilot playing it safe with extra height, instead of making an effort to rely on his own judgement.

Failure to recognise when too high after the final turn

Introduce opening full airbrakes after the final turn to check the situation (unless obviously low). Pilots should be encouraged to make an assessment during the final turn of how much airbrake they will need as they start to straighten up for the final approach, instead of waiting until the turn is completed at which point it is already too late. The use of the airbrakes during the final turn should be discussed and pilots should be encouraged to try it if they are too high. It should be emphasised that there is no reason to discourage any but the most inexperienced solo pilots from opening the airbrakes in the final turn, provided the glider is not already low (or slow).

Inability to sideslip effectively with full airbrake on the final approach

Sideslipping takes skill and practice. Plenty of dual instruction is needed to be safe, and then it requires constant practice on high approaches to be able to sideslip effectively.

Failure to recognise undershooting and to close airbrakes in time to prevent an undershoot

Instructors should demonstrate correct procedure again and pilots should practise aiming point technique. Flying dual, practise landings just beyond an obvious mark on the ground by manipulating airbrakes. Self-criticism is needed if any landing is even a yard short of the chosen spot.

Failure to allow sufficient speed for uphill slope

Ideally, have dual landing practice on uphill slopes. Otherwise, re-brief or think over all the aspects of misjudgements on slopes and the reasons for needing extra speed.

Failure to make a good hold off and landing because of eagerness to get down

Although often not practical, try to get dual experience at sorting out the landing after low final turns or upset approaches. It is important to be able to recover composure after stress, to forget the low turn, and to get on with making a good landing. Practise opening more airbrake during the hold off as a means of getting the glider down fully held off, but without such a long float. Being able to land safely in fields should be one of the ultimate aims in glider pilot training and it should not be left to the pilot to decide for himself when he is competent to fly across country.

Some thoughts on aerotowing accidents

Aerotow problems usually arise because the pilot ignores the possibility of something going wrong and is caught by surprise. Crossing the boundary, I always check the airspeed because I know that above 60 knots, if necessary, I can make a well banked turn of up to 180°, with virtually no loss of height and return for a downwind landing. This possibility is worth suggesting to more experienced pilots, but, of course, is not suitable for a beginner.

At lower speeds, unless there is plenty of height, a landing must be made somewhere ahead. Certainly during the first five hundred feet or so the pilot should be aware of possible fields ahead.

After a launch failure of any kind above two or three hundred feet, once the speed has been checked, it is best to turn off 90° or so in order to avoid going further from the field. In this position, the glider is on a base leg for any available field upwind and it is easy to look back and decide whether returning to the field is practical. On a normal tow, except for very low performance machines, the climbing angle of the towplane and glider is much steeper than the glider's gliding angle when flying downwind. So, in theory, the glider should be within easy reach of the gliding site. However, in turbulent and windy conditions it is always better to play safe and land into wind in another field, rather than to make a downwind landing.

Downwind landings

Every glider pilot should make at least one downwind landing during training in order to realise that there is no particular problem in making a safe landing as long as the wind is not very strong. In some circumstances it may be the best thing to do.

I once witnessed an incident that could so easily have been avoided if the pilot had considered a downwind landing as a possible option. He had never done one and always thought it a dangerous manoeuvre to execute. On this day he was gliding home to our airfield and only just made it back with less than a hundred feet as he arrived flying downwind over the boundry. Instead of carrying on and making the downwind landing without incident, he flew on to give himself room to land and then tried to turn around into wind for the landing. He was so low that a wing-tip touched the ground, causing a ground loop. He could so easily have hurt himself or irreparably damaged the glider but, in fact, he was very lucky and did surprisingly little damage.

It is important to realise that there is no particular danger in downwind landings on an airfield, apart from the possibility of floating too far and overshooting into the far boundary. This makes it important to use the airbrakes to ensure that you cross the upwind boundary very low as though you were attempting to land in the first part of the field. The other essential is to land well clear of any obstructions, because a wing can so easily go down and cause a bad swing as you slow down after landing.

The main point to remember on the tow is to hold position accurately. This means concentrating on the tow and only taking your eyes off the towplane for a brief moment. Rope breaks usually occur through inattention and getting badly out of position. They are probably almost as rare as engine failures, but there is one important difference. With a rope break, the climb out is at the normal towing speed when the rope breaks, whereas when engine problems occur the tow is usually slow and the climb is far worse than normal. If the rope breaks, the take off field should be within easy reach for a downwind landing, whereas a problem with the towplane's engine usually means a field landing is almost inevitable.

Towplane upsets

Over the years there have been a number of fatal towplane accidents caused by gliders getting too high and jerking the towplane into a steep dive. Although considerable effort has been made to develop an automatic release for the towplane, the problems are not as simple as they might at first seem and so far no really satisfactory technical answer has been found. Unfortunately, these accidents still occur from time to time.

Low tow position
The risk can be reduced by flying in the low tow position below the wake, but it still has some disadvantages and towing in this position has not been generally adopted in Europe or elsewhere. However, it is frequently used for long distance tows, because there is less of a tendency to get a slack rope during level flight in the low tow position.

In Australia, all launching is done this way, and for a time it was common in the U.S.A. The disadvantages, however, of the low tow position are as follows.

The glider must be flown through the wake in the turbulent air near the ground. (Some people think that this might be dangerous for inexperienced students, but it does not seem to cause any particular problems in Australia.)

It is impossible to watch the towplane and the ground ahead during the climb out so that in the event of a launch failure the glider pilot has to look for a field, whereas in the normal tow position he has a good view of the fields ahead all the time. There is also the additional hazard that if the rope breaks at the towplane end, it may fall over the glider, causing damage.

Normal tow position
Of course, there are also disadvantages in using the normal, high tow position and it is a matter of opinion which is best or easiest. Losing sight of the tow plane for even a second can be lethal and the glider pilot must always release immediately if this happens.

In one accident I witnessed, the take off was being made towards the glare of the sun. The glider pilot was dazzled for a moment and lost sight of the tug. He failed to release in time to prevent the towplane from being tipped over into the ground.

There are various contributory factors which can lead to a towplane 'upset' when towing in the normal (high) tow position. Many modern machines are not fitted with a nose release hook for aerotowing, but with one designed to be suitable for both wire and aerotow launches. With these, any jerk or sudden gust tends to result in a nose-up pitching movement, similar to the start of a winch launch. Unless this is quickly controlled, in a few seconds the glider can be far too high above the towplane.

The effect is accentuated if the c.g. is near the aft limit and, in some cases, it is doubtful whether there is sufficient elevator authority to stop the pitching once it has gone beyond the early stages. The only safeguard is to maintain the correct position carefully and to release at once if the glider is beginning to get too high in relation to the towplane.

A number of accidents and incidents have occurred with gliders such as the Olympia 463, K6 and K18, flown by relatively inexperienced pilots. These machines have lower stick forces than most training two-seaters and are not generally fitted with a nose hook for aerotowing. They have a marked tendency to zoom up into a steep climbing attitude if they are allowed to do so. Moreover, they are often flown by early solo pilots who do not have much experience of flying them or of solo aerotowing.

In an effort to prevent this kind of accident (which is almost always fatal for the tow pilot), the emphasis has been for pilots to keep their glider very low just after leaving the ground. It is possible that this has contributed to the risk of the glider zooming too high just after take off.

In windy weather, the effects of the wind gradient near the ground accentuate any movement up or down of the towplane and glider. If the towplane gains speed by flying close to the ground, when it noses up to start climbing, the effect of the wind gradient accentuates the climb so that the glider may easily be left flying close to the ground, in or near the wake and below the tug. Then, when the glider pilot recognises he is far too low, any quick movement to regain position takes the glider up through the same wind gradient, causing a sudden surge of speed and producing an unexpected and possibly uncontrollable gain of height. At the same time, the extra load in the tow rope accentuates the nose-up pitching movement on the glider (as in a winch launch). This slows down the towplane, leaving it at low speed below the glider and having its tail pulled up out of control.

Although it is vital not to get too high, there is no advantage trying to fly very close to the ground, except perhaps when taking off from a very short field. It is much safer to fly at five or even ten feet until the towplane leaves the ground. This makes it much easier to avoid pitching oscillations. It also makes it possible to watch the towplane instead of the ground and, as on a landing, looking well ahead reduces the tendency to over-control.

It is the speed with which the situation develops that causes the problem. Usually the tow pilot receives no warning of the danger. One moment the tow is quite normal and the next, his aircraft is diving vertically into the ground. So he has little or no time to release the glider, or to recover from the dive unless the upset occurs above about 500 feet, and then only if the rope breaks or the glider releases.

How can we help to prevent this kind of accident?

For a start, novice pilots should have some experience of aerotowing in single-seaters before converting to types which are not fitted with a nose hook, and gliders intended for inexperienced pilots should always be manufactured with a nose hook for aerotowing.

It is wise for inexperienced pilots to carry additional ballast to bring the c.g. well forward, making the glider more stable and increasing the stick forces. The nose heaviness will also provide additional down elevator power to help control any nose-up pitching tendencies.

The pilot must be vigilant on every aerotow and must realise the importance of being prepared to release at any point on the climb out should his glider get badly out of position. The pilot's left hand should certainly be near the release toggle all the time until the glider is at least 500 or 600 feet up. Pilots should also be briefed about the dangers of raising the undercarriage, closing the canopy window or fiddling with anything in the cockpit in case they are momentarily distracted or jerk the stick unintentionally during the initial climb out.

From the start, the need to release immediately if for any reason they lose sight of the towplane must be impressed on the students. The tow pilot can help by allowing his aircraft to climb away, gaining speed rather than holding it down close to the ground. Gradual changes of attitude make it easier for the glider pilot to follow in position behind the tow plane.

But it is the glider pilot who literally has the life of the tow pilot in his hands. Remember, do not hold the glider down too close to the ground, 5 to 10 feet is safer. Be ready to ease up to stay in position as the tug starts to climb. If you get out of position and if you find yourself too low, move up slowly in small steps, checking the movement every few feet. Don't try to move to the correct position too quickly. It is only rapid movements up that become uncontrollable. Release immediately if the towplane goes out of sight, or you become very badly out of position. Just concentrate on flying the tow smoothly and accurately and don't let yourself be distracted for a moment.

Low 'g' sensitivity

Everyone is aware of the sensation experienced in a lift as it starts to descend, and in a car when it goes over a humped-back bridge. On the ground the feeling only lasts a fraction of a second, but it can be more severe and prolonged during flight. Since we live at 1g for virtually all of our lives, the feeling of even slightly reduced 'g' is unusual and, for many people, alarming (it can be associated with nightmare dreams of falling). These are the sensations of reduced gravity or low 'g'.

Acclimatisation

The majority of students become acclimatised to these sensations after a few flights, but every instructor is aware that some students are particularly sensitive to these feelings and can develop a total abhorrence of stalling and pitching manoeuvres. Many give up flying altogether because of this. Others persuade their instructors to do the very minimum necessary and state categorically that they hate stalls. I often wonder whether these pilots would react safely and effectively if they suddenly got their aircraft into a stalling situation.

Most experienced pilots and instructors don't remember their own early flights and don't realise that sensations which cause discomfort on a first flight will not even be noticed by the hardened pilot or instructor.

At first, almost everyone dislikes the sensation of reduced 'g'. It is normal for this sensitivity to remain for a few flights and then gradually to disappear. After a little more flying experience, beginners' eyes interpret what is happening to the aircraft and the alarm signal is no longer sent on to the brain. For example, as the stick is moved forwards a little, the eyes see the nose of the glider moving down, and the brain expects the sensation and understands what is happening. As there is no cause for alarm, the brain suppresses the sensation at source. This is another reason to start off any flying training by emphasising visual references instead of the instruments.

If the reduced 'g' occurs because the air is turbulent, there is no visual sign of what is causing the sensation. This makes it more alarming for the beginner who gets no warning, just a horrible sinking feeling. After more flying the beginner will learn to recognise and accept that he need not worry about the .effects of these bumps. It is obviously helpful to make the first flights in smooth weather, with a clear horizon.

Because of the connection between vision and sensations, the latter are greatly amplified when visibility is poor, or when the pilot is looking in the cockpit, has no visual reference and is unaware of the exact movements of the aircraft. This is very noticeable with experienced pilots flying into cloud without the help of the instruments. After a very short time their sensations are heightened and they become worried. For this reason, in gliders it is important to avoid watching the instruments during nose-down pitching manoeuvres such as stall recoveries and when recovering into normal flight following a cable break during a steep winch launch.

Instinctive reactions to low 'g'

Some pilots are completely incapacitated by even gentle nose-down pitching movements. Less affected people will move their head back and push forwards on the stick. This response of putting the hands out and throwing the head back is certainly not a reaction learned during flying training. It is a very natural and fundamental protective instinct; babies respond in this manner if they are allowed to fall. In the same way, if an adult slips and is going to fall, his hands go out to stop himself hitting his face.

I have noticed the same response with sensitive people on their very first flight when they are trying out the elevator. As they move the stick forwards a small amount, causing only the slightest reduction in 'g', their response to the resulting sensation is almost always to move even further forwards, making the sensation worse. This is, of course, totally irrational. If doing one thing with a control gives you an unpleasant feeling, the normal reaction would be to stop doing it, or to move the control back in the other direction.

One possible theory about why some people are much more affected than others is that they may have had traumatic experiences of falling as a baby or a young child, and that this has further re-inforced their instinctive behaviour.

Why are the effects of these responses so much less noticeable in powered machines? Probably because of the very much greater stick forces and lower rates of pitch occurring in most light aircraft. These make it far less likely that they will dive vertically for hundreds of feet if the pilot pushes forwards on the stick. Gliders have very low stick forces and the lower flying speeds give them a very high rate of pitch.

Associating low 'g' with stalling

My experience with glider pilots has made me aware of many aspects of low 'g' sensitivity. Some survivors from 'dive-in' accidents have confirmed that they knew it was useless to try to pull out of the dive while they could 'feel' the glider was still stalled. This led me to think that some students may equate the feeling of low 'g' with the glider being stalled. If this happens, a pilot may mistake pitching or sinking rapidly in turbulence as an indication that the aircraft has stalled. In executing what would be a normal stall recovery, any movement forwards will, or course, increase the pitching, thereby making the sensation more vivid and encouraging the pilot to think that the aircraft is not recovering. This is a sure recipe for panic and will be fatal unless there is plenty of height.

I was once with a student who responded with a stall recovery when the glider hit some turbulence on the final approach. The glider dived almost vertically and I was just in time to pull back on the stick so that we hit the ground in a level attitude without any damage.

At least one double fatality has been caused in this way. It is obviously crucial that all instructors are aware of any student who has this problem, since it is so easy to be caught out, like I was. Since then, my instruction on stalls and recoveries has been modified to emphasise from the start that there is no sensation, only symptoms, of stalling.

Immediately after the first introduction to gentle straight stalls I demonstrate that in normal flight even a small movement forward results in the same sensation, the feeling of reduced 'g'. I take good care to emphasise that the sensation as we stall and recover is not a symptom and that it can occur in normal flight and in some cases when the aircraft flies through turbulence.

Hypersensitivity

Perhaps most interesting, but most dangerous, are the very small minority of students who are really chronically affected by this sensation. (At Lasham I estimated about 1 in 400 people making their first glider flights were very sensitive to low 'g'.) Fortunately, most of them try one flight and dislike it so much that they avoid flying again. To a few, overcoming their fears of flying becomes a challange.

I have flown with a number of people who, with the slightest lowering of the nose or the gentlest stall, look as though they are having an epileptic fit. They become quite unconscious of what they are doing for a few seconds, and yet insist that they want to carry on and learn to fly. With very gradual familiarisation training spread over many months of flying, some of these students have been completely cured. But if they are not spotted early in their training, they can be a real menace to themselves and to their instructors. These are the students who really do freeze on the controls and, with the stick held firmly forward, the instructor has to be quick and strong to prevent an accident.

The 'cure' is largely a matter of acclimatisation and a simple but thorough explanation of why the aircraft stalls and what causes the sensation. From then on the stall training must be continued, with a little done on every flight. The student must understand that nobody likes the reduced 'g' sensation at first, but that individuals differ in their reactions to it. Some are scarcely affected, whereas others need longer training to overcome their natural reactions. Young and old people may be affected and there seems to be no way of knowing who will have this kind of problem.

Experience has shown, however, that often it is the young and able students who are most likely to go undetected and have a low 'g' accident. I believe that this is because they do everything so well that they do not get excessive pitching movements in their training stall recoveries. As a result, they seldom experience much, if any, reduction in 'g'. Because they appear reasonably proficient, the instructors tend to give less practice to them than to the other students. It may be some months or even years later when, for the first time they over-correct from a practice stall, they experience a substantial reduction in 'g' loading. Then, if they have learned to associate the feeling with stalling, they will move forwards on the stick, making what they remember to be a normal stall recovery. This makes the sensation much worse and, believing the aircraft is still stalled in spite of their recovery action, they are liable to panic and become unable to think or act in time to avoid diving into the ground.

'g'-related landing accidents

There are other situations involving reduced 'g' which can be incapacitating. Reports about light aircraft landing accidents often say that the aircraft bounced or ballooned, pitched nose-down and then flew into the runway in a series of worsening crashes, smashing the nose gear and engine. Certainly, a low 'g' sensitive person is liable to become completely incapable of further thought once the aircraft pitches nose-down the first time. These pilots invariably demonstrate the basic response of pushing forwards on the stick and keeping it there.

The same kind of accident used to be common with gliders, and the pilots could never remember anything after the first bounce. They have become less common since the fully held-off landings have been taught. It is now likely that a student will experience ballooning a number of times while learning and will have learned to avoid moving forwards on the stick automatically.

In the past, many students were so petrified about stalling that they could not be persuaded to hold off properly for the landing. They would try to avoid a stalled situation near the ground by pushing forwards if the aircraft bounced. A person who is scared of ballooning will nearly always fly the aircraft onto the ground instead of making well held-off landings. This problem is accentuated by pilots being very tense and mis-timing the stick movements.

It is not unknown for quite experienced power pilots to be very sensitive to low 'g'. I remember an American pilot with about 200 hours, a twin-engine Commercial and full Instrument Rating who visited us some years ago. On his site check our instructor found he was severely affected by reduced 'g', although he had about 60 hours' solo gliding. When he was asked to do a stall, he became panic-stricken as the glider stalled, and it was obviously unsafe to allow him to go solo. He stayed the week and was given lots of extra training, but he was still unsafe when he returned to the USA. Although it may not have been related, within a month he had crashed on a bad weather approach, killing himself and his friend. Certainly, just a little low 'g' on the approach would have made things very difficult for him and I often wonder exactly what happened.

Surprisingly, there is usually less reduction in 'g' during an incipient spin or full spin than in a straight stall and, apart from the initial apprehension, these manoeuvres affect sensitive people less than normal stall recoveries.

Pilots who are frightened or apprehensive about stalling have not been properly trained and could be a risk to themselves and their passengers if they obtain their licence without overcoming their problem. So, every instructor has a special responsibility towards such people.

Pilots learning to fly the very docile 3-axis control microlight aircraft are also at risk. These all fly at similar speeds and have rather light stick forces like a glider. On the weight shift types it is difficult to give the student experience at low 'g' manoeuvres and the pilots may be badly affected without it becoming obvious. Fortunately, with weight shift, moving forwards causes a nose-up rather than a nose-down effect so that at least it does not accentuate the pitching movement and make the sensation worse.

I find it a little horrifying to think that some Commercial pilots flying large numbers of passengers may have had very little exposure to reduced 'g'. Few have gone through aerobatic training, and the modern tendency is to be happy with a few hours of stall avoidance training and little, if any, spinning.

It is even possible that some might be low 'g' sensitive and be at risk if a low 'g' situation suddenly occurs. What could happen if, for example, another pilot raised the leading edge flaps of a large aircraft by mistake? This would result in a sudden high rate of sink, with no obvious visual cause. A sensitive pilot could then be so confused that he would be unable to respond logically to the situation, particularly if it happened at night or in cloud.

Pre-solo testing

Most gliding instructors are aware of these probems and watch out for them in their students. Instructors should test every student before allowing them to go solo to make quite sure that they are not seriously affected by reduced 'g'. This does not mean pitching violently to get weightlessness or negative 'g'. The student can be asked to pitch nose-down gently from level flight and from diving and climbing attitudes. Most pilots who are sensitive find themselves incapable of doing this exercise and their reactions are obvious. In such instances they would need more training until an unexpected sensation does not cause a bad reaction. Perhaps this test should be used for all pilots, regardless of what aircraft they are learning on?

This is not the whole story about accidents associated with low 'g' sensations. Because I became aware of the problems when I first came into gliding, I wrote a booklet on the subject, called *Sub-Gravity Sensations and Gliding Accidents* (available from the BGA in the UK and SSA in the USA). Surprising though it may seem, although it is now well established that this is a serious problem with gliding, it is almost unknown in power flying circles or in the Air Force and it is taking many years to convince authorities. It is still probably one of the main causes of fatal gliding accidents all over the world.

Cloud flying

Fools rush in where Angels fear to tread

It is alarming to hear how many relatively inexperienced pilots seem completely unaware of the risks they take when pitting their skills against the forces of nature. They often think that if their flying is good enough, it is safe for them to press on in any weather conditions.

The performance of modern gliders makes it much easier and more likely for a pilot to fly himself into a potential death trap unless he uses his imagination or has already learned to have a healthy respect for the elements. The result has been a noticeable increase in the number of pilots who suddenly find themselves faced with a situation far beyond their control, usually a situation that they had not even considered at the start of the flight.

In most respects, using wave lift is far safer than cloud flying for attempts at Gold and Diamond heights. However, wave flying has its own problems which a pilot must understand and recognise if such flights are to be made safely. Similarly, if you are going to fly in a cloud, it is important to understand the possible hazards in order to avoid them.

Cloud flying, particularly in shower clouds, can be quite a dangerous pastime and on many days it would be totally irresponsible to risk losing a club glider by attempting to climb a large cloud.

Competence

The first essentials for any cloud flying in large cumulus are that the glider must be properly equipped for serious flying, and the pilot must be competent and experienced enough at instrument flying to be able to regain control from any attitude without having to use the airbrakes.

Because of the risk of a failure of the battery-operated Artificial Horizons, I always insist that pilots are competent to fly on the Turn and Slip Indicator before even trying a Horizon. Many pilots find that they manage safely on their first few short cloud climbs but that they soon get tired and lose their concentration. It is after they have lost control for the second or third time that the real difficulties appear. One or two short climbs in cloud do not prove the ability of a pilot to cope with the required longer periods of concentration and more varied conditions in larger clouds.

However, there are a number of risks to be considered by even the most competent pilot, and these are outside the pilot's control once the cloud climb has been started.

Getting lost

It is impossible for any glider pilot to make a high cloud climb and to be sure of his position. For this reason it is not acceptable to make climbs where the glider could possibly drift into Controlled Airspace. Unless frequent pin points can be obtained during the descent, errors in position of 20 miles or more can easily occur, and this factor alone limits cloud flying to days on which large clouds are isolated so that there are clear areas between them.

Icing

If the glider gets wet before taking off for a high climb, the airbrakes may freeze up and become unusable. This makes it vital for the pilot to be able to manage any loss of control due to stalling or spiralling without using them. Severe icing seems rare, but even slight jamming of the controls should be treated as a serious warning to leave the cloud immediately before all control is lost. Modern machines are blessed with a minimum of tail area and even a small coating on the leading edge of the tailplane may cause uncontrollable stability problems. Probably for this reason most of the glass fibre gliders are not cleared by the manufacturers for cloud flying.

Hail

Flying into hail or very heavy rain deliberately in search of lift is also an unjustifiable risk. Even in England, half-inch diameter hail stones are not unknown, and these will smash canopies and ruin the surfaces, causing very expensive damage and making it a matter of luck to get out of the area and down safely.

Lightning

In the past it was thought that the chance of having a glider struck by lightning in cloud was negligible. However, there is now ample evidence to show that this was an over-optimistic view. With gliders which climbed above 15,000 feet in cloud in the early 1960s, there was approximately one serious strike or electrical damage for every ten flights. In those days quite a number of Diamond heights were attempted in large shower clouds and cumulo nimbus, whereas very few are flown today because of the unacceptable risks involved. After an accident in which a pilot was killed by a strike, the remains of the aircraft showed the true potential power of nature. The main spars were burnt where the control cables had been melted away. It was obvious from this that in going into storms we were quite literally playing with fire.

The effects of electrical discharges on glass fibre and carbon fibre structures are uncertain, but it is clear that any moisture in the material would be turned to steam by a flash and would certainly cause delamination and very expensive damage. Clearly, therefore, we should take heed of these warnings and never enter clouds which are actively electric.

Hypoxia

The only safe policy is to have oxygen equipment available and to insist on its use for any attempts at Gold or Diamond Heights. At 15,000 feet, no enthusiastic pilot who is already suffering from the effects of lack of oxygen will be able to make the sensible decision to leave strong lift. Furthermore, people vary in their tolerance from day to day, and it is not safe to assume that because you have been to 15,000 feet or so without oxygen before, you will be able to do it again. The doctors tell us that elderly pilots and pilots who smoke should be aware that their tolerance to a shortage of oxygen is lower than younger people's or that of non-smokers. So, to be safe it would be wise to use it at any time flying above 10,000 feet.

There is a very real risk that even at 15,000 feet the pilot may become unconscious, or at least incapable, from the combination of cold and lack of oxygen. If the flight gets really 'exciting', there is also the possibility the pilot will become so frightened that he will begin to hyperventilate, and this can bring on hypoxia and unconsciousness very quickly.

Landing

In ideal weather conditions a field landing should present no difficulties and even in poor visibility, with a known wind direction, the risks are acceptable. But landing safely in torrential rain, with a squally and unpredictable wind, can only be a matter of luck for the most skilled pilot. If the cloud base is low, there is bound to be a risk of coming out under the cloud and being unable to reach an area where it is not raining. For a good chance of a safe landing, the ground must be seen from at least a thousand feet so that there is time to select a field and assess the wind. In sinking air even this would not be enough to allow for much choice and, of course, it assumes that the descent will be made over open countryside and not amongst hills or moorland. When the weather is showery, there is always a grave risk of the cloud base lowering to only a few hundred feet, and this can happen within minutes of the rain starting to fall.

Beware of snow showers, because they can reduce visibility to a few yards, making a safe landing impossible.

Common sense rules for cloud flying

1 Pilots should have experience at flying on the Turn and Slip indicator before using an Artificial Horizon, so that they can manage if the Horizon topples or becomes unusable.

2 These instruments should be switched on and checked before reaching cloud base.

3 Never enter cloud unless you are sure of your present position and are certain that there is no risk of drifting into Controlled Airspace.

4 The pilot's left hand should be on the airbrake lever during any climb in

cloud, ready to pull and open the airbrakes if the speed increases by more than 15 knots or so above normal.

5 Inexperienced pilots should only try cloud flying on days when there is no risk of large clouds developing, i.e. when there is an inversion preventing large vertical development.

Attempts at Gold Height (3000 metres gain of height)

1 The clouds must be sufficiently isolated to ensure that clear air can be found by flying out of the lift.

2 Check the forecast for risk of storms and do not enter large clouds if the freezing level is below 10,000 feet. A high freezing level greatly reduces the risk of shower developing.

3 The main cloud base should be at least 2000 feet above the highest ground in the region, the freezing level must be high and the visibility should be good.

4 If you are trying to go high, get on to oxygen and check it is flowing correctly before you need it.

5 If the glider does not have oxygen equipment, make a move to leave the cloud well below oxygen height.

SECTION 2

Moving on to other types of glider

One of the greatest hazards to a pilot can be his lack of current flying practice. In this section are described ways of getting back into practice and of improving flying skills by making better use of the time in the air.

Flying a new type of glider is always fun, but it worries many inexperienced pilots: there is always an extra element of risk if an unexpected situation occurs on the first flight in an unfamiliar machine. I have included help for those pilots trying out different gliders, and have suggested how to explore the handling of a new machine and how to minimise risks.

Flaps are described in detail for the many pilots who do not fully understand how to make the best use of them, and who may be nervous about their first flights in a flapped machine.

Another common cause of accidents is the inexperienced pilot who buys a glider which is not suited to his skill and experience. There are notes for pilots considering becoming private owners and on the types of glass fibre gliders which are suitable for early solo pilots.

Polishing your flying

During training, your instructor makes you practise and insists that you try to fly more accurately and efficiently all the time. But when you are a solo pilot, it is surprisingly easy to fly without any particular aim in mind, apart from trying to stay up! You need to make a point of setting yourself tasks to do in order to keep on top line and to improve your flying.

Here are some suggestions on things to practise and to try out whenever you have some height and time to spare, rather than just flying up, round and down as so many pilots usually do.

Getting back into practice

Whereas the inexperienced glider pilot needs to fly at least once a month to be safe, more experienced pilots can go much longer without always becoming badly out of practice. However, there is no doubt that we all fly better if we fly regularly and it is a good policy to fly whenever you have the opportunity. In some countries if you miss a chance to fly it may be weeks before the weather allows you another opportunity.

Every year at the start of the soaring weather we have what is sometimes known as the 'silly season'. This is when the pilots who have been hibernating during the winter months get their gliders out and start flying again. The gliding is often spectacular: poor landings, low final turns and generally sloppy flying. At many clubs it is compulsory for everyone to have at least one dual flight at the beginning of the season before flying solo again. Certainly, an emergency on the first flight after a long lay off provides the potential for an incident.

If you are out of practice, why not take a ride or two with an instructor and ask him to criticise your flying? This is a very quick way to get your hand in and learn what you need to practise.

Landings

You get a practice landing on every flight, but do you learn anything from it? If it is the first flight of the day for you, then it should always be the aim to make it an accurate spot landing. The first flight you make on any day is really the only one where your judgement is put to the test. On the following flights you position the final turn and approach relative to where you made the last one, i.e. if you kept too close and landed rather far into the field on the first landing, you will move back more on the next, remembering the positioning of the previous flight.

Of course, with field landings, every landing is a 'first time' and needs to be exactly right. You always hope that you will be able to select a large, easy field, but that may not be possible. Your very first field landing could even turn out to be the most difficult field of your whole gliding career.

Much depends on the wind strength as to how accurately it is possible to land. But even in the least conducive conditions, with no wind, you should be able make a properly held-off touch down within about two fuselage lengths of your chosen spot.

After the first landing, the things to practise are more variations in the approaches and landings, trying some steep and some shallow, but attempting to touch down accurately on the chosen spot. Always analyse how you could have improved your approach and landing and why you did not manage to touch down nearer to the spot.

With students and inexperienced pilots, it is usual to discourage them from making adjustments on the airbrakes during the hold off, apart from reducing the amount of airbrake if it is necessary to float to land further up the field. This helps stress the need to get the whole approach right if the landings are to be reasonably accurate.

However, as pilots become more confident about their landings, it is very important for them to develop the skills needed to co-ordinate the stick and airbrake during the final hold off, so that an even more accurate touch down can be made.

Many pilots undershoot or overshoot their chosen spot by large margins. Often they will comment that they did it deliberately, for some poor reason or other, or say that they could, of course, have touched down earlier if they had really tried. Usually they really believe this and do not accept that they have made a mistake. This is a dangerous way of thinking. You need to know how consistently and how accurately you can land; be honest with yourself and accept your limitations.

Whereas there is a definite minimum speed for rounding out with full airbrake, once the glider is in level flight close to the ground, with the right technique the airbrakes can be opened fully at much lower speeds.

When the airbrakes are opened, some lift is lost so that the glider sinks a few feet very rapidly. In addition, the drag of the airbrakes causes a more rapid deceleration. To prevent a heavy landing as the airbrakes are opened, a backward movement is needed on the stick to increase the wing's angle of attack to maintain the same amount of lift as before. When this is done, the combination of the lift loss and the extra drag result in the glider sinking gently and touching down almost immediately. This makes landing accurately on the spot just a matter of timing the opening of the airbrakes and co-ordinating the elevator movement.

To land on a spot consistently by this method, the round out and early part of the float must be made without too much excess speed and with less than full airbrake. Additional airbrake should be available to make the glider stop floating at the right moment. It is undesirable to finish the approach with very little airbrake, although even this situation, from the point of view of an accurate touch down, is better than full airbrake and too much speed causing the glider to overshoot the point.

Unless the wind is very strong, if it is obvious that you can reach the field, it is useful to open full airbrake for a few seconds immediately after the final turn to check that you can undershoot. It is suprisingly difficult to recognise an overshooting situation until often it is too late to get down without side-slipping and using full airbrake. Obviously if you have any worries about undershooting you should not do this. But you must get the final stages of every approach within the range of the airbrakes so that you have some control to prevent either under or overshooting.

In a field landing it often happens that on the final approach or even during the hold off you realise that the first part of the field is not as smooth as it is further along. Here you will need to reduce the airbrake to continue the float and then, as you get to the better ground, to re-open them to make the landing.

It is not satisfactory or acceptable, especially in a modern glider, to fly onto the ground by easing forwards on the stick. This will cause a bad bounce and balloon if the ground is rough and, combined with the much higher touch down speed, may result in a broken glider. Every landing should be made fully held off to ensure a low touch down speed.

I always think that it is criminal to undershoot the spot with some airbrake still on. It is equivalent to landing on the hedge because you did not close the airbrake, even though you knew that you were likely to hit it.

It is important to practise adjusting the airbrakes during the float and to 'kick' yourself hard if you ever land short of your point with brake still applied. It simply means that you have 'frozen' on the airbrake lever and have undershot when you could have saved the situation. This is the same as 'throttle arm paralysis' on a powered aircraft when the pilot undershoots and crashes his aircraft. He could have pushed the throttle forwards and avoided the accident by using the engine.

It is also worthwhile attempting the occasional no airbrake touch down to get a better idea of how far your glider will float. Be ready to open the airbrakes fully as it touches down to stop any bouncing or a gust lifting the glider into the air again.

Whenever possible, and especially if you are out of practice, choose a completely clear area on the landing ground and remember to prevent the glider weathercocking into wind at the end of the landing run. Landing with obstructions on the upwind side is particularly dangerous and is just the sort of error people tend to make when they haven't flown for a while.

If you are in good practice, it is fun to discover just how accurate you can be with a crosswind landing. Choose a line feature along the landing area, with a mark or line across for the touch down point. With a runway it is often possible to use the centre line and a selected spot. See how close to the spot you can get for a fully held off, no drift landing. Honing your skills like this is very enjoyable and will give you confidence if you ever have to land along a very narrow line such as a pathway.

I used to do this with my more experienced pilots using the Falke motor glider on the runway at Lasham. We took it in turns to see how close we could get. Most of the pilots were unconcerned if they were five feet or more to the side on their first attempts. Then, when I really insisted that they keep right on the centre line, they found they could do it if they tried hard. To achieve crosswind landing exactly on the spot without using the engine and in a strange machine offers a strong challenge even to the most experienced pilot.

Practise side-slipping

Every cross-country pilot should be competent at side-slipping. It is often the only sensible way of getting rid of extra height quickly if you are still tending to overshoot with full airbrake. In fact, it is unlikely that you would ever need to side-slip without full airbrake unless the airbrakes became frozen or jammed.

It is an important skill because even experienced pilots do occasionally make approaches which are far too high and which can be redeemed if they can side-slip quickly and accurately. Being able to side-slip, therefore, is a useful safety valve and has prevented many a nasty accident.

However, it cannot be denied that incompetent side-slipping and side-slipping close to the ground can cause accidents. It is a skilled exercise which needs careful instruction and supervision before attempting it on the approach with full airbrake.

Most beginners will find it difficult to apply the opposite rudder, because of their ingrained habit of using the stick and the rudder in co-ordination. It is also surprisingly difficult to hold accurate heading during a full airbrake side-slipping approach. You need to be familiar with the type of glider you are flying because each needs slightly different angles of bank and behaves differently when side-slipping.

Many types have a 'pot' pitot in the nose and the ASI indicates a false reading during side-slip. On some, the rudder overbalances badly and there is a bad trim change. Most only need a small angle of bank, as the rudders on gliders are not very powerful.

Normally you will want to use full side-slip for a few seconds rather than a small amount of slip for a much longer time. Provided that the need of slipping is spotted straight away, it should never be necessary to side-slip close to the ground. The slip is used just to get rid of the excess height so that less than full airbrake is required for the rest of the approach.

With most gliders, the easiest way to enter a side-slip and to hold the heading is to freeze the rudder central while applying the bank. Provided the approach path was correct beforehand, the adverse yaw as the aileron is applied swings the nose off to just about the right point to keep the glider on the correct path. The opposite rudder is then applied to hold that nose direction and to prevent the glider from turning.

Most beginners apply the opposite rudder too harshly and this makes it difficult to hold the bank constant. It is easiest at first to limit the rudder movement to half or three quarters of the full deflection and to start by applying the banking movement just before applying the rudder.

By all means practise side-slipping at height, but don't assume that because you can do it at height you will be able to do it accurately on an approach.

In most cases when it really matters, the glider will already be on the final approach with full airbrake when it becomes apparent that an overshoot is likely. So, this is the situation you must practise and be able to cope with. It is much harder than going into the side-slip from the final turn where it is easy to apply the opposite rudder and straighten up correctly.

Practise by coming round the circuit several hundred feet higher than normal, making the final turn well back but very high. When you are quite certain you will overshoot, even with full airbrake, apply full airbrake and start the final approach, keeping straight. Then, and only then, begin the side-slip and use up sufficient height to be sure that full airbrake will be more than adequate to get down for a spot landing.

With most gliders the attitude for the nose during the slip needs to be no higher than required to maintain the chosen approach speed. You may require a small backward movement in many machines to stop the nose from dropping.

The critical moment is just after the recovery from the side-slip. Most gliders are very reluctant to stall in the slip (try it some time), but if the recovery is made at a low speed, or the pilot forgets to ease forwards to prevent the nose rising during the recovery, there is a very real danger of stalling or of flying rather slowly as the glider encounters the wind gradient.

It is vital to check the actual flying speed the instant the side-slip is over and the ASI is back in normal operation. Usually, if the speed is low, you only have a few seconds either to lower the nose or to reduce the amount of airbrake to avoid a bad landing.

In a field landing, or whenever you are trying for a spot landing (which, of course, should be on every landing), the moment you find that you are having to keep full airbrake on continuously, you should start to side-slip and use up the excess height. Otherwise, any puff of lift on the approach will result in an unredeemable overshoot.

On every local flight that I make in a single-seater glider, I do some side-slipping on the approach to keep in practice. Usually it will be only for a few seconds, but it is the ability to do it instantly on demand that is so important.

You need to know about side-slipping in the aircraft that you fly. It is fun to do and needs to be practised regularly. However, do ask an instructor or a pilot experienced on your type of glider for advice or any adverse behaviour to look out for.

Cross winds

If you are out of practice, make a particular point of watching for cross wind effects on take-off and landing. Always be alert for a bad swing or a wing-tip touching the ground on take off and have your hand near the release, ready. Make a point of trying to keep absolutely straight rather than just correcting a swing when it happens. In this way you will improve your skills and prevent trouble on take off.

Explore the handling in steep turns

Time is always well spent when practising steep turns: not the classroom type where you pick up more speed and then go into the turn, but the sort you might use for thermalling.

If you are going to fly your glider efficiently while turning steeply in thermals with other gliders, you need to know how it will behave at the stall. You will never get the best out of it if you are worrying all the time about stalling.

You need to be able to get into the turn quickly and accurately, and to be flying within a few knots of the pre-stall buffet. On most gliders that will mean less than 50 knots, which you may think rather slow for a steep turn. However, don't look at the speed; try to go by feel and tighten the turn until you feel or hear the airflow start to break away around the wing-root.

Try pulling back harder until you reach the back stop on the stick and see what happens. Does the glider stall or just wallow about buffeting? Attempt this in a gentle turn as well, and in a gentle turn with a little too much rudder. This time it will almost certainly drop a wing, but just easing forwards a little will make a recovery.

Try some very steep turns and then some with about 40° of bank; try reversing the turn quickly, and making little centring moves. Of course, if there are thermals about, do all this in the lift, provided there are no other gliders sharing your thermal!

You should be able to go into turns and make centring movements without having to refer to the slip ball, yaw string, or ASI. Different types of glider behave slightly differently, so explore all the gliders you fly and adapt your flying accordingly.

Aerobatics

Aerobatics are an excellent way of improving your co-ordination and confidence, particularly if you aim to make them accurate and smooth-flowing.

Practising aerobatics and spinning will help to overcome any misgivings you may have about flying in steep turns at low speeds. It is all a matter of acclimatisation . . . and practice.

It is fun to practise pulling up into a climb and trying to establish an accurate, low-speed, steep turn. This can be put to good use in soaring conditions as a means of getting into the lift when cruising at a high speed.

Thermalling

Rapid progress across country is largely a matter of finding and using effectively only the very strongest of thermals.

You must develop the ability to find the centre of an area of lift quickly instead of losing it, and you cannot have too much practice and experience. To do well, you need to become sensitive both to surges of lift and to the feeling of flying out of it into the sink. Detecting the sink is particularly useful, because it enables quicker centring to be made. Why this is so and hints on how to centre quickly are given in the newest edition of *Gliding* (A & C Black).

The aim should be to out-climb every other glider nearby and not to be satisfied with just staying up, unless the conditions are very poor. This is a matter of constantly exploring out a few yards on almost every circle to try to find the best possible area of lift. Frequently this involves turning steeply at low speed to keep the radius of turn to a minimum and to make use of the narrow cores of lift. Remember, thermal soaring is more about staying in the strongest area of lift than flying at an 'efficient' angle of bank; it usually pays to turn steeply, as the small turning circle enables you to keep in the narrow cores of strong lift.

If flying across country is not practical and you are local soaring, it is better to practise moving from cloud to cloud or thermal to thermal without taking the climbs to any great height. For example, on a day with a 3000 foot cloud base, climb to 2500 feet on the first climb, then fly off leaving that thermal, using the airbrakes if necessary to come down to try to find another one at 2000 feet. If you are aiming to go back for a landing, only stay long enough in that thermal to get properly centred before moving off again down to 1500 feet and starting to look for the next bit of lift. Bring each search a little lower. In this way you will spend more time on the important part, i.e. finding the lift and getting centred quickly. Remember, too, that the thermals are smaller nearer to the ground, reinforcing the need for minimum speed, well-banked turns.

Even this only becomes valuable when you are below 1000 feet, by which time, of course, you will have moved closer to the gliding site or nearer to a suitable field if you are flying across country. At this height, if you do not make efficient use of any lift you find, you will be down.

Many pilots give up at 1000 feet when there is still a fair chance of finding something and getting away safely. At low altitudes, it is necessary not only to use the height most effectively to search, but also to retreat gradually to your position, off to one side of the landing area for a good base leg and an easy landing.

This is all valuable experience. If you do run into lift, you must assess the situation on each turn, being ready to break off for a normal base leg and approach. Of course, this is impractical on a site with a lot of power traffic or where a rigid circuit procedure is in force. But where it is possible, it is valuable to learn brinkmanship, because you also learn to reduce your feelings of stress under pressure and to make better use of thermals lower down where they are often smaller and more difficult to centre. At these heights, the first turn or so generally dictates whether you go up and get a climb, or go down for a landing. It is in these situations that centring skills are most useful.

When giving instruction in thermal soaring, I try to insist that students go on attempting to find lift until about 5-600 feet, and I very often explain my own thoughts and precautions as they do the flying. All the time during each turn it is essential to have a plan for the worst contingency and to know exactly what you would do if you suddenly lost 200 feet. In this way it is possible to use the lift low down with safety, provided that the thermals are not too turbulent. Then it is necessary to give up much higher.

Checking the compass

As you gain experience and begin to think about a first cross-country, local soaring provides a golden opportunity to check the compass for large errors and to get some practice at turning on to definite headings. You will find that the normal aircraft compass is quite useless unless you are flying straight and at a steady speed.

Experiment with the various compass errors. Heading north or south, try a little banking movement to see what happens to the reading. Then do the same on an easterly or westerly heading. Also try changing speeds. You will discover large errors flying near north or south with even small amounts of bank, and large errors on east and west if you vary the speed.

Compass errors are an awful nuisance and it is well worth finding out a little about them. You also need to become accustomed to thinking and using degrees, and deciding whether you need to turn left or right to change the heading. The easy way to remember it is that for a 'lesser' number of degrees, you turn 'left', e.g. turning from 350° to 320° is turning to a lesser number and therefore you turn left.

Turning point photography

If you are aspiring to fly competitions or to get your Gold and Diamond Badges, it is essential to take good turning point photographs. Like most things in gliding this takes practice and experience if you are going to avoid losing a thousand feet or more trying to take the picture of your turning point.

First perhaps, try taking the photograph with a hand-held camera. You will soon realise the difficulties and will not need much persuading to make yourself a fixed camera mount. A simple mount is invaluable, and it is best to set it up to get the wing-tip in the top corner of the frame. Then it is only a matter of banking the glider over until the feature is just below the wing-tip, steadying the glider and pressing the shutter. But you must be in the correct quadrant.

Until you are consistently getting the photos you want from inside the photographic sector, you will need to fly some distance beyond the turning point so that you do not have to be in a very steep turn or exactly positioned.

This is an ideal exercise to practise, using the camera without film. Select a local landmark on a 250,000 scale map and draw in the correct quadrant. It takes quite a bit of practice to orientate and get the right position for the shot, and this is something worthwhile perfecting during the winter or when you are just flying locally.

Many badge flights are invalidated by poor photography or by good photographs being taken outside the correct photographic zone. The majority of rejected photographic claims are due to impatience – the photograph is taken before entering the zone. So, take your time!

First flights in new types of glider

One of the most critical times in any inexperienced pilot's flying career is the first flight in a new type of single-seater glider. If you get a poor launch or something unexpected happens, you are at a great disadvantage and are likely to have a problem.

Therefore, make sure that you are in current flying practice and that you choose a straightforward day without a high wind, severe turbulence or a cross-wind component. Wait for another day if you are not feeling absolutely on top line. You need to be 'with it', because you can never guarantee that you won't have a launch failure or end up in a field instead of back where you started. You might need to draw on all your skills to manage safely in a strange machine.

Normally, you will have an opportunity to look over the machine and to sit in the cockpit beforehand to think about all the knobs and levers. The 'Maker's Handbook', although sometimes written in somewhat basic English, will give you an idea of the flying characteristics and flight limitations. It is also useful to watch how other pilots handle the glider.

If possible, get someone else to fly it before you to make quite sure that the ASI is working correctly. Obtain the approximate stalling speed, the normal thermalling speed and a sensible approach speed for the glider type from the

Cockpit layout of a Grob Acro 111

pilot. Also try to receive a thorough briefing from an experienced instructor or pilot who has flown the type in question.

Make a particular note of anything which is different from the aircraft you normally fly. The modern tendency to put the airbrake lever, flap lever, trim and undercarriage all on the left side of the cockpit can easily result in you pulling the wrong lever. A surprising number of gliders have been wrecked by pilots pulling the undercarriage lever or even the release knob instead of the airbrakes on the approach, usually on their first flight on type. Even on the ground you can do expensive damage by moving the undercarriage lever in mistake for the flaps or airbrakes. If you do this during a landing, there will not be time to realise your error.

If the glider has an unfamiliar type of airbrake or flap, it is vital to check their operation and to understand the system involved in locking them. Over the years there have been innumerable accidents and incidents caused by the airbrakes opening in flight. Although many gliders have a spring or bungee in the circuit to reduce the snatching loads at higher speeds on the approach, this is seldom powerful enough to prevent them sucking open if they are unlocked.

Most of the Glass ships have spring-loaded airbrake caps. These contrive to make the locking very stiff. The main point to realise is that if you cannot feel a positive lock, you are either not pushing hard enough or the lock is completely out of adjustment and too light to be effective. Don't be deluded into thinking that they are locked because they are flush with the wing surface. All airbrakes close fully before they lock.

Another potential disaster area is the canopy locking and jettison arrangements. These can be quite complicated and it is important that you understand both systems. It is possible that someone may have half pulled the jettison knob. So, with an unfamiliar type make quite sure that the locks are positive and always double check by trying to push the canopy up after locking it. Some emergency systems require operation of both the normal canopy catch and the jettison lever, and even then need a strong push up to get rid of the canopy.

Check the operation of the wheel brake. Even your first flight could end up with a field landing and, if the wheel brake lever is not in the usual position for you, your habits will catch you out as you claw for the non-existent lever in panic. Also, if the wheel brake is of the type that is applied automatically with full airbrake, remember that you should avoid touching down with full airbrake.

Unfortunately, a great deal of our flying is done by habit and this can lead to serious problems if anything goes wrong on the first flight in a strange machine.

If you are in current practice with aerotowing, a high launch is worthwhile for the first flight. Carry extra ballast in the cockpit unless you are well above the minimum cockpit load, as this increases the stability and makes the elevator less 'twitchy'.

Think carefully before take-off. Does the glider have the main wheel well ahead of the c.g.? If so, remember it will require a forward movement on the stick to get the tail off the ground, unlike most of the two-seaters. Also, it will need to be kept straight on take-off (see Swings and Roundabouts). Certainly, for your first few flights, your left hand should be close to the release knob, so that you can release immediately if you get into a bad swing or a wing-tip goes onto the ground.

One of the biggest hazards is overcontrolling just after you have left the ground. Remember, don't try to fly too close to the ground: 5 to 10 feet is quite all right and will make it much easier to smooth out any pitching which occurs before you have had time to get used to the light controls. Once clear of the ground, most gliders are very similar to each other and you should have no problems.

After releasing, slow right down, retrim the glider, and then raise the main wheel. If they are fitted, set the flaps for cruising.

Try circling at low speed and reversing the turn to get the feel of the ailerons. Then check it is clear below and attempt a straight stall, followed by a few stalls in very gentle turns. This will tell you if the glider has an obvious stall buffet and if it is likely to drop a wing during a stall when thermalling.

Before you go down into the circuit area, increase the speed to 60-70 knots and try the airbrakes to see how badly they snatch and how effective they are. Also try side-slipping at the approach speed to see if the rudder overbalances badly or the side-slipping is unusual in any way. This could be serious if you had to make a side-slip to get down into field on an early flight.

Rejoin the circuit with plenty of height, remembering to lower the main wheel if it is retractable. Look down and check that you are handling the right lever before moving it to the DOWN position. (Some undercarriage levers are forward for UP, and others are forward for DOWN!)

Finally, check the airspeed carefully and approach with an adequate amount of height and speed. Try to avoid an approach which ends up with a very small amount of airbrake. It is always easier to land with at least half airbrake provided that the speed is not too low.

Don't try to judge the landing attitude; just make sure that you are close to the ground and keep holding off until the glider lands itself. Make quite sure that you hold off fully. Gliders only bounce if they are allowed to touch down prematurely with excess speed.

If you do inadvertently end up with very little airbrake, or with excess speed, don't be afraid to hold off slightly higher than normal while you get rid of some of the speed. Try to get a small amount of airbrake on and keep the glider off the ground as long as you can, even if it floats a long way into the airfield. Be ready to open the airbrakes fully the moment the wheel touches the ground and then keep it straight and keep the wings level. Modern gliders are more prone to swinging than older aircraft and it is a little more difficult to keep the wings level, so don't relax until the glider has come to rest.

Ideally, take another flight straight away so that you can master any difficulties you may have experienced on the first flight. It will also help you to become more familiar with the glider.

Remember: modern gliders are more difficult than older gliders to operate in no-wind conditions. For your first flight, choose a day with some wind to make it easier to keep the wings level and to keep the glider straight. In the air, you will find all the modern machines very easy to fly but most are lighter on the controls.

Advice on using flaps

Apart from certain training machines and the Standard Class gliders (for which flaps are prohibited), all modern gliders are fitted with flaps. Their operation is basically simple, but they do add another complication to flying which the inexperienced pilot can do without.

One of the most likely causes of serious trouble on an early flight with a flapped glider is when the pilot becomes confused with the levers and pulls the flaps or undercarriage lever instead of the airbrake during the approach and landing. So, to prevent this happening to you, always sit in the cockpit and practise indentifying each control by feel. In flight, however, always glance down and identify the lever you want before using it.

In gliders, the ailerons are usually arranged to move up and down together with the flaps to change the effective camber of the whole wing. They can also be used as an extra aid to steepening the approach by being lowered to a much larger angle, thereby increasing the drag.

Modern aerofoils usually have a fairly limited range of speeds over which there is extensive laminar flow and very low drag. To put it another way, they work well within certain limited angles of attack. Keeping the same angle of attack, with the flaps and ailerons drooped slightly, increases the lift and so enables the glider to fly more slowly with the forward portion of the wing still operating efficiently. Similarly, an upward deflection of the flap reduces the lift without a change in the angle of attack of the forward portion of the wing, so keeping the wing efficient at a higher speed.

The result is a wider range of speeds with low drag, and hence higher performance. At the same time, the fuselage is kept much closer to the minimum drag angle for a much larger range of speeds and this produces lower fuselage drag. The result of this is very little change in attitude as you use the flaps to accommodate speed changes.

One way of thinking about flaps is as 'gears' on a car. Up until now you may have been flying an 'automatic' with only an accelerator (the elevator). Now you will have a gear lever (the flap lever) as well as the accelerator.

With the flaps in the neutral position, the glider can be considered a normal unflapped machine, except that the take-off and flying speeds may be slightly higher than without flaps. In most cases the flattest glide and the highest lift-to-drag ratio (Best L/D) occur with the flap in the neutral position. When the flaps are lowered to 5-8°, the main effect is an increase in lift, which in turn lowers the stalling speed slightly. The L/D usually suffers by a small amount, spoiling the gliding angle and increasing the rate of sink slightly, but enabling the pilot to circle the glider a little slower and therefore in reduced radius turns. This is of particular value with a glider carrying water ballast when it has a larger circling radius.

Lowering the flaps more than about 10° usually results in a little more lift but a considerable increase in drag. This would only be worthwhile with extremely narrow, strong thermals, which would otherwise be unsoarable at the higher speeds, or of course during landing.

The best speed ranges for a 15 metre flapped glider without water ballast might be as follows.

For cruising flight

Zero flap	42-55 knots in straight flight
Plus 8° (down)	40-45 knots climbing in straight flight
	40-50 knots in circling flight
Minus 5° (up)	55-75 knots
Minus 8°	70-Vne

For landing only

Plus 40°	Max. 70 knots (for the approach and landing)

The exact speeds for changing over may not be critical and in general it may be an advantage to lower the flap a little early when slowing down. Normally it does not pay to use the lowered flap except for circling flight, and there will be a definite penalty for forgetting and leaving flaps down at higher speeds in straight flight.

To make the most of the flaps it is necessary to keep one hand almost permanently on the lever and to adjust them as the speeds are varied in cruising flight.

Some machines have different flap limiting speeds for the various settings and these must be carefully adhered to. Others, such as the Janus, can be flown up to the normal Vne with any setting except for the landing position. Each type of glider will have slightly different recommendations for setting the flaps, but in principle the speeds are all much the same except when a large amount of water ballast is carried.

Use of flaps on take-off

Inexperienced pilots can make it easy for their first aerotow in a flapped machine by choosing a day with a reasonable amount of wind and setting the flaps to zero for the whole tow.

On a winch or car tow, the flaps can be set 5° down (or whatever is suggested in the maker's handbook) for the whole launch. This gives a better climb and reasonable handling in the event of a launch failure. The rapid acceleration on a wire launch gives ample aileron control.

In light winds on aerotow, it is wise to start with a negative flap position. This gives the best aileron control at very low speeds on the ground run. Even so, it is wise to keep the left hand near to the release toggle until full control is obtained. As soon as the tail is raised, the flap should be gradually lowered to plus 5° or so. This will help the glider off the ground.

On most machines this is a suitable setting for the whole tow. Be careful not to leave lowering the flap too long or to pull down the flaps too rapidly, otherwise the glider will leap up off the ground and get far too high above the towplane. A smooth movement back on the flap lever is all that is needed. If the notch holding the flap lever is missed, the lever should be held until you are several hundred feet up before you try to find it. The position of the flaps on tow is not critical and you don't want to start an oscillation by messing about with the lever too close to the ground.

Experimenting with the flap setting higher up on tow, it will be noticed that the glider flies more nose-down with positive settings, giving a better view ahead, but that the aileron control deteriorates slightly. The ailerons become heavier with more aileron drag and adverse yaw. This is particularly noticeable when larger downward deflections of the flaps are used.

Unless the tow is very fast, any negative setting will result in the glider tending to drop into the wake of the towplane.

Why negative flaps for take-off?

When the first high performance glass-fibre machines arrived, it was not long before we found out that the aileron control at the start of the take-off run was noticeably worse than in the earlier gliders. The word soon spread around that using negative flap was the answer to the problem.

I was rather sceptical at first and continued to recommend the zero setting, because it seemed likely that the actual range of movement of the ailerons might be reduced by the upward deflection. I thought that it might just be the impression gained by the pilots using the negative flap after experiencing a bad swing or ground loop on an earlier occasion. It is surprising how much quicker pilots can react to a wing drop after such an experience.

One day, I was sitting in the cockpit of a PIK20D just after landing on a very windy day when I realised that it was an excellent opportunity to experiment with the flaps and aileron power. Facing into the 30 knot wind, I found that it was impossible to raise the wing-tip off the ground with any positive flap setting. With negative flap settings, however, full aileron lifted the wing off the ground immediately and gave me good aileron control. This was such a convincing demonstration that I just had to find out why the negative flap was such an improvement.

The explanation to this question is an interesting one. The very small wing-tip chords on modern machines, and the very low speeds during the start of a take-off, mean that the wing-tips are operating close to model aeroplane conditions. When the glider is sitting on the ground, the angle of attack of the wing is well below the normal stalling angle for the aerofoil. However, the very low airspeed and small chord result in a greatly reduced stalling angle. With the wing at about 8° to the airflow, any large deflection of the aileron results in the airflow separating at the tip, with a resultant loss of effectiveness. As the speed increases, so this effect diminishes, and lifting the tail results in an immediate reduction in the angle of attack and better control with less aileron drag.

The effect of these very small tip chords has some other interesting implications. With a 15 metre flapped machine it is common to have extension wing-tips to increase the span to 17 metres. As the wings are tapered, the wing-tips become extremely small, and this makes them rather inefficient at low speeds.

Carrying water ballast to increase the cruising speeds has the advantage that it gives an effect similar to increasing the chord of the wing-tips and so improving their efficiency. As a result the best gliding angle of most of these machines may well be improved by a few points when they are carrying the extra weight and are flown at the revised best speed. (However, the extra speed increases the rate of descent slightly.)

Many glider designers would prefer to start a new 17 or 18 metre span Championship Class which would allow them to design for that span and to have larger wing chords at the tips. They claim this would give a worthwhile increase in performance at a low additional cost. They all agree that little improvement is possible through refinements or by stretching the 15 metre machines beyond 17 metres.

The earlier 25 metre Open Class machines also had problems because of the small sizes of their wing-tips. Here the difficulties are associated with circling flight at low speeds. Because of the huge wing-spans, the difference in wing-tip speeds in a turn is significant and results in a pronounced overbanking tendency. This can only be controlled down to a certain speed before the inner tip becomes so inefficient that the bank becomes uncontrollable. These gliders have the slight disadvantage of having to be circled with a little extra speed to be properly manageable.

For this reason the tip chord on the ASH25 was increased to improve the handling at very low speeds in circling flight. This causes a slight deterioration in performance in straight flight, but an improvement in the turns.

Approaching and landing

A small downward deflection (5°-8°) has little effect on the gliding performance and can be applied at any point on the circuit in preparation for the landing. Remember to lower the nose to maintain the same speed. More flap than this will definitely spoil the gliding angle and so should not be used until you are sure that there will be ample height for the base leg and approach.

If the glider has both flaps and airbrakes, *always* select the amount of flap required for the particular approach *before* unlocking and using the airbrakes. This is to avoid the need to take your hand off the airbrake lever and the risk of the brakes opening themselves.

As the flaps are lowered, the glider has to be flown more nose-down and the glide steepens. The airbrakes can then be used normally while the pilot carefully monitors the airspeed to ensure it is maintained. The ailerons usually become mechanically stiffer as the flaps are lowered into the landing position due to the flexing of the wing, making the hinges bind.

If the glider (e.g. PIK20D, DG202, ASW20) is fitted with powerful airbrakes and flaps which can be lowered to large angles, it may be unwise to use more than a limited amount of flap. This is because of the serious deterioration in control when the ailerons are deflected to large down angles. The combination of flaps and airbrakes gives superb approach control and it is unlikely that full flap and full braking will ever be needed for the landing.

Where trailing edge airbrakes are combined with the flaps as one unit (e.g. on a Vega, Mosquito, Mini Nimbus, Nimbus 2c and Ventus), again the flap setting is made first. This sets the aileron droop before the airbrake lever is pulled to operate the flaps as a trailing edge airbrake.

It is debatable with these types of flap/brake how much flap (if any) to lower for the approach and landing. Using the airbrake will automatically lower the 'flap' considerably and the advantage of good aileron control might outweigh that of a slightly lower approach and touch down speed. Positive or landing flap should only be necessary when the approach or touch down speed is critical, e.g. for landing in a very short field. When landing in a large stubble field, on the other hand, the few extra knots of touch down speed will do less damage than a groundloop as you lose lateral control! Experiment with various settings within the safe confines of your gliding site – the difference might surprise you.

These flap brakes usually increase the lift slightly, making a reduction in the airbrake during the float a doubtful proposition. Reducing the amount of airbrake in such a case can result in a heavy landing unless there is plenty of speed.

If the wind is very light, it may be a good idea to raise the flaps to improve the aileron control as the glider slows down after landing. This also reduces the lift, making the wheel brake more effective by increasing the weight on the wheel.

With a powered aircraft on the approach, it is considered most unwise to raise the flap once it is lowered, because the loss of lift causes rapid sinking. Although not recommended as a general practice, in gliders the landing flap can be raised, provided that the glider is not flying too slowly and the flaps are not moved up beyond the high lift setting of 5°-10°. The sinking effect can be eliminated by raising the nose slightly at the same time as the flap is raised. This is worth practising at height, just in case you ever lower the flaps too soon and find yourself short of height. At low speeds it would be dangerous, because there would be a risk of sinking and stalling.

A few designs, such as the 1S29D and the Schweizer 135, have flaps without the interconnection with the ailerons. These are fine for landing, but are probably of doubtful value when raised or lowered in cruising flight. The 135 is unusual in that the Vne with the flaps deflected upwards is less than the Vne for zero flap. This is because of the change in the lift distribution when only the centre of the wing has a flap. With the flaps deflected upwards, for instance, the centre of the wing will have reduced lift and the outer portions of the wing will be making more, creating a greater bending moment as well as much higher induced drag. The great advantage of having the flaps and ailerons deflecting together is that the lift distribution remains very similar for all flap settings, so keeping the induced drag to a minimum.

What kind of glider should I buy?

The experienced pilot needs no advice on which glider he should buy, but I am often asked for help by early solo pilots contemplating joining a syndicate or buying their first glider. Obviously the amount of money available is the main consideration for most people: should they buy a cheap, low performance machine which they could afford by themselves; or, should they form a syndicate with one or more other members and buy a more modern glass machine?

A number of people I know have bought a Tutor, or a similar very low performance glider, and then later, when it's too late, have realised its limitations. Novice pilots who have been accustomed to flying K13s and K8s or modern machines soon find that it becomes a bore to keep making circuit flights while their friends are up soaring most of the day. The occasional climb to 3000 or 4000 feet, though exhilarating and something to boast about, in a low performance open cockpit glider is a freezing experience that soon becomes tedious and ceases to be much fun. Most of these gliders spend almost all their days sitting in their trailers or at the back of the hangar collecting the dust. Even if you are not interested in competitive flying, there is no doubt that you will almost certainly find a share in a better machine more satisfying than owning a low performance glider by yourself.

There are still bargains to be had amongst the older wooden and metal gliders, many of which are described in detail in *Derek Piggott on Gliding* (A & C Black). Many are available at surprisingly low prices. If you will be flying from a small or very rough gliding site, I still consider it is a wise move to own one of those older and slower machines for a season or so before going for glass. However, the pleasure of owning a share in a really beautiful machine with much higher performance is undeniable, but, of course, it will cost more.

Two-seaters

For the lucky pilot who can afford any type of glider, there is also the possibility of buying a two-seater and using that for solo flying. This looks very attractive at first sight, but there are a number of disadvantages and I would not recommend it for your first machine. Once you have tasted the superb handling and ease of rigging of a modern single-seater, it becomes difficult to be enthusiastic about a two-seater.

The majority of two-seaters are heavy to rig and are also quite hard work to fly. This is a major drawback when it comes to cross-country flying; most privately owned two-seaters are flown within range of the gliding site because of the sheer effort involved in a possible retrieve. Experience has also shown that where soaring is concerned, inexperienced passengers find the constant circling both boring and sickness-inducing.

ASK21 glass fibre two-seater training glider

Blanik all-metal two-seater

Australian ES65 Platypus glass fibre two-seater

Grob Acro 111 trainer and ASK13 two-seater

French Marianne two-seater

After a short time in the air, two pilots in a two-seater often become very frustrated and disgruntled with each other because each one is itching to take over while the other is flying. For the majority of pilots, soaring is a solo occupation and any criticism or distraction is unwanted and uncalled for. If the weather is soarable, both pilots want to be doing the flying.

However, the latest very high performance two-seaters compete on equal terms with the top Open Class machines and have glide ratios of nearly 60:1. These are proving irresistable to many of the top pilots because of the advantages of having two sets of eyes and two brains to do the flying. These are definitely not going to stay flying locally. 60:1 is over 11 miles per thousand feet of height lost! However, they are not suitable for beginners or for initial training.

The investment

If you haven't seriously considered private ownership, you may not realise what a good investment a glider will be. History shows that a glider's value is held or even increased year by year. Unfortunately, a number of this class of glider get written off or are badly damaged every season. This means that there is always a ready market for such aircraft and even after a few years you will not be left with an unsaleable machine.

The costs

It is never a good idea to analyse the cost of your flying too accurately. However, being realistic, unless your syndicate can use your machine for at least 100 hours a year, the cost per hour will be far higher than the cost of paying normal club fees for using a club glider. The attraction of private ownership, especially in the UK where weather conditions are erratic, is that you can always fly on those very few days when the conditions are really good, and that you do not need to be at the gliding site at dawn to get your name on the flying list.

The major annual costs involved are the loss of interest on your capital, the insurance premium necessary to protect your investment, and the cost of the annual C of A inspection. Insurance rates for a Bronze C pilot are likely to be about 8% of the value and will drop when you have completed your Silver C. The cost of the annual inspection for the C of A depends on the condition of the glider, but you could save money by helping with the inspection rather than having it all done professionally.

Syndicates

If you cannot afford the glider you would really like, it is always worth considering enrolling another syndicate member. If you choose carefully, you might find someone who doesn't fly much, or who only wants to fly on days when you cannot get to the gliding site.

Flying ability

The average Bronze C stage of pilot should be able to manage these gliders without difficulty, provided that he can get at least a few launches in a glass two-seater to become accustomed to the more demanding speed control and lighter elevator forces of the modern machines. In any case, you should always consult your CFI to see that he agrees with your choice.

In most cases, once you have made a few flights to get used to the lighter controls, you will find the modern machines both easier and more docile to fly than the training gliders.

Gliders reviewed

The gliders can be divided into three categories:

older glass fibre gliders
modern 'Club' class gliders
competitive high performance Standard Class gliders.

The earlier glass fibre machines I have chosen to review include the ASW15, Open Cirrus, Standard Cirrus, Club Libelle, Astir CS and Sport Vega. Because almost all of these are 15 metre Standard Class machines, there seems very little point in quoting specific details for each type. I have not included any of the flapped 15 metre gliders. True, they may have slightly lower landing speeds, but the complication of both a retractable undercarriage and flaps, together with the move onto a glass machine, may be too much for some beginners. I have included a warning about the PIK20b and IS29d. All of them were designed with large safety factors because of the then 'new' materials. As a result, they are very strong and unlikely to suffer structural problems in the future. However, buyers should be especially cautious about checking the surface finish and the cockpit limitations, since many of these gliders are likely to be at least fifteen years old. Refinishing a glass machine is a most time-consuming and expensive business.

I have also included notes on the Libelle and Phoebus C which are, in my opinion, only suitable for 100+ hour pilots who have a considerable amount of cross-country experience, including a number of field landings.

Older glass fibre gliders

The ASW15
In good condition, this has a very high performance, with a claimed best glide ratio of 38:1 at about 48 knots. It has quite powerful top and bottom surface airbrakes, making it relatively easy for field landings.

Whereas most gliders have no tendency to swing unless there is a cross wind, the ASW15 has the almost unique problem of a definite swing on take-off caused by the offset tow hook. It is important to start the take-off run with full rudder against the probable swing and to have the wing-tip runner on the down wind wing-tip. The worst situation is aerotowing in a light, following cross wind from a hard surface or runway. The tail skid offers little or no resistance to swinging and it is easy to swing badly and ground loop.

At other times it is no problem, but on all modern machines with a forward main wheel it is sensible to start the take-off run with the left hand on the release toggle so that the cable can be released if a wing drops.

Compared with the glass two-seaters the ailerons of the ASW15 are

ASW15

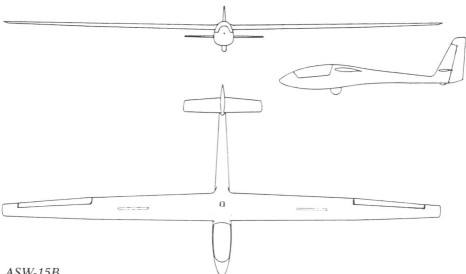

ASW-15B

incredibly light and seem to snatch slightly in rough air. The elevator is also light, but after one or two flights these features will not cause any difficulties.

The Open Cirrus

This is a 17 metre machine with good handling, large cockpit and acceptable airbrakes. It is totally outclassed now as an open class machine, as it would have to compete with the 25 metre span Nimbus 3s, ASW22s and ASH25s, all of which have glide ratios of over 1:55. However, for regional competitions

Open Cirrus

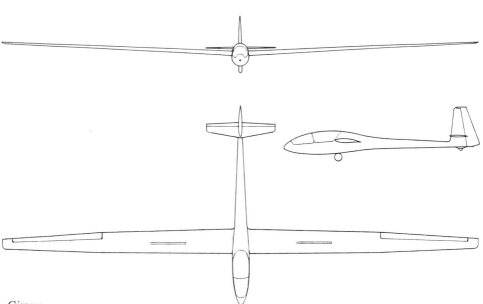

Cirrus

which employ a handicap system it is still competitive, having a best glide ratio of about 43:1 in good condition. Being of a larger span, the Cirrus does not have quite the rate of roll of a 15 metre glider, but it has good handling, is docile and is very suitable as a first glass machine.

The Standard Cirrus

Early versions of the Standard Cirrus were rather under-braked and might be a problem for early field landings. The later Cirrus 75 has an improved wing and better airbrakes, and a few Standard Cirrus have been modified to have a double area airbrake blade similar to that on the Pirat. This appears to be a

Standard Cirrus

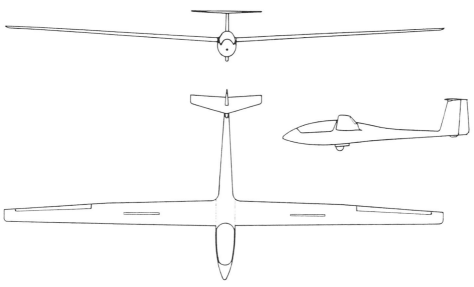

Standard Cirrus

worthwhile modification, as it considerably improves the power of the airbrakes.

The all moving stabiliser and spring trimming make it sensitive, if not 'twitchy', at higher speeds. With the c.g. near the aft limit, inexperienced pilots may run into pitching problems, so to improve the stability the initial flights should be made with extra ballast in the cockpit to bring the c.g. well forward. Pilots should be carefully briefed to avoid overcontrolling, particularly just after take-off on aerotow.

In all other respects the Standard Cirrus is a nice machine, with good handling and stalling, and a competitive performance. It is only suitable for the very competent Bronze C pilot and is perhaps a better second glass machine.

The Hornet

The Hornet is a 15 metre Standard class machine fitted with trailing edge airbrakes. For some reason it did not sell well in England, but it is very popular in Australia and many other countries where it is often used as a first glass machine. It has good handling and flying characteristics. In later models carbon fibre was used for the wing spar to reduce the weight and make it more competitive.

The trailing edge airbrakes are powerful enough, but they increase the lift slightly when they are opened. This makes the Hornet less 'forgiving' than those types with normal airbrakes. Reducing the airbrake setting during the hold off to float a little further up the field can result in landing even shorter as the extra lift is lost by closing the airbrakes. (This also occurs with the Club Libelle, Mosquito, Mini Nimbus, Vega and Ventus.) Apart from this, it is a very nice glider with a good performance.

105

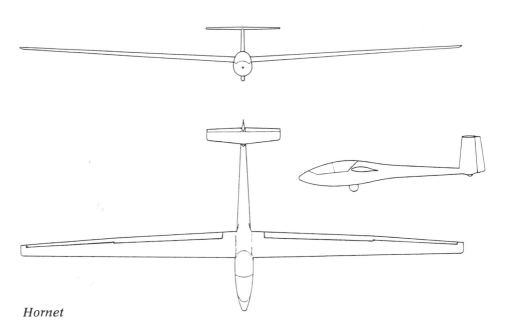

Hornet

The Club Libelle

The Club Libelle, like the Hornet, was made by Glassflugel, one of the finest manufacturers of glass fibre machines. Experience has shown that the Club Libelle is suitable for a first glass machine. Frankly, I was surprised that it did not cause problems; beneath its docile stall is hidden a fairly pronounced wing-drop which may have been the cause of several serious stalling accidents. With

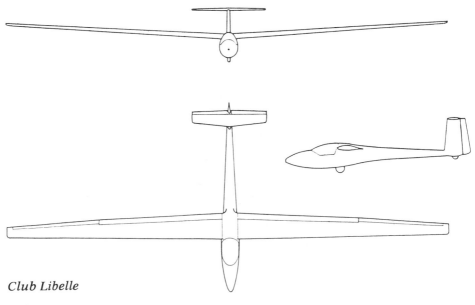

Club Libelle

106

a claimed performance of 35:1, a Club Libelle has made many fine flights in the hands of the Imperial College pilots and, to my knowledge, it has never been damaged by their inexperienced pilots. However, like the Hornet, it has trailing edge airbrakes which increase the lift slightly, making closing the airbrakes at low speed near the ground unfeasible.

The Astir CS and variants
This is a well-proven, easy to fly machine that is suitable for the average pilot. The earliest version has a larger cockpit than the pointed nose Astir 77, and has very much better lateral handling. Why this is the case I am uncertain, but later

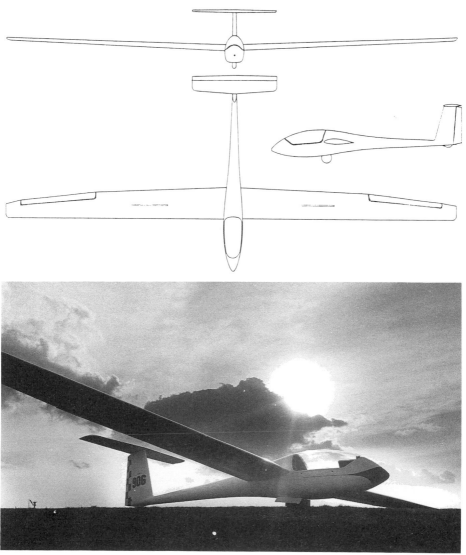

Astir CS

models do seem to have a little more sweep back than the earlier ones and this may increase the lateral stability, thereby reducing the power of the ailerons. Fly before buy, I always say!

Production aircraft have a large number of alloy castings for the various fittings. In particular, the main fuselage load carrying frame is a casting and this seems to break rather too easily in a heavy landing. If you are buying an Astir, get the frame checked for damage by a competent inspector before you hand over your money. Some of the very early production machines have wooden main fames which are not so easily damaged.

I have owned a share in an Astir CS for many years and find that, although the performance is well below the latest Standard Class machines, it can still be competitive and fun to fly.

The Sport Vega

The Sport Vega was designed as a club version of the original flapped 15 metre Vega. It has a fixed main wheel which does not protrude as far out as the retractable one. This reduces the ground incidence of the wing and so improves the aileron control during the ground run. The combined cruise flaps and airbrakes of the original design have been replaced by plain, trailing edge airbrakes.

At one time it was thought that trailing edge airbrakes might be less expensive to design and offer a better performance than normal airbrakes. Certainly, they leave the top surface completely sealed right back to a point where it is unlikely that any laminar flow can still exist. By hinging them carefully, the operating loads can be very low and without the usual snatch which occurs with the other types of airbrake. However, as is often the case,

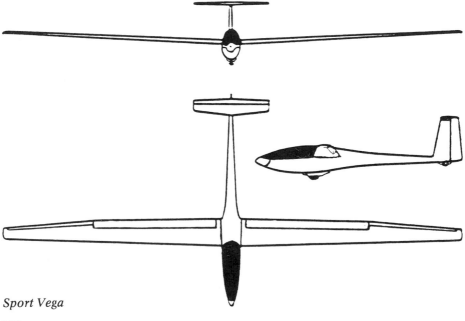

Sport Vega

Sport Vega

avoiding one problem leads to introducing others, and most designers seem to have gone back to the normal type for the latest machines.

The Sport Vega is the only glider I have flown whose trailing edge airbrakes do not increase the lift and reduce the stalling speed slightly. At first, to me this seemed ideal; it was only after several years of intensive operating with a number of these aircraft that I came to the conclusion that the trailing edge airbrake is less desirable than other types of brake. If ballooning occurs during a hold off, so that the glider is desperately short of flying speed, closing these airbrakes does little to help the situation. Closing the trailing edge airbrake only reduces the drag, whereas closing a normal airbrake increases lift, reducing the stalling speed as well as reducing the drag.

So, although they have a powerful braking effect on an approach, this type does not give a wide safety margin in such a situation. Also, opening the final part of normal airbrakes results in an immediate sink and touch down. With the trailing edge type, the extra drag from the airbrakes has a gradual slowing down effect, making it more difficult to judge just how far the glider will float.

Early Sport Vegas suffered from poor inspection standards, but modifications have turned this aircraft into a very acceptable first glass machine which is quick and easy to rig, easy to fly, and capable of good soaring flights.

Not recommended for inexperienced pilots

The Libelle
The beauty of the Libelle is the light weight of the wings and the ease of rigging and derigging. However, it is *not* for you unless you have already made a few field landings and are an above-average pilot. Although it is nice and easy to fly, the airbrakes are ineffective compared with those on most other machines – an extra 5 knots on the approach and you will be in the far hedge or the next field! Because of these airbrakes, you must be able to side-slip quickly and accurately

Libelle

while using full airbrake on the final approach. With less experienced pilots, it is inevitable that the occasional approach will end up a little high or fast, and only a quick side-slip can prevent an overshoot and an expensive accident.

The Libelle suffers a serious loss of performance and buffets badly unless it is flown accurately. This is probably due to the sharply pointed top of the fuselage which causes a breakaway of the airflow if the glider is flown with the slightest slip or skid. Having a short, stubby fin and rudder, the Libelle is also not as directionally stable as later machines, and this makes it more difficult to fly accurately than most other types.

In the air it is docile and pleasant to fly, but the poor airbrakes make it unsuitable for an inexperienced pilot. Larger pilots may find the cockpit a very snug fit, as the top is rather narrow.

The PIK20B

This is the earliest version of the PIK20 and is a flapped 15 metre Standard class machine. At first sight it looks a good buy, since it is less expensive than most 15 metre machines. Instead of airbrakes it uses plain flaps for approach control. Although these are very effective, because of their large area, their operation is so different from normal airbrakes that there is a serious risk of breaking the glider through operating them incorrectly.

Raising the flaps near the ground by mistake may result in a broken glider, and this is what most pilots will do quite instinctively if they are undershooting slightly and have been used to closing the airbrakes. Moreover, if approaching in a strong wind gradient and becoming too slow, there is nothing that can be done with the flaps to prevent a heavy landing.

Lowering the flaps fully involves several turns of the handle and it is sometimes difficult to choose the correct direction. It can be left at the top or bottom of a turn so that a forward movement may result in either more or less flap. (This problem can be largely avoided by always leaving the flap lever at the top of the movement so that any subsequent movement starts in the same direction as it would with a normal airbrake, i.e. pushing forwards to reduce the amount of flap.)

Proponents of this type of flap claim, quite rightly, that they result in much lower landing speeds and steeper approaches. However, the advantage is offset by their lack of flexibility. In my opinion, normal airbrakes are far easier

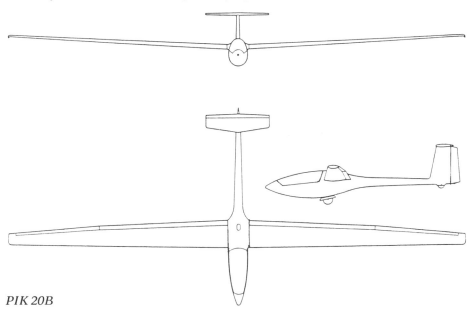

PIK 20B

to operate, and they are safer because of the extra lift available when they are closed. They are certainly not for the average pilot who has only used airbrakes and who may so easily react instinctively to an undershoot situation. I would never recommend any glider like this to an inexperienced pilot. Airbrakes are so much more 'forgiving' and make approaches and spot landings much easier than flaps. It should be noted that the PIK20d and e models have both flaps and normal airbrakes, and that these criticisms only apply to the early PIK20b model.

The Phoebus C
The Phoebus C is another early 17 metre glass machine and has a slightly better performance than the Open Cirrus. However, the airbrakes are ineffective, making it unsuitable for inexperienced pilots. The construction is largely a sandwich of glass and balsa wood; with ageing, the balsa tends to shrink and swell in places, spoiling the surface smoothness. There is also a tendency for the main wooden frame, to which the retractable undercarriage is attached, to fail with a heavy landing, and this is an awkward and expensive repair. More recent designs use a synthetic foam filling between the glass fibre skins instead of balsa wood. These hold their contours much more accurately and do not soak up water and swell like wood.

The cockpit is rather small and the rigging is finicky. The ineffective airbrakes mean that it is vital the pilot can side-slip accurately. I flew one in a regional competition and enjoyed the excellent climbing performance. However, I did have to use full airbrake and side-slip on practically every approach!

Modern club class gliders
This glider group consists of those glass fibre machines deliberately designed for inexperienced pilots, and also those which, by small modifications, have been made more suitable for these pilots than their competition sister ships. Absolute performance has taken second place to good handling at low speeds and, to avoid complication and expense, they usually have a fixed undercarriage. In most cases the cost of these machines is kept to a minimum by reducing the use of carbon fibre and eliminating water ballast tanks, etc.

They aim to have lower stalling and circling speeds, and good, 'forgiving' characteristics. The ideal 'club' glider should have control forces more comparable with the average glass two-seater so that pilots can use it as a step between the two-seater and the top performance machines. Of course, it must have powerful airbrakes to make it easy for initial field landings.

The majority of the top Standard Class machines meet most of these requirements for a 'club' glider, except for the elevator control forces. However, the higher touch down speeds make them less 'forgiving' of a heavy landing, and the higher circling speeds make the radius of turn larger. This in turn means that thermalling is more difficult for the beginner.

The ASK23
The ASK23 was designed specifically as a 'club' glider to suit pilots trained on the ASK21 two-seater. The performance is good, with a best glide ratio of well

Phoebus

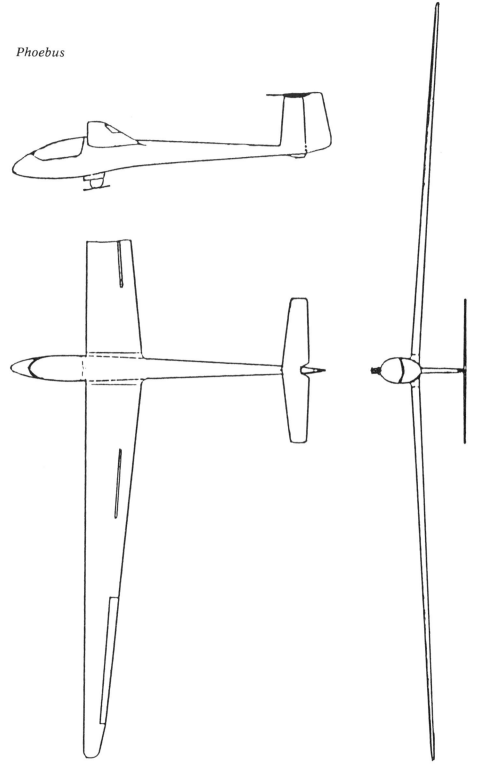

ASK23B

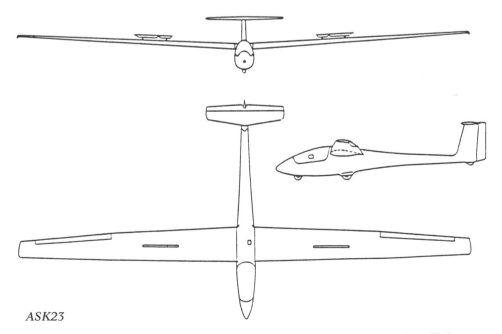

ASK23

over 30:1, making it suitable for early cross-countries and 300 km flights are possible on any good day. It is simple to fly, has no vices and has good airbrakes.

The ASW23 has the main wheel located just behind the loaded c.g.; it also

114

has a nose and tail wheel. This arrangement makes it easy to keep straight on the ground and simple to make a smooth landing. Provided that it is held off so that it lands on the main wheel, it is unlikely to bounce. The arrangement is also good for ground handling, because the empty glider is almost balanced on the main wheel, making it easy to raise the tail for turning by applying a little downward pressure on the nose. Like most modern machines, it has no tail handle which means that lifting the tail and moving it forwards is awkward.

The ASK23 is very light on the elevator at low speeds and care must be taken to avoid pitching oscillations just after take-off. For some reason, there seem to have been more trouble on aerotows with pilots overcontrolling and flying into the ground just after lift off with this machine than with most others, even those which seem to have just as light, or in some cases even lighter, stick forces.

It is difficult to analyse just why this is the case. It might be that the position of the main wheel is a little further back than on some of the other similar designs. This in turn might make it slightly more difficult to lift the nose wheel so that pilots tend to bring the stick further back to help the glider leave the ground. Then, when the glider has gained enough speed to rotate, it leaps off the ground suddenly. If the pilot is worried by this, he may be too vigorous with his correction to prevent the glider moving quickly up far too high above the towplane. It would therefore be easy to set up a PIO (pilot induced oscillation), involving the glider pitching up and down violently and flying back into the ground, or very close to it.

To prevent a PIO, it is best to make only a gradual backward movement on the stick on take-off and not to pull it right back, so that it is easier to feel the moment the nose wheel leaves the ground. The pilot should then watch the towplane and try to fly level at about 5-10 feet, rather than a few inches above the ground.

As a stepping stone towards flying a glider with a retractable undercarriage, this type of nose wheel undercarriage has the disadvantage of allowing sloppy landing habits to develop unnoticed. It is very easy to make what feels like a good landing; no problems occur unless the glider is hardly held off at all so that it is flown onto the nose wheel at high speed. Then it is bound to bounce badly. A pilot who is not used to having to hold off fully during landing may run into trouble when flying machines fitted with a retractable undercarriage. With the wheel well forward, these aircraft bounce and swing more easily.

Apart from the slightly 'twitchy' elevator on take-off, the only other disadvantage of the ASK23 is the cost of repair if the fuselage ever gets badly damaged. The construction is the usual Schleicher sandwich, as in the ASW19 and ASW20. It is extremely strong, but is expensive to repair. I have known of a fuselage damaged in the nose which would have cost more to repair than to replace with a complete new fuselage.

The GROB 102 or CLUB III

This is the 'club' version of the Astir series and can be fitted with either a nose wheel or the normal main wheel ahead of the c.g. In both cases there is a sensibly sized tail wheel to make ground handling easy. The alloy castings of the earlier Astirs have been replaced with welded steel fittings.

The Grob has proved to be a very popular glider with all of the features desirable in a club machine. The handling is excellent and, being a little lighter weight than the other versions, it seems to have slightly lower circling speeds than the normal Astir. The best glide ratio appears to be in the 33 to 35:1 range, making it suitable for early cross-country flying. Although the controls are much lighter than those on the two-seater Grob 103 Twin Astir and Twin Acro, it is an easy transition from one to the other for early solo pilots.

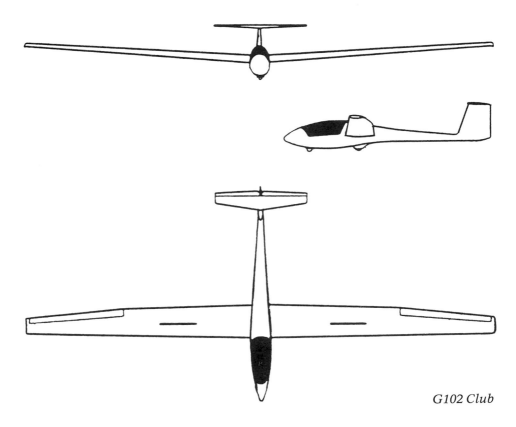

G102 Club

The SZD JUNIOR

The Junior is perhaps the least known of all the 'club' gliders, but it has many excellent features and has much the same best gliding angle as the ASK23 and Grob 102, although this is at a lower flying speed.

The most striking and advantageous feature is the huge main wheel fitted with a disc brake. It reduces landing shocks and prevents damage when landing in rough fields. With a claimed glide ratio of 35:1 at 43 mph, the Junior is nearly 10 mph slower than other machines and this makes it particularly suited to thermalling in small, weak thermals. The lower speed is also an advantage for winch launching on a small site and ensures a really high launch.

This machine is much closer than many other gliders to my own idea of a good club aircraft. In my opinion the lower circling speeds are a great advantage to the inexperienced pilot, and the chance of damage is always

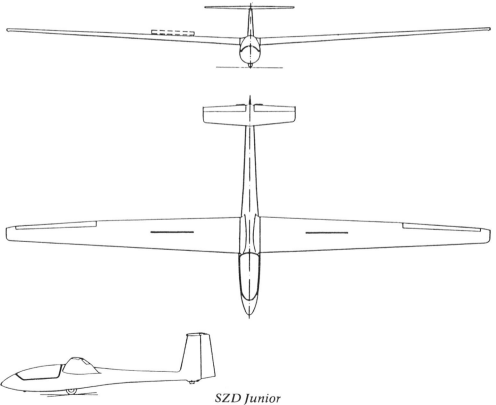

SZD Junior

greatly reduced by lower landing speeds. This is why the K8 and the K18 were so successful and popular in the clubs.

The DG100 and DG101

The DG100 started life with an all-moving stabilizer and consequently very low stick forces. The earlier version has a rather narrow cockpit, but the low-cut canopy gives the pilot wonderful visibility. The performance is comparable with, if not a little better than, the Standard Cirrus. Like the Cirrus, this is a nice machine for the slightly more experienced pilot. Later versions are fitted with a normal tailplane and elevator, making them more stable, but still very light on the controls.

The DG101 is a more recent version with a wider cockpit, a forward opening one-piece canopy, and the fixed tailplane and elevator in place of the all-moving stabilizer. It can be fitted with a retractable main wheel and water ballast as optional extras.

The cockpit seems to have become more or less standard in the DG200 and the DG400 (self-launching motor glider) and is a definite improvement on the early model which was uncomfortable for larger pilots. The visibility is exceptional, because the sides of the cockpit canopy are much lower than in most other designs.

This is a nice handling glider with a very good performance, making it competitive with many of the Standard Class machines. Unfortunately, the elevator is very light and quite different from any of the present breed of two-seaters, so some caution is needed converting onto it.

Accurate circling is particularly easy and the only word of caution needed is to explore the side-slipping at height before trying it on the approach. With up to about three-quarters of the rudder deflection the side-slip is perfectly normal, but with all the rudder applied suddenly, the yawing movement goes to an extreme angle and then the nose drops as control is lost. This could be disconcerting on your first field landing, but only means that the amount of

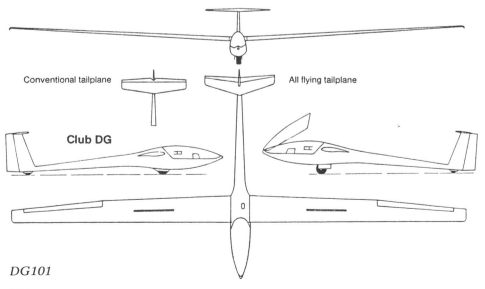

Conventional tailplane

All flying tailplane

Club DG

DG101

DG101

rudder used in a side-slip should be limited to about three-quarters of the available movement. In practice, side-slipping would seldom be necessary, as the airbrakes are very effective.

The side-slipping characteristics of the Janus C two-seater are rather similar, so it is possible to see this effect with an instructor if you can get a flight in a Janus. However, with the Janus, the rudder control loads are very high when the rudder overbalances, making it difficult to push the rudder straight again to get back to normal flight. In contrast, the rudder loads on the DG are light and the side-slip is easily kept under control once you have experienced the problem.

I envy the pilots flying any of the DG series: all the aircraft are a joy to fly. But perhaps the DG101 is for the pilot who has already flown a few hours in a K6E or another type of glass machine.

The DG300 Club

This is a simplified version of the DG300 which was a high performance Standard Class machine using a 'blown' wing.

With a 'blown' wing, air is leaked out through hundreds of tiny holes in a line on the bottom surface just ahead of the point where separation would occur. This makes the boundary layer turbulent so that it sticks to the surface, preventing early separation and a laminar bubble. Almost the same drag reduction is possible by fitting a 'tape' turbulator to the Club version.

DG 300

The DG300 Club has very good handling and stalling characteristics and is altogether a suitable machine for an inexperienced pilot. Originally it was intended to have it cleared for advanced aerobatics. A retractable under-carriage and water ballast can be fitted at a later date if required.

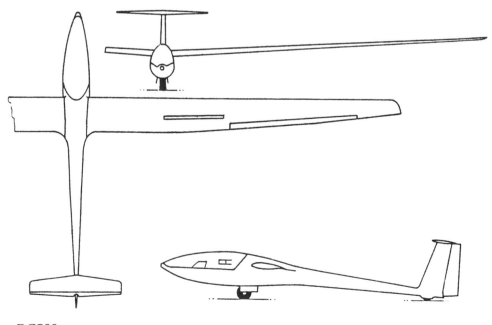

DG300

The IS29d and IS29 Club

In my opinion, this is a machine for the experienced pilot and is not suitable for the average pilot with less than about 100 hours' flying experience. Even then, because of its sharp stalling characteristics, it must be treated with more than normal respect below about 800 feet or so.

This is an all-metal design from Romania and for the past few years has been built in the same factory as the BAC111 airliners. The standards of workmanship, corrosion-proofing and inspection have greatly improved in recent years, and there is much to be said for a metal glider if you have experience with metal work. It can be picketted out all summer in the same way as a light aircraft, which means that daily rigging and derigging are avoided. It also needs very little maintenance.

One year, I was lucky enough to be lent an early, flapped IS29d for a Euroglide competition. I had a most enjoyable few days chasing the glass ships. It climbed well, but was usually beaten by the Standard Cirrus in any long fast glide. The flaps of the early model were disappointing and not an obvious advantage, except when used on landing. The Club version has no flaps fitted, but has more effective airbrakes. They both have an air strut to provide extra shock absorption for the main wheel during the ground run. This gives a wonderfully smooth ride over the roughest ground. However, like the Blanik shock absorber, if it ever leaks and loses pressure, it needs special equipment and adaptors to re-inflate it. When this happens, you will probably wish it had plain rubber blocks as shock absorbers like the old wartime Mosquitos had.

The IS29d has an all-moving stabiliser with anti-balance tabs which produce a reasonable stick force and stability. The general handling is excellent, with very crisp control right down to the stall. However, the stall warning is almost non-existent and it is very much a case of one moment you're flying happily

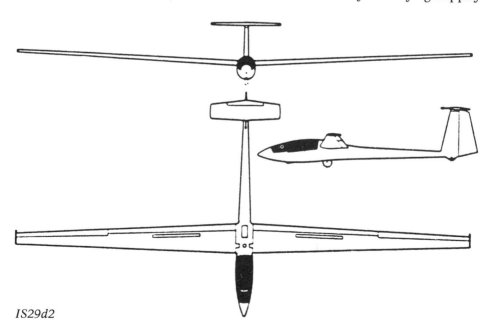

IS29d2

IS29D, an all-metal single seater

and the next you've rolled over past the vertical and are about to spin. This may be satisfactory for training jet jockeys, but is not acceptable for people flying for fun!

The later version, the IS29 Club, has additional washout and no flaps. The rigging is also better. Unfortunately, although there is a reasonable stall warning, the wing drop is still very rapid compared with that of any other glider in production. The IS29 simply is not a club glider and I would suggest that CFIs have a friendly word with any inexperienced pilots thinking of buying one.

One of my competent aerobatic instructors had a few exciting moments doing simple aerobatics in the Club version. Pulling up into a loop the aircraft flicked into a very nose high position, tail slid, and then fell into a normal dive. After years of normal loops, it came as quite a surprise for the pilot to be left with no horizon in sight and nothing on the clock, wondering what would happen next. This is yet another indication that the stalling characteristics are unusually sharp for a modern glider.

Other Club Class gliders

The Pegasus Club and ASW19 Club are fixed-wheel versions of the standard model and are also suitable for Bronze C pilots. I have not had an opportunity to fly the club versions, but they don't appear to be modified apart from having a fixed main wheel.

Competition Gliders

This group of gliders is amongst the top competition machines of the Standard class at the time of writing. They are all suitable for inexperienced pilots of about Bronze C standard, with the proviso that the pilots have flown several other types of solo machines and have some experience in a modern two-seater glass fibre glider.

These gliders are all characterised by their very light elevator control. This makes it only too easy to overcontrol and set up a pitching motion, particularly just after take-off on the first flight. Once again, I would advise lifting the gliders up to about 5-10 feet on aerotow instead of trying to keep very close to the ground. Keeping too close is a recipe for pitching badly on the initial few aerotows. The other controls are also very light, but light and powerful ailerons seldon cause any problem. In fact, if anything, they make the flying easier.

Because of the forward wheel position and the rather low wing-tip clearance on most of this class of glider, low time pilots will have to be careful to keep straight and prevent the wing-tips touching the ground in a light cross wind. Remember to keep that left hand down near the release until the tail is up and you are sure that you have everything under complete control.

The retractable undercarriage should not cause any difficulty. Experience shows that the most likely cause of landing wheel up is forgetting to raise the wheel after release. Then, when intending to lower the wheel before landing, to move the lever and raise it by mistake.

Since quite serious and expensive damage can occur on a wheel-up landing, it seems sensible to fit a warning device. It is certainly good sense to make sure that the cockpit side is clearly labelled to indicate the 'down' position and it is always wise to glance down to check that you are on the correct lever. There have been a number of accidents caused by the pilot pulling on the undercarriage or flap lever, instead of the airbrakes, on the approach.

The Jantar Standard

Much has been learned about glass fibre construction and finishing since the early days. Some of the old machines are prone to some surface finish deterioration and so a very careful inspection of the finish is particularly important to avoid buying a heap of trouble. (This is true of any older type of glass fibre glider, or any machine which is more than about 5 years old, and of any glider that has been left out in all weathers.)

The latest Jantar Standard 3 is a direct descendant of the original model which went into production in 1973. The Jantar is a thoroughly practical glider, with a best L/D of about 40:1 and very good high speed performance. Flying against the Standard Jantars in Australia, I found them markedly superior to the Standard Cirrus in the straight glides at about 80 knots. However, this could well have been because they were flying with full water ballast and had a higher wing loading.

The general handling is straightforward, the stall is similar to most glass two-seaters and the airbrakes are powerful enough to give confidence in early field landings.

Although not quite as good as the very latest in Standard class machines, the Jantar Standard makes a very good interim machine for the pilot aspiring to enter competitions seriously.

SZD-41 Jantar Standard (photograph courtesy of Robert Bryce-Smith)

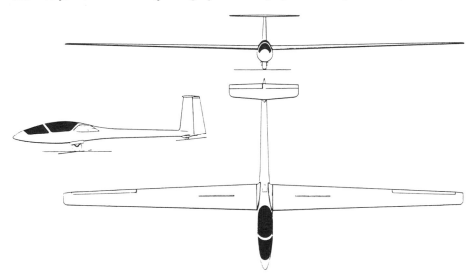

The ASW19

This design superseded the ASW15 and incorporated carbon fibre for the main spar booms to save weight and to enable use of a thinner aerofoil. It is a truly great design and is very suitable as a first glass machine for any well trained solo pilot.

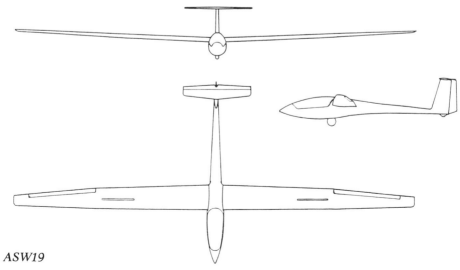

ASW19

Like those on the ASW15 and Club Libelle, the ailerons on this machine are so light that I always have the suspicion, for a moment on take-off, that they may be disconnected. In very rough weather they feel on the verge of snatching. I am sure that after one or two flights this feeling would disappear, but don't be surprised if you get the same impression as you make your first flight in it. Personally, I prefer to have a more positive feel to the ailerons.

Like the ASW15 and all the Waibel/Schleicher designs, the ASW19 has the very tough (but rather expensive to repair), double-moulded skins sandwich construction. However, it is a beautiful design and one chosen by the BGA for their instructor cross-country training.

The Pegasus

This is another excellent glider. It is very similar in handling and performance to the ASW19, but has perhaps a more progressive feel to the ailerons.

For a number of years Centrair, the designers and constructors of the Pegasus, built components for the ASW20 before branching out on their own, first with the Pegasus and later with the Marianne two-seater. Centrair has since been taken over by a larger French company who are still producing the same range of gliders.

The latest model has a tail water ballast system to compensate for changes in the c.g. with varying amounts of water ballast, but this is of no importance to the inexperienced pilot who will want to fly it with the c.g. well forward at first.

The question of buying French, German, or Polish aircraft revolves mainly around the possible delivery dates and the exchange rates.

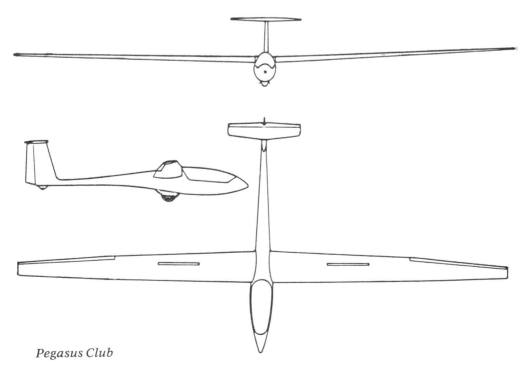

Pegasus Club

Pegasus

The LS4

When first produced, the LS4 offered the highest performance of all the Standard class machines. It has superb handling and stalling characteristics, and extremely powerful airbrakes.

One clever feature is the positioning of the undercarriage and airbrake lever

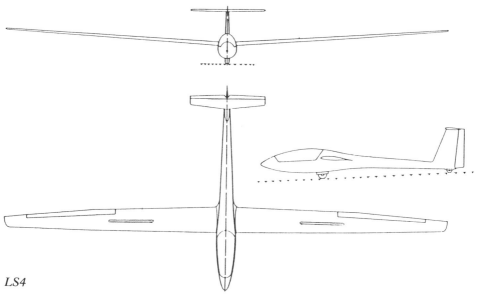

LS4

127

LS4

together on the left-hand side of the cockpit. The arrangement is such that it is difficult to get at the airbrake lever with the undercarriage in the up position. As a result, the pilot cannot forget to lower the wheel before landing.

Compared with some of the other designs, the clearance between the bottom of the LS4's fuselage and the ground is rather small, and the aircraft sits on the ground at a very shallow angle. This might be a problem when flying from a rough site and landing on stony ground, although I have never heard of anyone actually having trouble.

The Discus

This is another classic design from the Schemp Hirth factory. At the time of writing, the Discus is still the favoured competition machine in the Standard class, although it is suitable for any well trained solo pilot.

I had the pleasure of flying a Discus during a Lasham Regional competition and I found it a real joy. The multi-stage swept leading edge to the wing, which seems to be the latest adopted style, was originally introduced by the American, Wilf Schuman. Within a short time the German Akafliegs had checked the principle, and the Discus was the first production machine to incorporate it. The idea is to induce a slight outward flow in the boundary layer of the top surface of the wing, thereby reducing the normal inflow caused by the flow around the wing-tips. By doing this, the induced drag can, theoretically, be reduced slightly, because it weakens the wing-tip vortices.

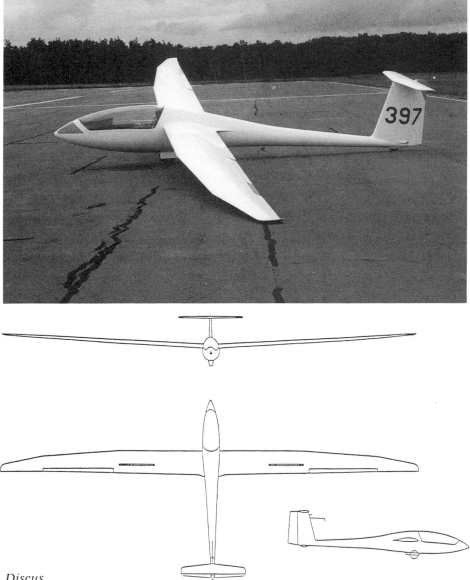

Discus

Whether this is, in fact, the reason for the success of the Discus is open to argument, but it certainly performs well and is thoroughly enjoyable to fly.

When the idea of the swept back leading edge was first mooted, I thought it might cause tip stalling in the same way as other forms of moderate sweepback. But the stall is very docile and it is only if you attempt to make it spin fully that the Discus behaves a little more positively than most of the other designs. If really provoked, it will spin fully with quite heavy pilots; the recovery, however, is excellent.

129

A good feature which I hope will become standard practice if not a requirement for every future design, is that all the controls are automatically connected when rigging the wings and tail.

Decisions, decisions!

So, which of these lovely machines would you try to buy? There is not much to choose between them for handling and general flying. They all have about 40:1 or above best gliding angles, but this will not automatically make you win competitions.

Experience shows that you cannot hope to be really competitive until you have been flying gliders for three or four years. Up to that time it is unlikely that you would find much advantage in carrying water ballast or in buying the highest performance machine available.

Delivery times for new gliders are often one to two years, so it is probable that you will buy what second hand glider you can have without a long delay. In terms of cost, remember that the glider is only part of the outfit. To make the most of any machine you need a minimum of reliable instruments, with good total energy compensation for the variometer. You also need a parachute, a barograph, and a trailer for storage and for those days when you don't get back to the site.

One big advantage of buying a used machine is that it will be ready to fly. There is a considerable amount of work involved in fitting instruments and radio, etc for a new machine, and in fitting out the trailer.

Of course, by the time this book has been printed there will be other new types of glider available; in the quest for better and better performance there may have to be some sacrifice in handling characteristics. It would therefore be wise to consult instructors and experienced pilots about the newer types to make sure that you are not going to buy a machine with unforgiving stalling characteristics which might prove dangerous for a pilot of barely Bronze C experience.

SECTION 3

Better gliding instruction

Safety in any kind of activity is largely dependent on the standard of instruction. This section is intended to broaden the outlook of both the instructor and the student pilot.

The instructor has the greatest responsibility in seeing that his students have a clear understanding of all hazards in gliding and of how to avoid them. Much depends on the formation of good habits in the very early stages. Section 3 is devoted to ideas on instructing and how to make it more interesting and effective. Some of these suggestions have already been implemented world-wide, while others may be controversial but worth considering.

Student pilots will find the information interesting and useful, because it should explain some of their problems and how their instructors try to overcome them. I have often found that students can gain a great deal from listening to instructor-training discussions. Advice for the new instructor is always good advice for the student pilot.

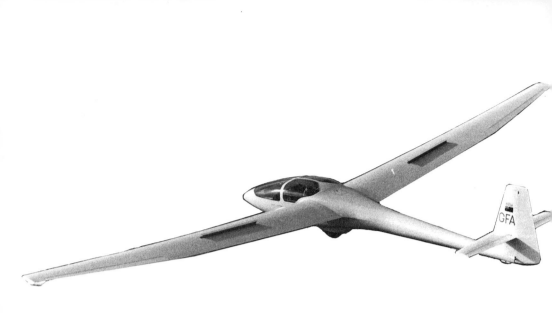

Notes for new instructors

During the first few months of instructing, every new instructor is at risk from incurring minor damage when teaching landings. If the approach and round out have gone badly wrong, a good landing is unlikely and it is always safer to take over and save possible damage.

Remember: it is no crime to take over control too soon. Gliders can be damaged if you leave it too late!

Making your mark with a new student

Unfortunately, in most gliding clubs students are likely to fly with a number of instructors and this slows their progress considerably. Your first flights with a new student give you the opportunity to win his confidence and respect of you as an instructor. He will naturally be a little apprehensive at the outset, especially if he knows that you have not been instructing very long. It is important to give him a useful lesson so that he will try to fly with you again in preference to another instructor.

However, if he is at the circuit planning stage and is working towards solo, you will probably not have much advice to give or anything new to teach in the air. You will be watching to see how he flies and, in particular, whether he recognises what is going on and whether he makes sensible decisions when they are needed. So, you may complete the flight, or flights, having contributed little, other than allowing him to gain experience.

Don't just sign up his progress sheet and log book and say goodbye. Find something about which to make a little lesson that he won't forget. For example, perhaps you have just seen another glider doing something unwise, or the conditions are especially interesting or unique. Spend five minutes explaining such things and make him feel that you really do care about teaching him. Then he will go away appreciating your help, even though the flights may have been no more than further practice and experience.

Keep within easy reach

The inexperienced instructor is faced with many new problems. While concentrating on teaching the student, he must pay attention all the time to the need to be able to get back for a safe circuit and landing at the gliding site. Students have an uncanny knack of losing extra amounts of height just when you need it most. So, always give yourself an extra margin of height.

Be ready for the student who turns left when you tell him to turn right on the base leg. On a windy day this can easily put you into an impossible position to reach the field.

Never fly for more than a few seconds directly away from the airfield without checking your position and the angle to the field. Ideally, get into a position from where you can watch the field all of the time before you start height-losing exercises, such as steep turns or stalling. It is only too easy to make two or three stalls and to find yourself too far away from the field and embarrassed by having to scrape home with little or no height to spare.

In the early stages point out why you have suggested getting nearer to the field. Later, when he is more advanced, ask the student to make the decision and emphasise that there might be sink on the way back so that it is prudent to allow for the worst. There are likely to be occasions when you see other aircraft just get back with no real safety margins or when you get into that position yourself. Use every incident as a lesson and make sure that you emphasise that you or the other pilots were lucky not to run into sink because it could so easily have meant landing out with very little choice of field.

Always keep within easy reach and make your student aware of the need to 'play safe' all the time. Only allow your student to make poor decisions if you are quite sure that you have the height to rescue the situation if the worst happens. Then explain carefully how the whole situation could have been avoided by taking action earlier.

If your student is likely to be running short of height, keep a careful check on the airspeed. Being low is one thing, but running short of speed and height is quite another.

Always keep an alternative plan in mind.

Cockpit checks

Watch for the student who says the checks out loud but does not really do as he says. For example, students frequently say 'Controls full and free movement', but they do not move the controls through the whole range or check that they are actually moving.

You may think they have done their checks properly, but the airbrakes may still come open on the launch. It is a good habit to glance out sideways to check them on every flight. It is even more embarrassing to have the airbrakes open if you have not spotted that they are out!

On take off

Having a wing drop onto the ground on take-off is not serious if the ground is fairly smooth and the grass is short. However, be ready to release if it happens in windy weather on rough ground or long grass.

As you leave the ground, always be prepared to stop the student overdoing the forward pressure on the stick. You have to be very quick to stop him from flying the glider into the ground. This is most likely to happen after he has climbed away too steeply on a wire launch or has got too high on aerotow, and also when you have just emphasised the need to prevent the error happening again.

Teaching landings

In the early stages, students need prompting and help to get the final turn in the right position and to straighten up in line with the landing run. Don't expect them to be able to fly straight. This is almost the last thing a student learns to do because it requires such good co-ordination.

The instructor will need to stop any oscillations caused by lack of rudder and badly co-ordinated movements; this should be done at about 50-100 feet. If you explain that you are only helping and are not taking over control (and tell him clearly when you take your hand off again), there should be no confusion. It is quite impossible for a student to make a safe landing if the glider is swinging violently.

Demonstration landings

It is important to realise that you should not demonstrate a perfect landing by rounding out and holding off close to the ground. If the student tries to do this he will almost certainly fly you into the ground. Instead, you need to start the round out a little higher than normal and the hold off needs to be a foot or two instead of inches from the ground. This is because if the student attempts to get much closer than that, the glider is bound to touch down the moment it starts to sink. If it is held off a foot or two higher, the student has time to spot the sinking movement and then start his backward movement to hold off again.

When the student is learning to land, it is the instructor's job to see that the approach speed is adequate and to arrange things so that at least half airbrake can be used for the last 50-100 feet. The airbrakes give you your reserve of energy and you will need it if the student balloons badly or gets the landing all wrong.

The worst problem for both the student and the instructor occurs when the initial round out is left too late. If this happens, the instructor cannot tell if the student is going to make the necessary control movement in time or to fly the glider into the ground. The student will snatch back the stick and overdo the movement. Since this is usually caused by looking too close, it is important to emphasise the need to 'look well ahead' on every early landing.

In fact, on every early landing, it is best to remind the student of all the vital requirements. These are: look well ahead; relax; be very gentle with the stick movements; and be ready to start the round out in time and not to leave the initial movement too late. It helps to cue students when to start the round out, but remember to allow a little time for them to react. Later, this talk should be cut down to a reminder to look ahead and not to leave the initial check too late.

A common error with inexperienced instructors is to use up too much height on the approach so that the last part has to be done with little or no airbrake. This makes it much more difficult for the student to learn to land and leaves you no reserve energy to cater for ballooning, etc.

135

Ballooning

Inexperienced instructors usually tend to reduce the airbrake setting too early when the student balloons the glider. This makes it balloon even further. Unless the approach has been very slow, or the ballooning occurs after the glider has been held off for some time, the moment to reduce the airbrake is just as the glider has started to sink. This prevents a heavy landing. If the airbrakes are closed unnecessarily, it makes the elevator control more sensitive and this increases the likelihood of the student ballooning.

Be ready to reduce the airbrake immediately if the approach is very slow and the glider balloons up, and take over straight away to ensure a safe landing. Avoid this situation whenever you can by checking the speed several times on the approach and telling the student to lower the nose a little to correct it. Always use an approach speed which gives you ample speed for the round out.

A late check, or the student moving forwards on the stick as the glider starts to balloon, are the two points which can catch the instructor out or cause him the most worry. If you let the student get apprehensive about ballooning, he will tend to drive the glider into the ground. Keep emphasising the need for gradual backward movements on the stick to make the round out. Even on the first attempt every student will push forwards if the glider balloons up a little. Be ready to stop the forward movement, as you will break something if you hit the ground with any drift.

If, with a normal approach speed, the glider balloons more than a few feet, the student should be told to hold the stick still for a moment. When the glider starts to sink again, he should ease back to stop the descent and hold off for the landing. While this is going on, you must reduce the amount of airbrake as the glider starts to sink; not before, or you will simply go higher!

You can tell the student that he should never make a forward movement during a landing. The landing involves a gradual backward movement. This may have to be stopped for a few seconds if the glider balloons up a few feet, but it is then continued during the hold off until the glider sinks onto the ground in spite of the pilot making a backward movement.

It is only when the glider balloons up to 20 or 30 feet that there is time for him to move forwards a little to start a completely new approach. Even then, it requires an almost immediate move back again to stop the glider from flying into the ground.

Emphasise these points: don't move forwards if the glider balloons a few feet; just hold still, wait, and then ease back as the glider starts to sink again.

In the later stages of training, when the student is making the judgements and using the airbrakes, remember to have your left hand very close to the airbrake lever and be ready to stop him from opening more airbrake if he has ballooned up or held off high. If it has been necessary for him to reduce the amount of airbrake because of ballooning, make sure that he cannot re-open them again until after touch down. If the airbrakes are re-opened, the glider will sink rapidly and even closing them quickly will not save you from a heavy landing. Remember, if you end up with no airbrake at low speed, you have no reserves left and it is wise to take over to make quite sure that you do not balloon up again.

Drift landings

Choose a clear landing area for the early landings and keep emphasising the point that whenever possible landing in a restricted area is to be avoided. Landing elsewhere, or further into the field, is preferable.

Stress the fact that no pilot, however skilled, can guarantee to land absolutely accurately and that landing between obstructions and, in particular, behind obstructions is most unwise. In gusty weather, any severe gust may make the glider balloon, and reducing the airbrake will then be necessary to prevent a heavy landing. If there is an obstruction ahead, this could mean having to take violent avoiding action to prevent a collision. Do not ever rely on the wheel brake. Explain that glider wheel brakes are generally rather crude and can let you down.

Steering

You must teach steering on the ground, i.e. using the stick and rudder completely independently on the ground run.

Crosswind landings

A drift landing will normally do no harm, provided that it is fully held off so that the touch down is made on the main wheel. Most students will be mesmerised by the drift near the ground and will tend to forget to make the round out if they are busy trying to sort out the drift.

In the early stages, whenever it is possible it is better to angle the approach across the landing area to reduce the effects of the cross wind. Always emphasise the need to concentrate on making a proper round out and hold off even if the glider is drifting. Any drift at the last moment can be corrected by the instructor kicking it off with the rudder just before touch down. This need not interfere with the student's landing and can be explained afterwards.

Later in the training it is important to make the student realise that if the glider is drifting towards something, the drift can only be stopped by banking away. Applying the rudder merely swings the nose and the glider will not have changed direction. (This makes an impressive demonstration when the approach is long and low with very little airbrake. Apply the rudder, keeping the wings level, and show how the nose swings but the glider hardly changes its direction at all.)

Remember that even the slightest angle of bank the wrong way (out of wind, wing down) will result in very large amounts of drift, whereas even a little bank into wind will usually stop the drift altogether. The crabbing method of cross wind landings is only useful for more experienced pilots, because it relies on split second timing for the rudder movement. However, the instructor should always be ready to kick the rudder to swing the nose out of wind if some drift becomes apparent at the last moment.

Eventually, every bit of skill and knowledge relating to flying safely must be passed on to the student. Personal experiences and anecdotes, and explaining

137

things you have seen, are more easily remembered by the students and help to make your instruction more interesting.

Safety at the launch point

Every instructor has a special responsibility for safety and must make sure that visitors and new members are briefed about the main hazards at the launch point.

Quite apart from accidents involving damage to a glider or aircraft, there are many hazards and many ways in which a person quite unwittingly can be hurt or can contribute to a serious accident at the launch point. Most of these can be prevented by good supervision and a few words of help and advice.

Newcomers and visitors should be carefully briefed about helping with even the simple things, such as holding a wing-tip, or where to push and pull on a glider.

Whenever winch launching is in progress, it is vital to brief them about the hazards of standing on or near any winch cable, particularly if there is a glider about to be launched. There is always a possibility of the spare cable becoming tangled with the one being used so that it and its parachute are whisked off at 60 miles an hour, taking anything in its path with it.

If a visitor or an inexperienced student is being briefed about the launching signals, make a particular point of explaining the STOP signal and emphasise that if anyone calls 'Stop!' that signal must be given immediately.

Many newcomers don't realise just how quiet a glider can be and that they do not always land accurately in the normal landing areas. Every open area on a gliding site may become a landing area in an emergency and everyone must be made aware of the need to look carefully downwind and all around for gliders and other aircraft landing.

They should also be told that when crossing a landing area it is better to stand still and let the tow pilot or glider pilot take the avoiding action than to dodge about or run across their path at the last moment.

The cable dropping area in front of and to the sides of the winch is especially dangerous. A cable parachute may look quite harmless as it comes down, but even the shackles or launching rings could kill if they fell on someone's head.

Towplanes and motor gliders are also potentially dangerous and there are still occasional incidents and accidents caused by people walking in front of aircraft or into propellors. Usually they occur when someone goes to talk to the pilot when the engine is running. Everyone should be told of the danger of touching propellors and that, if they ever go to an aircraft when the engine is running, they should always approach the cockpit from behind the wing and never in front of it.

It is also important to emphasise that on a gliding site most powered aircraft will have a tow rope hanging down behind them as they come into land and that at 60 miles an hour the rope and rings are lethal.

Always keep an eye open for newcomers to the launch point. They are a constant worry and must be briefed or looked after until they understand what is going on.

Teaching look out

When I was instructing for a period in the USA, it was very noticeable that many of the experienced pilots that I was teaching to glide had to be re-taught to look around as they flew. It is no wonder that in the crowded airspace, collision is an ever present hazard, with an average of about two mid-air collisions a month involving all types of aircraft. Of these, apparently 70% occur below three thousand feet and within about five miles of an airport, and about half occur in situations where one aircraft is overtaking another. This makes one suspect that either the pilots are failing to look out at all, or they are not looking round before they turn.

It is my impression that the average glider pilot has a better look out than the average power pilot, and that some of the pilots of big jets seem scarcely to bother at all. (Fortunately, they fly in completely controlled airspace and are closely watched by radar.)

Good look out

Glider pilots are encouraged to have a constant look out by needing to spend most of their time analysing which clouds are forming and where the best lift is likely to be. Also, of course, other gliders nearby are giving away useful information by the way they are climbing or, when cruising between thermals, by their changes in attitude as they dive to speed up through sinking air and pull up in any lift.

There is certainly a higher element of danger in competitive soaring where the pilots are often flying within a hundred feet or so of each other while circling to use a thermal. However, the risks can be kept to an acceptable level if every pilot keeps a good look out all the time.

Danger signs

Of course we all know that anything which appears to stay in one position on our windscreen is likely to kill us if we don't move out of its way. Also, anything which appears level with our horizon is at our height. But this all assumes that the pilot is actually looking out and that when he looks out he recognises what he sees and whether it constitutes a hazard.

Forming habits

Unfortunately, once a pilot has learned to fly it becomes extraordinarily difficult to establish the habit of a good look out and this applies regardless of the type of aircraft. Even the occasional nasty scare doesn't seem to have a lasting effect once habits have been formed.

The ideal is for the initial look around before commencing a turn to be totally automatic. This is not difficult to obtain provided the pilot is taught the correct procedure right from the start.

Look for the habit

Watch the pilots you fly with and, if you are an instructor, next time you fly a student just ask for a turn and attend carefully. What do you look for? Are you satisfied when he goes smoothly into a co-ordinated turn, or is there something else you want to see?

It seems that many instructors are quite happy if the turn is good. They think that the look out will come, like the co-ordination and other skills, with additional experience. Nothing is further from the truth. The maddening thing about the look out habit is that the more flying the person has done, the harder it is to change his ways. With a beginner, even after two or three flights, it is a real problem to change bad habits and is utterly hopeless unless the instructor makes a special point of tackling the problem. The only way is to ask the student to make turns and then to stop him unless he looks around first. This becomes very tedious for both the instructor and the student, but it works . . . eventually. However, there is an easier way.

Establishing the right habit

Habits, such as the look out, can be taught on the first flight; they last for ever if this is done properly. It is an exercise that the student can perform well right from the first flight and this is good for morale at a time when perhaps the student is finding the handling tricky.

Immediately after showing the basic effects of the controls, why not let the student have a go at really flying the aircraft? Teach him to turn instead of bothering about that straight and level flight. Clearly, at this stage a student can make more progress by using the controls to make proper turns than he can by learning to make the very minor control movements needed to hold the aircraft straight and level.

Establish the look out habit you want right from the start. Talk him round a few turns, something like this: 'First of all, look right around and behind you before each turn. (Not just a glance to the wing-tips, but right round.) Then look ahead and check that the position of the nose is correct against the horizon. Apply the bank with the stick [and rudder together if it's a glider or old fashioned aircraft] . . .' etc. etc.

For the next few turns talk him through each one, prompting him the way you want it done: 'Look around first, then look ahead. Apply the bank.' etc.

Don't let him apply the bank while he is still looking around (like you do), but make him take his time. One of the major problems with both beginners and experienced pilots learning to fly gliders is that they are always in too much of a rush to get into a turn. As a result, they miss the really valuable clues to the accuracy of the entry to the turn and only spot that the nose has dropped or risen long after it has happened. Looking ahead, they can see the attitude, the angle of bank and, when they become more experienced, any adverse yaw.

Don't fuss too much if the nose gets badly out of position as he looks around, or if it takes him a few seconds to settle down before he applies the bank. All of this will improve with practice.

The most important aspect of flying is to establish the right habits.

Setting the trap

After three or four turns I always set this trap: I just ask for a turn and keep quiet. I watch what the student does. Usually, you will find that the habit is already established and that he looks round properly before starting the turn. If by any chance he doesn't look around, pull him up immediately with a sharp 'Stop!' Then insist that he looks around properly before starting the turn.

Continue reminding the student on the trip until the look out habit is established. It will save endless trouble in the long run and it may save your neck at some time later when you meet up there in another aircraft.

At the start of each of the next few flights I always try to re-establish the habit by talking the student through the actions for the first few turns so that he is reminded of what to do and never makes a turn without that initial look out. For your sake and his, don't let good discipline slip.

Priorities

Of course, if on that first flight you insist on trying to show all of the effects of controls, such as trim changes, and changes of feel and response at varying speeds, the whole business of flying will look complicated to your students and some may even be discouraged from continuing with their training.

Re-think your priorities. Are those details of instruction you introduce on a first flight really important at that stage? Isn't it more important to establish the look out habit before anything else?

Simplifying the instruction

When I first started training gliding instructors, I used to tell them that to be successful it was 90% a matter of knowing how to set about it and how to lay out the instruction into flights which could be easily digested by the average student. The other 10% was largely psychology and flying ability.

At that time we were teaching on the old Slingsby T21b and T31 two-seaters on winch launches. Even the most able instructors were finding it difficult to teach effectively on the 4- and 5-minute flights. I would advise them that if they followed a standardised sequence, the majority of their pupils would learn quickly.

The secret to instructing on such short flights is to break down the instruction into easy stages. Trying to teach planning and judgements at the same time as teaching co-ordination and general flying is too much for the average student.

Inexperienced instructors still find difficulty in fitting meaningful training into four-minute flights, and I have even been asked by experienced power instructors how I manage to include teaching turns as well as the effects of controls in a fifteen-minute flight from a two thousand foot aerotow.

Because of the lack of engine noise in a glider, instruction can be far more intensive, with the student actively turning one way or the other almost continuously. It is very noticeable, however, that when longer flights are possible, the pace of the instruction is reduced without the instructor being conscious of the fact. When short winch launch flights are the norm, the ideal flight time seems to be between 10 and 12 minutes. Certainly, after about 15 minutes, the average beginner is beginning to lose attentiveness and co-ordination.

Watch what happens using an aerotow with a student who has been flying on short winch flights. Whereas the instructor would normally make use of every foot of spare height before joining the circuit, immediately there is more time in the air the student happily joins the circuit several hundred feet higher, without considering using up the excess by practising more turns, etc. In terms of instruction, much of the extra height and time are often largely wasted.

Of course, it is useful to make use of any thermal activity by talking the student into the lift. But it is not economic to make long soaring flights. I seldom let my students climb to more than two thousand feet before moving them on to find another area of lift. Even after only a few flights, I explain how we are searching and why we are making corrections to our circles to centre in the lift. By doing this I hope gradually to make them more aware of the whole art of soaring, besides teaching them how to handle the glider efficiently.

I have a personal rule when with a beginner never to take over to thermal. Usually, if you do take over you don't find a usable area of lift, or by the time you have got up a little and have handed control back to the student he is tired or has lost interest and is more interested in getting down before he is sick.

The major objective in any sequence of instruction is to make the task of the student as easy as possible by starting with the simple, basic essentials and then adding to them item by item until he has a complete mastery of the subject.

In order to simplify learning to glide, the instruction is best divided into two stages: the *handling stage* and the *planning and judgement stage*. This is a great help to both the student and the instructor.

Stage 1: handling

This is the basic stage and concerns the development of co-ordination and the ability to take-off, land and turn the glider. It does not have to include any judgements except for the round out and hold off for the landing.

The early flights can be made with very little reference to the airfield or to the circuit pattern and procedures, and this greatly simplifies matters for the beginner. It enables him to concentrate on the flying without having to think about the positioning of the aircraft.

Turning and straight flight

With this system, while the student is practising his turns, the instructor is talking him down into a good position off to the side of the landing area, ready for the approach and landing. This gives the maximum amount of time and height to be used for turns. With a winch launch, the practice turns can be continued right down until the glider is opposite the landing area ready to turn onto the base leg.

Turning is the basis of all gliding and soaring flight, and the more turns that are made the quicker the necessary habits of using the stick and rudder together become established.

Practising straight flight in smooth air involves very few control movements and is impossible until the co-ordination is well established. Therefore, it is much more efficient to concentrate on practising turns.

Straight flight is really a form of negative turning. To fly straight, the stick and rudder must be used to bring the wings level each time the glider is tipped by a gust or a bump. Straight flight should be avoided as much as possible on the early flights because it looks so easy, but in fact it is very difficult. Students find it demoralising when the glider persists in yawing from side to side and they are unable to stop it. Success in any exercise is important to keep the students' morale high.

Speeds

At this stage it is also undesirable to mention actual speeds or to teach the use of the A.S.I. Flying by attitude alone reduces the work load for the student and makes it easier for him to learn to spot small changes in attitude and to hold the glider in steady flight. It also avoids the tendency of the student to chase the airspeed and to spend too much time watching the instruments instead of looking around.

On early flights, attempting to watch the airspeed indicator in addition to the attitude is dividing the beginner's attention when he is still trying to become accustomed to the various control movements. The problem is not helped by the fact that flying a steady speed requires flying in a constant attitude.

Landings

Care must be taken not to waste a single landing. Every landing should be either a meaningful demonstration or an attempt by the student.

During demonstration landings it is best to tell the student not to worry about positioning and planning for the approach or to take any notice of the airbrakes. The instructor should explain that these will be done for him and will be introduced later once the landing has been mastered.

After one or two landings, the instructor can talk the student down using a fixed amount of airbrake for the final fifty feet or so. Ideally, this should be between half and full airbrake to provide additional evergy to cater for ballooning or holding off rather too high. In the event of bad ballooning or a high hold off, the instructor can then reduce the amount of airbrake to allow the student a second try to get a good hold off and touch down.

Landings are often almost wasted by the instructor allowing a situation to arise in which he has to take over because the final turn is very low, instead of telling the student to turn in to land earlier and perhaps land further up the field. I used to say that the instructor should offer to pay for half the cost of the flight every time a landing was wasted because there was insufficient time for the student to take over control. Certainly, every landing that the student cannot execute means one more flight before going solo.

The student will need some help with straightening up on to the approach and with stopping any swinging which may occur because of lack of co-ordination. If the instructor checks the oscillations for the student at 50 to 100 feet, there is not usually enough time for them to start again before the landing. This gives the beginner a chance to concentrate on the round out and hold off and enables him to have a go at the landing long before co-ordination has become established.

Ballooning

In the event of ballooning or holding off high, it is important not to sound anxious. It is very difficult to teach a person how to land properly if he is scared of ballooning. Anxiety about ballooning results in the aircraft being flown onto the ground instead of being held off to lose speed.

In actual fact ballooning is a useful fault, because it gives the student time to recognise the situation and to be ready to continue the hold off after allowing the aircraft to sink a little more. Also, the contrasts between a gradual descent and gaining height, and vice versa, are more obvious. Eventually, the pilot must learn to recognise a movement up or down of a few inches.

It is vital that every student learns to resist the instinctive reaction to ballooning, which is to move forwards on the stick. This usually results in the aircraft being flown into the ground and the instructor has to be very quick to prevent possible damage.

Just occasionally students make good landings from the first attempt and never experience problems with ballooning. In these instances the instructor must contrive to cause it to happen so that the student learns to resist the instinctive movement forwards. Otherwise, at some future date, perhaps flying solo, a gust will cause the glider to balloon up a few feet and the pilot will unwittingly push forwards and drive the aircraft into the ground.

This way of teaching the landing, with the instructor using the airbrakes, makes learning much easier because the student is not involved in having to make changes in the airbrake setting near the ground when things go wrong. The timing of the reduction in the airbrake needed when a landing does go wrong is not easy and trying to teach that, in addition to the hold off for the landing, is too much for most students to assimilate.

If at a later stage of training the landings deteriorate badly, it is often best for the instructor to take over the operation of the airbrakes from the student for a few landings until they are re-established.

It is important that the instructor does not unwittingly or deliberately change the airbrake setting during the hold off to produce a smooth, soft landing each time. It is very tempting to use the airbrakes to do this, but the round out and hold off must be made with stick movements. It is only too easy to have the student get the aircraft flying level a few feet up, and for the instructor then to open a little airbrake to bring it down closer to the ground and to close the airbrakes slightly to reduce the rate of descent so that a smooth touch down occurs. Clearly, the student will learn nothing if the instructor does this and will only get the wrong idea about how to land. This could produce no attempt to hold off with a gradual backward movement on the stick. In addition, this style of landing makes it almost impossible to make a spot landing and can result in a high speed touch down, with the tail high.

Aiming points

During the process of learning to land it is important to try to get the landing along a clear area, without drifting to the side, and not on a spot.

Don't give the student an aiming point or even mention aiming points at this stage, otherwise he will try to get the glider down instead of attempting to hold it off properly.

Aiming points and spot landings should only be introduced much later in the training and only after the student has taken over the operation of the airbrakes. Then, as before, the aim in the landing should always be to hold the glider off the ground for as long as possible to ensure a proper touch down at low speed, even if it overshoots the chosen spot.

Although towards the end of the training I explain and demonstrate aiming point technique to every student, I do not expect them to use it to make precision approaches. They are usually unable to see the subtle changes until they have more experience, probably not until after solo. Unless they happen to have a very long approach, they don't have enough time to spare. However, they can use the method to confirm when they are reaching the field safely and also when they are clearly overshooting and should use full airbrake.

Demonstrations

The instructor must use discretion when deciding whether to take over and demonstrate. On short winch flights it is especially easy to use up most of the flight doing a demonstration, which means that the student hardly get any of the flying. Demonstrations should be used initially to explain how a manoeuvre is performed and to set an example. However, it is a waste of time to give demonstration after demonstration and it is far better to let the student have a go as soon as possible after the first one.

After the student has had a few tries at a manoeuvre, it is often worth another quick demonstration to clarify a point, but remember: it can be very demoralising to be shown how badly you are doing.

Sometimes a student will have forgotten what he is supposed to be trying to do. For example, with the first part of a winch launch, it is easy to forget what it should look like. It happens so quickly that it is difficult to know if the occasional good climb away is skill or just luck. So, after a few goes at the take-off and launch, the student is more receptive to a further demonstration and it is useful to give one.

Where the student is doing well and is getting a little complacent or even overconfident, it may be a good idea to show him that it is still possible for him to improve and that it is still worthwhile trying. This is one of the few times when an instructor has an excuse to show his student how well he can fly.

Synchronised patter
I spent many years teaching RAF instructors how to synchronise their flying and patter, and it was only after teaching in gliders that I realised that this is not the ideal way to instruct in any aircraft.

Exactly synchronised patter does not work well. Because of the time it takes for the student to hear the instruction, understand it, and them to focus attention on what is being done, most control movements have happened long before the student is ready to see them.

'Pre-patter'
When demonstrating, the instruction needs to be given ahead of the action and in the form of a warning of what to do, or what to watch for, or the control movement to feel. Then the action itself can be cued by saying 'Now', or 'Like this'. It is easier for the instructor as well as for the student.

This technique is particularly important for demonstration landings where the student is following through on the stick and rudder, and where the all-important initial backward movement is so tiny.

High on the approach, or even on the base leg, the warning instructions can be given like this: 'On the approach you will need to look well ahead, about a hundred yards or so all the time. When the aircraft is getting down to around 20-30 feet or so (about the height of a double-decker bus), you will feel me make a very tiny backward movement to start to level off so that we end up flying level about 3-4 feet above the ground.'

'Now, there is the landing area ahead; look well ahead and keep gliding down steadily . . . lower, lower . . . I'll tell you when I start the tiny backward movement . . . [that was the pre-patter] . . . not yet – not yet – now'.

'Now we are level and I must keep the glider flying. As it tries to sink, I move back, back, back, until it lands itself.'

Because the hold off is a continuous action and the timing is not so important, it can be synchronised. But the student would certainly miss the crucial moment when the round out was started if the instructor synchronises his talks with his control movements. The landing might well be completed by the time the student had realised what he had to look for.

It is quite unnecessary to mention the use of the airbrakes during these early landings. Provided that they are operated smoothly by the instructor, there will be no significant change of trim.

Similarly, when teaching turns the instruction needs to be ahead of the action, particularly in any demonstration. Errors on the first one or two flights, such as letting the bank become too steep in turns, can be avoided by a few words spoken before the situation develops and this usually avoids the necessity to interfere or take over.

Following through on the controls

It is important to realise that getting the student to follow through on the controls can be confusing and unproductive. For example, on a bumpy day the instructor's normal reaction to the glider being tipped into a bank is so quick that the student will be confused by the movements made on the controls. If the left wing drops, the instructor will correct it with the stick and rudder almost before it has gone down. The student may, therefore, be puzzled, since he may think that the left wing dropped because the instructor moved the stick and rudder to the right. Usually the instructor's movements are so fast that they are impossible for the student to follow or to recognise what is being done. For this reason it is almost useless to try to teach aerotowing by this method.

Following through completely masks the all-important control pressures. Only the movements can be shown and, unless the visual sense is brought into play, it is unlikely that the student will have much idea of the actual movements made.

With turning, after the student has been shown what the turn should look like by watching ahead over the nose and feeling the instructor's control movements, it is always worthwhile doing a further demonstration, with the student watching the stick and rudder pedal movements to help to form a mental image of them. But it is only when he is given the freedom to try himself, with the instructor's hands and feet right off the controls, that effective learning is taking place. Obviously in the early stages the instructor must make sure that the student does not become scared by getting too much bank in a turn or by stalling the aircraft. This can usually be avoided by keeping ahead with the talking rather than interfering.

Phrases to avoid when instructing

Phrases such as 'Centralise the stick', 'Use left aileron', 'Use opposite stick and rudder to straighten up out of a turn', 'Watch your airspeed', 'Keep 50 knots', 'Pick your landing point', etc. should be avoided, because they don't help and can be confusing in the early stages. If the approach is getting slow, 'Lower the nose for a little more speed' is better. (If there is insufficient time or height, a reduction in the airbrake setting can be made without comment to allow a normal round out and hold off to be made at the lower speed.)

One of the hardest things for every instructor is to avoid mentioning points which are not essential. It is only too easy to start talking about lift and sink,

147

wind gradients and the hundred and one other things which are common knowledge for the more experienced pilot, but which are a complete mystery to a beginner.

Stalling

It is largely a matter of opinion at what stage it is best to introduce stalls. Certainly, it is unwise to show them on the first one or two flights while the student is still very sensitive to any pitching motions. I prefer to save them until later so that I can introduce them as a means of showing the student that he is making progress. This is particularly useful with a slow learner.

If co-ordination and landings are not progressing well, the student may begin to get bored with turns and become disheartened with his progress. This is a good time to introduce something new, i.e. stalling, rather than to continue concentrating solely on the turns and landings. If progress is already satisfactory, introducing stalling can be left until later, when it is useful for putting the student into a slightly unexpected situation for rejoining the circuit.

Obviously if an inadvertent stall occurs at any time, then the subject must be introduced right away so that there is no mystery about the loss of control. Otherwise, it may be a traumatic experience and lead to a fear or dislike of stalling.

Beginners tend to get very tensed up about stalls and spins unless the initial introduction is made carefully. Contrary to all you may have read in books on instructing, it is best not to brief about stalling and its causes before the initial lesson. A pre-flight briefing about stalling will have many students in a state of nerves before you even get off the ground.

The best way to introduce a beginner to stalling is to make no mention of stalling at all beforehand. Up to this point the student has been learning to turn, practising the look out and the co-ordination of the stick and rudder, and trying the landing and perhaps the take-off and launch.

When I am about to introduce stalling I ask the student to make several well banked turns so that I can check that the area below is clear of other aircraft and is suitable for the exercise. I also silently check that the height is adequate and that there is nothing loose in the cockpit. Then I take over control, saying: 'I have control. Those turns are going well, so I'm going to show you something new. Just sit back and watch. I'm going to show you what happens if I hold the nose up a little higher than the normal attitude. Watch; I've brought the nose up a little and you will notice it getting quieter as the glider loses speed. Now you will feel a slight shaking and the nose is gradually dropping. Now I have eased forwards a little and the glider is back in normal flight. That was a stall.'

With this method of introduction most students are amazed that the stall is so docile, and a typical comment is: 'Is that all there is to a stall? I thought it would be far worse than that!' Contrast this with the student who has been thoroughly briefed and who is in a state of nerves by the time the instructor has gone through his checks just before starting to demonstrate a stall.

This first stall is always very gentle and is followed by several more with further detail and with the student following through on the controls. It is important to emphasise that a large movement is not required to recover, just a relaxation of the backward pressure or easing forwards on the stick to allow the glider to recover. It is really a matter of allowing the aircraft to unstall itself, rather than making a large or rapid movement forwards on the stick.

On this flight I always introduce the subject of reduced 'g' (see page 70) and demonstrate very gently that the feeling of reduced 'g', although sometimes occurring during stalling and recoveries, is not a symptom or indication of stalling; it occurs at any time the aircraft is pitching nose-down and sometimes when the aircraft flies through turbulent air.

I never attempt any serious instruction on this first lesson. In most cases after landing I give a brief explanation of the causes of the stall and the way in which it can be recognised and prevented. I also mention the need for the checks before practising stalls (explaining that I did them as we circled before showing the first stall).

I also suggest that the student should now go and read about stalling. I think that it is important for most people to read about flying as well as to have the instructor explain things. Some people have good aural memories and others good visual memories; teaching is most effective when conducted in a multi-sensory way.

From this flight on, almost every flight should include some stalling, bringing out the various symptoms and progressing to stalling in gentle turns and more complete stalls with the nose higher. This leads on naturally to stalls with a wing drop (incipient spins) and, finally, following a comprehensive explanation, to full spins and recoveries.

Spinning
Whereas stalls and incipient spins in which one wing drops at the stall need very little technical explanation, full spinning does need an explanation before the first demonstration to describe why and how it happens and the logic behind the recovery. It can be a frightening experience if it is not discussed beforehand, and it may remain a mystery, worrying the student for the rest of his flying career.

Spinning is perhaps the only exercise which I believe should *always* be introduced by a careful ground briefing. Virtually all other manoeuvres are best introduced in the air first and then discussed afterwards, when the student has a much clearer idea of the problems.

Stage 2: teaching circuit planning and judgement

There is little point in trying to teach much about positioning and judgement unless the student has reached the stage of being in charge of the airbrakes. Operating the airbrakes is not a matter of learning how to pull the lever, but of learning to judge when and how much to use on each individual approach and landing.

The student is ready to start using the airbrakes himself and to take over planning and judgement once his landings are reasonably consistent and any ballooning is limited so that the instructor is not having to alter the settings of the airbrakes to correct the landing.

However, some of the concepts involved in the planning can be introduced

149

on earlier flights once it is obvious that the landings are progressing well and that the student has mental capacity available to start to make judgements.

Angular judgements

The concept of angles in relation to the nearest landing area is surprisingly difficult for some people to grasp and needs to be demonstrated on the ground before trying it out in the air. For most situations the positioning needs to be such that the nearest part of the field is at an angle of about 20 to 30° downward from the horizon.

Once I have explained this kind of angle, I ask the student what he thinks about the angle as we join the circuit and at various points. This soon shows up whether the idea of angles has been understood. Of course, this angle only works if there is sufficient, or more than sufficient, height for a good base leg. If the glider is lower than normal, the angle to the field must be much steeper, otherwise the final turn will be dangerously low. Extra height is seldom an embarrassment on the downwind leg provided the angle is about right. It just means a longer base leg and more time to make the necessary judgements as the excess height is burned off with the airbrakes.

For the first two or three circuits I try to set up situations in which there is ample height for a good, long base leg so that there is extra time for discussion and, where necessary, prompting.

Briefing

Once again, I seldom brief students about circuit planning until I have introduced the subject in the air. The initial two or three circuits help to make the later comprehensive ground briefing easier to understand and more meaningful.

About this time is also the ideal stage to discuss launch failures, etc., so that if they occur the student can have a go at dealing with them without help.

Teaching decision making

After the first few of these flights, I aim to allow the student to do all the planning, only making occasional hints or giving him alternative plans of action, and always trying to get him to make the decisions. There is seldom only one satisfactory solution or choice of action and it is important for the student to understand the options and to learn to choose the best one for the situation he is dealing with.

Teaching circuit planning is one of the most difficult stages of training and a common fault is for the instructor to tell the students what to do instead of encouraging them to make the decisions. It is only too easy to revert to saying, 'Turn now' and 'Open the airbrakes now' rather than making the student do the thinking and make the decisions by saying, 'Don't leave the final turn too late. You decide when to turn' and 'Remember, if you think you are unnecessarily high, do something about it; you can either move a little further back or use up the height with the airbrakes: you decide.'

Judgement of heights

Most students and early solo pilots rely far too much on the readings of the altimeter during the circuit. It is a good idea to mask off the altimeter between about 150 feet and 500 feet during all the basic training so that the student becomes accustomed to judging the base leg and approach. Once this habit is established, it is unusual for students to revert to using actual heights at a later date when they are landing in fields where the height of the ground is not known accurately. Heights above 500 feet are much more difficult to judge, but do not matter very much anyway, provided the normal angle to the edge of the field is being referred to and maintained.

I never mention any actual heights below about 500 feet; instead I try to relate the height to nearby trees or buildings and suggest that they try to think of the situation as being 'about right', 'unnecessarily high' or 'getting too low', rather than a certain number of feet above ground. After all, this is what matters – not the precise measurement of feet or metres.

Thinking aloud

It is a distinct advantage to ask the student to comment on his thoughts aloud throughout a circuit, because this enables the instructor to see how much the positioning and planning are down to good luck and how much to good judgement. I always tell my students that giving a running commentary as they fly will save them many launches towards going solo. When the student verbalises his thoughts, the instructor has a much better assessment of why decisions and actions are being taken.

Forming judgement

One of the disadvantages of all aerotow training is the tendency to make individual training flights. Single flights make learning to land or to make circuit judgements very inefficient. Towards the end of the training, whenever possible, the launches should be limited to varying heights between 800 and 1500 feet, even if this seems expensive and uneconomical for the student. Perhaps the ideal would be either a mixture of aerotow and wire or, better still, motor glider flights.

The judgement of the final stages of the circuit and approach is best learned by making groups of four or five short flights whenever this is possible. Perhaps on the first one the student comes in far too high and lands well into the field. In trying to correct the previous error during the next, he may be rather too low. By the third, therefore, he should be somewhere in between and beginning to form some judgement. Obviously a single flight each day is almost useless in helping a student gain the relevent experience. By the time he comes to fly again it is difficult for him to remember what happened on the previous flight.

Launch failures and cable breaks

There is often a tendency to rely on briefings instead of practical experience in dealing with launch failures. This can be very dangerous because, without experience, the student may not recognise the situation and may therefore make the wrong decision or no decision at all.

With winch cable breaks, it is important to give the student experience at the 'awkward' height, where a decision has to be made. This is particularly true on smaller sites where in some conditions the situations can be very critical. If these are not dealt with during training, they will eventually occur during solo flights. Unless this training is adequate, the possibility of a problem may be so unnerving that the less confident student may give up flying altogether in preference to flying with the constant worry about it.

Since launch failures are bound to occur from time to time, however well the equipment is maintained, it is important to practise cable break procedures during the training. Again, it is a matter of good decision making, having a clear understanding of the possible situations and having practical experience to reinforce any briefings.

Use of briefings

With flying instruction it is most unwise to rely on a briefing to cover a significant point and particularly one dealing with an emergency situation. Any briefing should always be followed up with instruction in the air and, later, with a test to see that the lesson was properly absorbed, for example, a simulated cable break at a height requiring judgement and a correct decision, or placing the student unexpectedly in a situation where the glider is a little short of height to see if he recognises this and takes the necessary decisions to avoid a dangerously low turn.

It is tempting to think that because the students can make consistently safe circuits they are fit to go solo. But the real test is whether they are making the correct decisions when the circuit is not perfect and when they are faced with emergency situations.

Flying speeds on the circuit

Variations in circuit procedures

In many countries where launching is by aerotow it is normal to pick up the approach speed as the glider joins the circuit at 800 to 1000 feet. This means that the whole of the downwind leg is flown at a high cruising speed so that the effects of areas of strong lift and sink are greatly reduced because of the short time that the glider is in them.

This style of circuit procedure is often adopted by instructors and pilots coming into gliding from power flying. Although it may simplify the initial training, the pilots do miss learning to recognise developing situations and dealing with them satisfactorily. It also means giving up any possibility of using lift once the circuit has been commenced so that many opportunities of climbing away and continuing the flight are missed.

Where only relatively low winch or car tows are available, starting the circuit at 800 feet or so leaves little or no height for searching for a thermal. This results in a drastic reduction in soaring. But, perhaps of more importance, the pilots never get any experience of thermalling safely at lower heights and of learning to judge when to break off and organise a safe approach. Such situations arise during field landings after misjudgements of height; the pilot who has always flown the whole circuit at the approach speed and has never used thermals at lower levels can be at a great disadvantage when things don't go completely according to plan.

Provided that the pilot has been used to joining the circuit at various positions, from the safety point of view there is no need for a formal downwind leg, although it does give the pilot a further period in which to view the field for slopes and obstructions. A safe landing should always be possible if the glider is well to the side of the landing area with an adequate amount of height for a good base leg.

The normal cruising speed for most gliders is too slow for safe flying below 3-400 feet for the final turn and approach. This makes it important to establish a suitable speed beforehand, but it is still a matter of controversy amongst instructors when and where this increase in speed should be made. When the glider is flying slowly, there are a number of good reasons for picking up extra speed before turning onto the base leg and very few, if any, for leaving it until the base leg itself.

Planning safety margins

For safe flying in a glider, it should be the norm to plan to have some height in hand for the majority of the circuit and to require the use of some airbrake to use up this excess on the base leg. Without this reserve, the pilot relies on normal sink at all times.

It helps to have a realistic idea of the glider's performance in terms of miles per thousand feet and loss of height per mile in no wind. At 25:1, a glider will go 3.8 miles per thousand feet and lose about 270 feet per mile. Yet it is not uncommon to see gliders still wandering about well upwind of the winches at a height of 600 feet or so with almost a mile to fly to a landing. This means that there is little or no height in hand to cater for any extra sink on the way back to the landing area.

On a busy airfield or gliding site, additional height on the circuit can also be useful to allow for the possibility of flying the glider faster than normal in order to get further ahead of another aircraft or to widen the circuit and delay making the approach to allow the other machine to land first.

In training, often far too much emphasis is put on having the 'right height'. This encourages the students to try to arrive for the base leg at exactly the height needed, instead of having a margin in hand. This, in turn, leads to short base legs with little time for judgements and for insufficient height to allow for the final turn to be far enough back for a reasonably long approach . It is much easier to organise the circuit with plenty of height so that a longer base leg is possible. Then the excess height can easily be reduced with the airbrakes, ready for the final turn.

In most gliders the stalling speed is increased by about 3-4 knots when the airbrakes are opened and the effect of even a slight error allowing the nose to rise for a few seconds can result in a large loss of speed due to the extra drag of the airbrakes. Therefore, if the airbrakes are going to be used on the base leg, it is essential to have more than a normal cruising speed so that they can be used without hesitation and without the delay needed to gain more speed.

Normal cruising speeds are really only adequate for average angles of bank in turns at height, and not when near the ground on turbulent days. At any time when a sudden height loss would be serious, extra speed should be maintained to reduce the chance of an inadvertent stall in the event of an error in speed control or a loss of speed due to turbulence.

Speed control

Speed control on a modern high-performance machine is more difficult than on most training aircraft, because of the much lower stick forces and because very small changes in attitude result in large changes in speed.

When flying in poor visibility or amongst high ground it becomes impossible to judge speeds accurately by the attitude. It is therefore particularly important to form the habit of getting the glider properly trimmed and of checking the actual airspeed readings every few seconds during the final stages of the circuit and approach.

Effects of sink and loss of airspeed

Perhaps an even more important reason for extra speed during the last stage of the circuit is that it reduces the loss of height caused by flying through sinking air.

At low speed the glider is far more vulnerable to lift and sink than at a high speed. Any sudden loss of height when flying slowly below 4-500 feet could leave the glider 'low and slow' and in an impossible position both to pick up the necessary speed and to make the final turn for a safe landing. When flying slowly there is a very real risk of losing the height so quickly that the glider becomes too low to allow time or height to pick up speed for a safe turn in to land. You may think that you can gain speed when sink is encountered, but it is already too late to pick up speed when the strong sink is recognised visually or by the variometer or altimeter readings.

Often the highest rates of sink occur because of horizontal variations in the airflow in windy or thermic weather conditions. A loss of three or four knots of airspeed due to what can be considered as a gust or lull in the wind will cause an immediate, rapid loss of height as well as a critical airspeed. Horizontal gradients are common close to thermals and this is what makes attempts to soar at low altitudes especially hazardous.

In spite of flying into strong lift, an immediate turn can often result in the glider losing several hundred feet and becoming semi-stalled. This is the probable cause of many stall and spin accidents on cross-country flights when the pilot is tempted to thermal at low altitude rather than go in to land. Even what appears to be good lift must be ignored unless you can afford to lose two hundred feet, drift downwind and still be certain of reaching the landing area.

Apparent versus 'real' height

While flying slowly, the pilot can easily be deluded into thinking that there is still plenty of height and no need for concern. Although he may be several hundred feet above the ground, in reality he may already be desperately low on energy. If he turns without gaining speed, he is liable to stall and spin; if he gains the extra speed needed to avoid stalling, there will be a considerable loss of height and he will be faced with a dangerously low final turn.

This kind of hazard can only be avoided by picking up the extra speed earlier while there is plenty of height so that the glider is never flying low and slow.

Once the speed has been increased and is being maintained, the height remaining is 'real' height available for manoeuvring. If necessary, a turn can be made immediately without the need for a further loss of height to gain speed.

Provided that there is adequate speed, in these situations a well-banked turn is safer and takes a shorter time to complete than one with a gentle angle of bank. This reduces the height loss and also the effects of drift in windy conditions. (In normal air the optimum angle of bank for the minimum loss of height is 45°, much steeper than most pilots would ever use on a low final turn.)

Running into sinking air at low altitudes was a common cause of accidents in the T21/Tutor era and is still a problem creator with many of the slower microlight aircraft. Numerous incidents and accidents used to occur simply because the speed was allowed to get too slow on the base leg and the glider just happened to fly into sink or bad turbulence. There is no second chance with a slow aircraft.

In those days pilots were made well aware of the dangers of continuing to fly slowly at low altitude. The extra 10 knots or so in the cruising speeds of modern machines has lessened the effects of sink, but the risks are still there for the pilot who persists in flying slowly all the time.

It is vital to recognise and accept that the glider is running short of height if this *is* actually the case. Otherwise, the pilot may instinctively try to stretch the glide to conserve height, with the possibility of ending up low and slow. In situations like this it is important to make a point of lowering the nose, picking up the extra speed and retrimming at a safe height. From then on the speed must be maintained to allow for a turn into the landing area when that becomes necessary.

Beginners often tend to retrim and pick up the extra speed and and then, a few moments later, let the nose come up so that they are back at their normal cruising speed again.

Minimising the work load

Leaving the preparation for landing or the downwind check until the last moment can result in the pilot having too many things to think about, and thus in serious overloading. It is then that it is easy to make mistakes in judgements and flying techniques.

Picking up the speed earlier reduces the work load on the base leg. All the vital actions and downwind checks can be completed without rushing, and this allows more time in which to retrim and settle down at the chosen speed. The extra speed gives a greater margin of speed above the stall and must therefore make the turn on to the base leg far safer. This is a definite anti-stall and spin precaution.

A little more time spent on the base leg is an advantage to everyone. Even

Nimbus 3 flying . . .

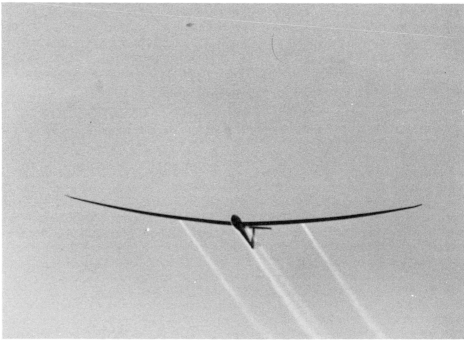

. . . and later jettisoning water ballast before landing

experts can find themselves under a high work load. Flying a new type of glider, jettisoning the water ballast, setting the flaps and remembering to lower the wheel leaves little time for judgements, particularly if the pilot has left his decision height rather late.

If the preparation for the landing is done earlier, the base leg only involves: checking for any other traffic; watching the landing area and the airspeed; and deciding when and how much height needs to be thrown away to put the final turn in exactly the ideal position and height in relation to the landing area.

Effects of excess speed

If the full approach speed is put on very early during the circuit, the extra loss of height must be allowed for, otherwise it may make a normal circuit into one where the glider has to be turned in early to avoid running out of height.

A high speed also makes the timing of the turn onto the base leg much more critical. On a windy day the ground speed may be over 100 m.p.h.; if the turn is started only a few seconds late, the glider may be so far back that the landing area is scarcely in gliding range on the approach.

In windy weather, increasing the speed up to a full approach speed of 60 or 65 knots before the base leg may create some extra problems for the pilot. Speeds of much over 60 knots will make it difficult for beginners, because there is so much less time in which to make judgements and to adjust the height.

For all normal conditions I would recommend that a minimum approach speed is used for the turn onto base and for most of the base leg, but that the final increase to the approach speed is best left until just before the final turn.

Except in very stable, smooth conditions, any glider flying below 400-500 feet at less than 50 knots or so is at risk. If it flies into strong sink or turbulence, the loss of height might leave it in a dangerously low and slow situation. In fact, below these heights any strong sink could put the glider into an unredeemable position within seconds.

Approach speeds

Minimum approach speeds

I always suggest to my students that they choose a speed which allows for a normal hold off and slight float using full airbrake throughout. This enables them to make a safe landing if they are overshooting slightly and need all the airbrake to prevent a bad overshoot. Later, when they are more experienced, I explain the advantages and also the hazards of choosing a lower speed.

Most pilots would agree about what is too slow, because it results in the need to close the airbrakes to avoid a heavy landing.

Allowing for strong winds

The actual approach speed is largely dictated by the wind gradient and turbulence existing at the time. It can be argued that there is nothing wrong with the pilot electing to make his approaches 5 knots faster than other people do. It merely means a longer float which can be allowed for by moving the aiming point back a little.

What is not acceptable is for the pilot to choose a speed which is too slow, or to choose one speed but to fail to achieve or maintain it because of poor speed control. This can be dangerous, because sooner or later he will end up flying far too slowly or at the wrong speed for the prevailing conditions.

Obviously plenty of extra speed is vital in rotor conditions or on a hill site with a bad curl over, and at any time when there is a very strong wind.

Dangers of judging speeds

Unfortunately, much of our flying becomes semi-automatic and, unless we make a conscious effort to check what we are doing, things can go seriously wrong.

It is important to cultivate the habit of checking the actual airspeed during the base leg and approach. The pilot who 'judges' his approach speeds will end up breaking the glider when landing on an uphill slope. The illusion of approaching too steeply will invariably make him reduce his angle of approach and so run out of speed for the round out. Extra speed is always needed for an uphill landing; it is wise to remember that when landing into wind, the wind gradient will be much more pronounced than over a flat field. Special care is always needed to keep checking the airspeed in these cases. Extra airspeed is soon lost during the uphill hold off and any visible slope has a drastic shortening effect on the length of the ground run. Usually, even on a gentle upslope, the glider will only run for one or two fuselage lengths.

Special cases

In most training gliders, establishing a suitable speed for the last stages of the circuit will be a matter of gaining extra speed. However, on some high-performance machines it may be a matter of slowing down to a suitable speed.

A few older glass fibre types, such as the Libelle, have rather ineffective airbrakes and therefore need low approach speeds. However, it is still sensible to have extra speed for the last part of the circuit and base leg. The speed can then be gradually reduced after the final turn to obtain the selected speed just before the round out.

Conclusion

Leaving the preparation for landing or the downwind check until the last moment can result in having too many things to think about and serious mental overloading. This is believed to be a common cause of poor judgements and landing accidents in fields.

The speed should certainly be increased for all flying below 4-500 feet and before the turn onto the base leg. This makes it far less probable that sink will deposit the glider low and slow, and makes misjudgement of the height available for the final stages of the circuit less likely. It also makes the turn onto the base leg safer because of the bigger speed margins, and it reduces the work load on the base leg so that accurate speed control is easier.

It is always a better policy to have something in reserve rather than to try to be one hundred per cent right with judgements on the circuit. You can always use up height when you want to, but you cannot regain it.

During training, pilots must learn the habit of maintaining a sensible speed and repeatedly checking the indicated airspeed whenever the aircraft is down below five hundred feet or so and particularly on the base leg, final turn and final approach.

The final turn

The analysis and explanation of the faults in the final turn form one of the most important and interesting parts of a glider pilot's training. The cause of inconsistent approaches can usually be traced to bad positioning or poor flying during this turn. The instructor should analyse carefully the conduct of the flight prior to the final approach, and identify any handling or judgement errors that might have contributed to such a poor approach. An inexperienced instructor who fails to look beyond the approach itself may pass on 'incorrect' advice to the student, who may become confused on subsequent flights when this advice fails to work. This is especially true when the student is flying solo and the situation is seen from the ground. Never jump to conclusions about the causes of a low final turn. They are usually the result of a poor decision earlier in the flight and are seldom done deliberately.

The first essential is to commence the turn high enough to allow a reasonable length of straight approach. At this stage of the circuit the pilot should not refer to the altimeter, since it may be sticking and over-reading by several hundred feet. Unless the approaches are always over open country, the student should be made to learn to judge by comparing his height with nearby trees or buildings. Thinking of the height in feet is misleading and unnecessary, and may easily cause the pilot to check his estimates by the altimeter. This results in lack of confidence and misjudgement when the altimeter is unable to give the exact height above the ground.

It is usually undesirable to have an excessively long approach, because variations in the wind and the effects of turbulence, downdrafts or the wind gradient may cause the glider to undershoot the field. If the approach is twice as long as normal, there is twice the time for these effects to occur and therefore twice the chance of them affecting the approach seriously.

On the other hand, a very short approach with a low final turn cannot be tolerated. A low final turn usually results in the pilot having to open the airbrakes at high speed close to the ground and experiencing difficulty in making a spot landing.

The ideal at most gliding sites is to complete the turn by, as a minimum, about twice the height of very tall trees (much higher in windy conditions) and in a position which allows for an average of about half-airbrake.

The student must learn to use his judgement about how far it is safe and necessary to go beyond the downwind boundary to allow enough room for the final turn and approach. In very windy weather, the final turn will need to be completed almost over the boundary of the landing area. However, on a calm day the turn must be some way behind it if the landing is to be made in the same position.

When the final turn is completed in the wrong position or at an inappropriate height, an undershoot or overshoot of the desired landing point may be unavoidable. If undershooting, any attempt to stretch the glide by easing up the nose during the approach will result in a loss of speed and, subsequently, a steeper glide path in a semi-stalled condition. This is particularly dangerous in turbulent air, when a gust or the wind gradient may stall the glider. In any case, the glider will land heavily and undershoot more than if a normal approach speed had been used.

If overshooting, diving off excess height will not have the desired effect unless very powerful airbrakes are fitted. Height and speed are more or less interchangeable, and diving results in extra speed. This has to be used up by floating level just above the ground; the glider floats almost the same distance as it would have glided at the normal approach speed.

At first, every student has some difficulty in making a well co-ordinated and steady final turn. This is due to the nearness of the ground distracting their attention from the handling of the aircraft. The stick and rudder movements are generally becoming co-ordinated after about a dozen flights, but during the final turn the rudder is often forgotten and the turn suffers accordingly. After further experience this problem tends to solve itself.

There is also a distinct tendency for the student to allow the nose to drop in the final turn. This is usually because the pilot has applied bank and rudder, but has failed to apply any backward movement to prevent the nose from dropping during the turn, or has judged the attitude of the glider relative to the landing area rather than the horizon. Sometimes this is caused by worrying about stalling in the turn, although in reality there is plenty of speed. A backward pressure is required for every turn; the greater the bank, the greater the backward movement for an accurate turn. The final turn is no exception, and this movement is essential, otherwise a slipping or diving turn will occur.

Excess rudder, or forgetting to reduce the rudder once the turn is established, is also a reason for the nose tending to drop. Since the stick and rudder movements have become semi-automatic, some over-ruddering in the final turn is almost certain to happen. This is because with the higher airspeed compared with soaring turns, there will be less adverse yaw and therefore less rudder will be needed during the entry.

There are several reasons for being too low after the final turn, besides starting it with insufficient height.

If the final turn is started rather too soon so that only a very small angle of bank is required, the height loss will be greater because of the extra time spent in the turn. A well banked turn is completed much quicker, leaving more time and height for the straight approach, and makes the positioning of the final turn much easier.

In order to finish the turn at a particular position, an allowance has to be made for the amount that the turn will bring the glider forwards towards the landing area. Most inexperienced pilots make the error of positioning themselves on the base leg, without allowing for the effect of the turn, and so finish by straightening up far too close for a spot landing. Much more room will be needed for a gentle turn, because of the larger radius.

On the base leg it is necessary to leave room for the turn to be completed well behind the landing area instead of directly over it. (You are flying a glider and not a helicopter!)

It is important to realise that if the glider is getting rather low on the base leg, a well-banked turn should be made *immediately*, if necessary landing across the landing area instead of directly along it. A gradual turn started at the same height would result in the glider running out of height while turning.

Excessive speed in the turn has a similar effect. The radius of turn is increased and more height is lost because of the higher rate of descent. In this case, the glider is often very low as it crosses the boundary, but with the extra speed it floats so far that it usually overshoots the landing place.

In a very strong wind, the drift will foreshorten the turn so that the glider does not gain much ground towards the landing area. The pilot must learn to assess the wind strength and how much room is needed for the turn. He must also try to plan the approach so that the glider is lined up exactly with the chosen part of the landing area as it completes the final turn. No further turns or adjustments in direction ought to be necessary before landing.

If the glider is too close to the landing area on the base leg, the landing will be an overshoot. The use of the airbrakes during the turn cannot correct this mistake and may result in the glider running out of height altogether. Airbrakes should only be used before or during the turn if it is clear that the landing area is within easy reach and if the turn would otherwise be completed higher than necessary for a normal approach.

A common cause of ending up too low in the final turn stems from starting the base leg a little short of height. This inhibits the pilot from moving back sufficiently to allow room for the final turn and puts the edge of the landing area at a steep angle. From this position looking down at a steep angle the pilot concludes, quite correctly, that he will overshoot badly. This encourages him to open the airbrakes during the turn which is already on the low side. The result is usually an unnecessary, dangerously low turn. In this case, the pilot has mistaken being too close and looking down steeply at the landing area as indicating that he is too high. In fact, he was already low and used up even more height by opening the airbrakes. Taken to extremes, he used the brake and could have collided with the ground; without the airbrake he could have completed the turn safely.

In summary, the airbrakes should only be used before or during the final turn if there is more height than is necessary to complete the turn and have a normal approach. This is best judged by comparison with trees, etc. nearby. The final turn must always be completed within a safe height.

Often it is not obvious exactly why a particular final turn and approach went wrong. It is only too easy for an onlooker, however experienced, to misinterpret the reasons for it happening. This is no help to the student who has probably frightened himself and does not want to repeat the same mistakes again.

Causes of a low final turn

1 Failing to recognise that the glider was low on the downwind leg and failing to shorten the base leg by turning early and cutting the corner to conserve the remaining height.

2 Making a 'nice square base leg' when already short of height, instead of cutting the corner to the final turn.

3 Starting a very gentle final turn rather than flying on a few more seconds to allow for a steeper turn. The gentle turn results in a greater height loss and the glider will still be turning while very close to the ground.

4 Using the airbrakes on the base leg without analysing whether there is actual height to spare.

5 Using the airbrakes during a low final turn after misinterpreting the steep angle as indicating too much height.

6 Over-ruddering during the final turn. Like using the airbrakes, over-ruddering creates extra drag and height loss, and helps to cause the nose to drop during the turn. If the over-ruddering is not recognised, the pilot will instinctively stop the nose from dropping by easing back on the stick, thereby causing a further loss of speed. (This is the classic way of spinning from a turn.)

7 Allowing the nose to drop during the final turn, causing excess speed and extra height loss.

Causes of overshooting

1 Keeping too close to the field on the downwind leg so that the base leg is too short to allow time for corrections.

2 Failure to recognise excessive height on the base leg and to move further back or use the airbrakes to throw away the excess.

3 Making a rigid base leg instead of a flexible one.

4 Failure to move back during the base leg to allow room for the final turn.

5 Insufficient room with a gentle final turn, bringing the glider into a position too close to or over the landing area before completing the final turn.

6 Allowing the nose to drop during the final turn so that the increase in the radius of turn puts the glider too close to or over the landing area. The extra speed then results in a long float and overshoot.

7 Late and half-hearted use of the airbrakes. The pilot recognises that airbrake is needed, but in spite of being high only uses half-brake or less to begin with. Very soon the glider is too high to get down even with full airbrake.

   (If the approach looks good, try full airbrake immediately after the final turn to check the glider is not going to overshoot. Use full airbrake to throw away the excess height quickly so that the final part of the approach can be made with less than full airbrake.)

Experienced pilots only
8 Failure to recognise that the glider is too high to get down, even after using full airbrake.

9 Failure to side-slip when it is first apparent that continuous full airbrake is likely to be necessary for the approach.

Causes of undershooting

1 Base leg too far back for wind conditions.

2 Total misjudgement of wind strength.

3 Failure to maintain chosen speed on the base leg so that the glider is adversely affected by sink or turbulence.

4 Excessive braking on the approach, resulting in a very low, no airbrake and low speed final approach.

5 Failure to allow for any extra loss of height during the last fifty feet or so due to wind gradient when using aiming point technique.

6 Trying to approach close over obstructions and not allowing for their turbulence.

7 Failure to maintain sufficient speed on the approach to penetrate a strong wind.

Teaching aerotowing

It should be the axiom of all flying instruction that a student should never be taught a method of overcoming a problem which requires bad flying techniques.

It appears that some quite experienced gliding instructors are still attempting to convince their students that the best way to keep behind the towing aircraft is by using the rudder. Some time ago I flew with a rather bewildered student who had just spent a week on a course where all of his instructors had emphasised this method. It seemed contrary to all he had read and been told before, and it is not surprising that he was in a state of confusion.

Aerotowing is probably one of the more difficult exercises to teach successfully; perhaps some instructors try too hard to give advice which will result in a miracle cure for problems that are usually overcome by a little more practice.

If all training is done by aerotow, instructors are naturally keen to get the student to do the launch himself. However, it does require a fair degree of handling skill and no attempt should be made until basic co-ordination of the controls has become established.

Many experienced instructors leave towing until near the end of the training, knowing that by then it will only take five or six tows to reach a good standard. Like most exercises in gliding, very little can be learned by the student following through on the controls or by just watching the instructor. It is practical experience, trial and error, which really enables students to learn and become competent.

The average near-solo student and the person with a few hours of basic training in a motor glider are ideally placed to start aerotowing, and should not need to be driven around the sky by an instructor.

Most of the problems with aerotowing seem to be due to the weight and inertia of the present two-seaters. Certainly, they do not occur on the solo machines. In the 'good old days', up to the time of the Eagle, Capstan and K7, it was policy to send off quite inexperienced solo pilots on their first ever aerotow on the Olympia (single-seater). Of course, a careful briefing and ideal smooth and clear conditions were essential. Hundreds of pilots were converted to aerotowing this way without serious trouble and without any dual instruction on towing.

When a two-seater is used, a good standard has to be achieved before it is safe to allow the student to go solo. At Lasham we found that it was easier to send them off in the Olympia than to ruin their morale in a T21b or Eagle which were heavy and not easy on aerotow. It always took five or six tows before they had mastered the art of keeping in position with these older two-seaters.

I am not advocating going back to those methods, but am merely trying to point out that aerotowing cannot be all that difficult. Perhaps our instruction is not very effective.

The take-off itself, unless there is an appreciable cross-wind, can always be done by the student. On the first one or two attempts, the instructor will want to be ready to take over or help during the climb out until there is enough height to give a margin of safety in the event of a rope break.

Instructors should note that whereas some gliders tow perfectly satisfactorily on the normal winch launching hook, whenever a nose hook is fitted, it should be used. On some types it is not always possible to maintain control of the glider on the rear hook and on these types a broken release spring in the nose hook should make the glider unserviceable for aerotowing. The problems on the rear hooks seem to arise more from swinging out to the side than by getting too high.

One advantage of dual instruction is that it is not necessary to brief the student on all aspects of aerotowing before the first attempt. A few well-chosen words are usually of more use than a comprehensive briefing at this stage. The detail can be filled in during later tows.

Most students experience a few problems on the first one or two tows, and the instructor should always explain that this is normal and that aerotowing is a knack which is usually acquired after a number of tows. If the instructors don't do this, the students tend to become rather despondent with their first efforts.

During the vital actions, the trimmer should be set a little further forward to help prevent the tendency for the glider to climb. Emphasise that the airbrakes must be correctly locked, since you jeopardise the tug pilot as well as yourself if they come open on the launch.

Explain that because of the slow acceleration on aerotow the stick can be held in the position to get the glider into the flying attitude straight away: stick right back with the older types, and forward with the modern 'taildraggers'. With gliders fitted with a forward skid, the take-off run will be far longer if the skid is kept on the ground unnecessarily.

Tell the student to watch ahead at the towplane and not at the ground, and not to pull the glider off the ground. Emphasise and explain the need gradually to make the attitude of the glider more nose down as the speed is gained so that it does not climb too high above the towplane. More and more forward movement will be needed to hold the glider from climbing as the towplane accelerates after leaving the ground.

Stress the fact that it is not desirable to try to keep down close to the ground; a height of about 5 to 10 feet is fine. But it must not, on any account, be allowed to get much more than this. Look ahead at the towplane and not at the ground; keep straight and keep the wings level. It is important to be ready for the moment the towplane begins to climb and to follow it up, maintaining position. Otherwise, it is easy to be left below it and to have difficulty in keeping the wings level in the turbulent wake.

Because of the speed on tow, all the controls become more effective. The elevator in particular becomes much more powerful and care must be taken not to overcontrol. It is wise to move up or down in small steps, a few feet at a time, rather than attempt to correct a low or high position in one movement. Moving downwards must be done gradually, otherwise the glider will tend to gain speed, making the rope go slack. Moving upwards always puts a higher load on the rope for a few seconds and if it looks as though there will be a jerk on the rope as it becomes tight, avoid moving up until the jerk is over. If you don't, you may break the rope or a weak link. There is always a tendency for the glider to zoom up slightly as the rope becomes tight and this should be anticipated by a tiny forward movement as it happens.

The ailerons become much heavier and the key to keeping position behind the towplane is to make very positive aileron and rudder movements as soon as a wing starts to drop. The wings must be kept level or parallel with the towplane's to stay behind it.

If a wing drops, the glider begins to move out to the side almost immediately and this usually starts a swing to and fro from side to side. The solution for an inexperienced pilot is to stop attempting to get back in line and, instead, to bring the wings level and to wait for the glider to come back on its own. It does no real harm to sit out to one side and, if the wings are level, the glider will tend to move back into the correct position. If necessary, a tiny banking movement can be made using the stick and rudder normally, but this should be followed by a small, momentary banking movement the other way as soon as the glider begins to move.

Eventually the correction should involve a co-ordinated turn towards the right position, followed by another turn the other way as the correct position is reached. This requires good timing and co-ordination, and will be quite beyond any beginner.

Using rudder alone to keep behind the tug not only constitutes poor flying technique, but it also leads to a poor standard of towing as the pilot becomes more experienced. It will only work in gliders which have stronger lateral stability. Otherwise it may result in sliding out to the side even further.

Corrections should always be made with the stick and rudder together. Emphasise the fact that when a wing drops, the student must use the stick and rudder together, making a firm movement and getting the wings level again as quickly as possible.

In reality it is doubtful whether anyone tows successfully using the rudder alone and it certainly results in higher drag than correctly co-ordinated flying. It also tends to create problems in ordinary flight when the habit of using the rudder to initiate moves is obviously a serious error.

On very many types of glider, including the Bocian, K7 and K13, the overbalance or change of rudder loads in slipping and skidding flight adds to the student's problems. If he forgets to use any rudder and is trying to keep the wings level with the ailerons alone, the glider yaws and the rudder is moved the wrong way by the airflow. This can be most confusing (even if the student is an experienced power pilot), because it feels exactly as if the instructor is interfering with the controls.

Of course, the instructor must keep his hands and feet off the controls unless he is actually taking over to help correct a bad situation.

The instructor

The first essential is for the instructor himself to be competent. He must be confident that he can rescue any extreme situation in which a student may suddenly find himself.

A useful test of competence is to try to move quickly from position to position or, better still, ask another instructor to put the aircraft to extreme positions and practise recovering. (Don't forget to tell the tug pilot before the flight!) An instructor should also be able to prevent a serious snatch and the risk of a rope break when recovering from a position with a big bow in the rope.

After the student has had some practice, the instructor should leave the student to try to rescue himself. It is unnerving for the student if the instructor shows signs of being scared!

Finally, it is of little benefit to the student if he is allowed to swing wildly from side to side, and it can even result in the instructor having difficulties himself in getting back into position.

Judging the towing position

Always start by explaining a method of judging the positioning in relation to the towplane which is suitable for poor visibility. Probably the best method is by keeping in position in relation to an imaginary line along the fuselage of the towplane, extending back to the glider. The normal tow position above the wake is with the glider just above that line. This is a good method because it works for all types of towplane, regardless of the power.

Positioning the fin or tailplane of the towplane against the cabin or wing to spot changes in the view of the towplane is another method but, of course, it requires learning a new view for each type of towplane.

Once a good position has been reached, maintaining position can also be accomplished by picking a spot on the glider's canopy or, if the nose is long, on the top of the instrument panel and keeping that on the towplane. However, this is not easy if the canopy is close to the student, although it works beautifully for the instructor in the back seat of the glider.

Only resort to methods which require the horizon if all else fails. Otherwise, the pilot will have difficulty later when he is being towed on a hazy day with no horizon. Most pilots eventually use a combination of many methods, often without actually knowing which ones!

Most beginners find that after three or four attempts they begin to get the knack of spotting what is happening and responding quickly on the controls to hold the towplane in position. Once the knack of timing the corrections is acquired, the tows become easier.

Instructors should remember that it is concentrated hard work on aerotow. Always take over for at least half a minute in the middle of each early tow to allow the student to look round and relax. Otherwise, you can expect the tow to deteriorate as the student tires and loses concentration. Also, if the tow is a high one, the student may be exhausted by the top of the tow so that the rest of the flight is of little value.

Releasing

During the Second World War, we were taught to slacken the rope before release on the heavy Horsa troop carrying gliders. But this was because the rope ends had very solid plugs of steel to fit into the release hooks which were in the leading edges of the wing on either side of the cockpit. On release under tension, the plugs could swing together into the cockpit and this made it a good idea to relax the rope by getting a little high and then lowering the nose before the release so that the rope ends dropped well below the glider.

However, this is not a good idea with the very clean gliders flown today. If you do this, you may find that after release, the rope end is thrashing about near your nose. A canopy was smashed this way some years ago and other pilots have had the tow rope over the wing, which could be very dangerous.

It is also unwise to put an extra load on the rope to make it more obvious to the tug pilot that you have released. Firstly, you may overdo it and pull his tail up, or, secondly, you may either break the rope or find that it is difficult to release at all. Releasing under extra tension is usually the cause of those knots which appear in the tow rope near the glider end.

Make a special point of releasing correctly from tow. Many pilots become sloppy after a while and actually start to turn off before they pull the release. If they pull the knob, but don't manage to release the rope, they will not be able to stop their turn and will topple the towplane by pulling its tail to the side and then up. This is hair-raising for the tow pilot and can be very dangerous for both towplane and glider.

Teach the students: (a) to check that they are clear to release and turn off, and (b) to release first, see the rope go, and then to make their climbing turn off to the side. They should slow right down, almost to the stall, before retrimming and checking that they can see their airfield or gliding site.

If this is done, there is absolutely no possibility of a hazard between the towplane and glider, whichever way either of them decides to turn.

After towing at 60 knots or so, all students have a tendency to fly far too fast after release unless the glider is slowed right down and retrimmed correctly. After the noise of the tow, even 50 knots sounds slow and, unless the trimmer is re-adjusted, the stick forces are also very deceiving. Get the students into the habit of checking for the airfield as soon as they come off tow.

If you fly abroad, some aviation authorities insist on the glider making a left (and some, a right) turn off, with the towplane turning the other way. In fact, the only real hazard is the lunatic tug pilot who, when the glider releases, pulls up into a stall turn. The tow pilot should always check that the glider has actually released, before starting to descend, and should never pull upwards.

Remember that all difficulties are solved by a little more practice and that almost every beginner doubts his ability to learn to do it. The ability to see the movements and correct them quickly comes after a few launches; gimmicks, such as using the rudder alone, do very little to help, and may cause endless problems at a later date.

Teaching other pilots to fly gliders

These notes may prevent unnecessary and irrelevent instruction being given by a gliding instructor who has little or no experience on powered aircraft, or who may be uncertain about training someone who has thousands of hours on powered machines.

What to expect

A pilot who has been flying 3-axis micro-lights, light aircraft or even large jets should not really have a great deal of trouble converting onto gliders. However, he will certainly resent being treated as an absolute beginner and being shown the basic effects of controls! Don't think this is an exaggeration. It is quite common for experienced gliding instructors to be given lesson 1 on the effects of controls by power instructors when they go for their first lesson on a light aircraft.

Try to find out from the start about how much training they will need and explain this to them. Power pilots can usually begin at the stage of circuit planning and judgement, because after the first few landings they are quite ready to take over the operation of the airbrakes and do the planning. The co-ordination will certainly need quite a lot of working on, but that can be done during the flights at the same time as the circuit planning.

Occasionally you will meet poor pilots and will wonder how they ever managed to fly safely and get a licence. They are usually people who have only flown one type of aircraft and have just about managed to master that. Put in a different machine or a glider, they are completely thrown, and they are often shattered to find that they really cannot manage at all. Some pilots find it difficult to accept that they have much more to learn about flying and give up gliding when they find that it is not as easy as it looks.

Differences in handling

Most powered aircraft differ from gliders in their shorter wing span and higher flying speeds. Their control forces may be considerably heavier and the longitudinal stability much stronger, which means that they are hard work to fly unless they are retrimmed for every small change of attitude and power. They have flaps but not airbrakes, and because of the shorter wing span, their rate of roll is much better, making the ailerons crisp and effective. (If you haven't ever flown a powered aircraft, try to get a short flight with an instructor to see for yourself what it is like. Most glider pilots find the average modern light aircraft very easy to fly and land.)

Unlike teaching a beginner, it is worth spending time briefing a power pilot before flying. It is useful to explain the adverse yaw, the need for stick and rudder co-ordination and the reasons for having to hold off bank yet leave a little rudder on during the turns.

Aerotowing

Apart from ex-Service pilots, very few people have ever flown in formation and therefore aerotowing is a new experience. So, it is a good idea to demonstrate the first tow and to let them try the second one when they have the feel of the controls and a better grasp of co-ordination. However, on the first tow it is valuable to show them the low tow position and the effect of flying through and in the slipstream. I also like to show them the best position for towing and the upward limit that I want them to respect.

Aerotowing is difficult until the pilot has established some stick and rudder co-ordination; therefore, few pilots will manage the very first aerotow and it is demoralising for them if they swing about all over the place.

Using the rudder

Immediately after releasing and trimming the aircraft, it is worth demonstrating the adverse yaw. This is insignificant in a powered aircraft and most power pilots do not even know that it exists. You don't need to explain the basic control movements; just show the large swing of the nose when the aileron alone is applied. It is also worth demonstrating that once the glider is in a turn it needs virtually no rudder, and that the fairly large amount of rudder used during the start of the turn should be reduced as soon as the aileron movement has been made to check the banking movement.

Point out that, as with all aircraft, a backward movement is needed during every turn.

Ask the pilot to try the rudder control and to feel the loads change as the rudder overbalances. You will have to explain this, as it does not occur on normal powered aircraft. Then quickly demonstrate the stick and rudder movements for a turn.

Look out

Try not to embarrass the pilot by having to point out that he has completely omitted to look around before starting a turn. This can be avoided by pattering through the first few turns as though he was a beginner so that he cannot fail to look around. Many power pilots have lapsed into bad habits, but don't realise it. They will be genuinely surprised to discover that they don't have a good look out habit and should be more than willing to put it right.

Pilots are bound to have problems with the stick and rudder co-ordination and will often forget the rudder altogether. After a week's break they will have reverted to their old habits and will need more help, because the new system will not have become established.

Most power pilots are not accustomed to using such steep turns, or such high rates of turn as are employed on gliders. Instructors should therefore make them use plenty of bank.

Stalling and spinning

They will be interested to see the stall, but may be so out of practice at stalling that it could be wise to demonstrate one, emphasising the small movement forwards or relaxation of the backward pressure on the stick. They may have been taught to move forwards quickly and this may put you into a steep diving position, frightening them and perhaps you, too!

Very few pilots seem happy if the glider drops a wing and many will never have done any full spinning, but that can be left for later flights.

Don't be surprised if you meet some power pilots who are terrified of spinning. Work gradually from stalls to incipients, and finally to full spins. The rest of their flying may be perfect, but they must be confident about spin recoveries before they go solo in a glider. Otherwise, if you put it off and let them go solo, they will never combat their worries.

Don't do any full spins without a careful briefing unless the pilots have executed plenty before and are obviously happy about them. Even then, perform a demonstration spin first, with the pilots following through. (A full blooded spin recovery for some aircraft will make a training glider turn upside down and go off Vne.)

Initial landings

It is usually best to work the airbrakes for them for the first two or three landings. Otherwise, there is too much to explain and for them to master. They will almost certainly round out and hold off far too high, in spite of being reminded that there is no long undercarriage. Tell them that: the landing is just the same as in other aircraft, except that it is much nearer the ground; after the round out, the glider must be held off just like any other aircraft.

In spite of being told, powered pilots' first landings are always held off high and will end up touching down tail first. Explain that this does not really matter, but is caused by the high hold off and by the stick being snatched back instead of being eased gradually backwards as the glider sinks the last few inches.

Give them a definite approach speed to maintain and arrange the approach so that plenty of airbrake is needed. A glider landing is rather like a flapless landing in a powered machine. The speed and control response does not decay as quickly as on a light aircraft landing with the flaps down. This is because on light aircraft the high induced drag from the short span wings results in a rapid loss of speed and the need to bring the stick back very much quicker than in a glider. All that is required for a glider is a smooth, gradual backward movement until the glider practically lands itself.

Warn all pilots against pumping on the stick during the hold off. Many power pilots do this. It isn't good flying and it will cause trouble later when on a more modern glider with light control forces. Just occasionally you may find pilots who have not been taught to hold off properly in their powered aircraft.

After several flights, most pilots will be making good landings, although you may still have to persuade them to get down closer to the ground for the hold off. Then introduce the airbrakes, trying them out to get the feel at height before using them on the approach. On the first few attempts with the airbrakes, encourage the pilots to set them and keep them still for the last part of the approach and for the landing. Mention that their function is similar to that of a throttle. Push it forwards to go further; pull it back to steepen the approach.

Flexible circuit planning

Power pilots are used to having a rigid circuit discipline and making square circuits. Spend time briefing them about circuit planning, emphasising that it is sometimes necessary to do unconventional things such as landing in a different direction because of running short of height.

Explain that the base leg does not have to be square with the landing run and that it should be used for the positioning of the final turn. During the base leg pilots will need encouraging to make slight turns away or towards the landing area to adjust the positioning, as well as to open the airbrakes to use up excess height when necessary.

You will notice that at first they will always start their final turn far too early so that a very gradual turn is needed to line up properly with the landing area. This is because they are accustomed to a much larger radius of turn due to the higher approach speeds in their powered aircraft.

Conditions

Power pilots are not particularly aware of the effects of strong winds; the wind gradient effects are less for powered machines than they are for gliders because their approaches are so much shallower.

It is important for power pilots to have experience flying the glider in both light and strong winds, because of the large differences in the positioning necessary for a safe approach.

Teach the pilots all you can about centring techniques and how to search for lift under the cumulus clouds. They are not learning to glide in order to do circuits. It is important to convey the need for well-banked turns and to show them that getting into the core of a thermal requires quite steep turns. If other gliders are in the thermal (which might unnerve them), this is a good time to reinforce look out.

Most power pilots will tend to rely too much on the ASI and altimeter and very little on their judgement. They are used to being told when and where to land and are not in the habit of making this kind of decision themselves. So, ensure that they get enough practice at problem circuits, running out of height and cable breaks. If they fly well, there is always a tendency to make assumptions about their awareness and to send them solo too soon.

Safety and glider aerobatics

For sheer beauty there is nothing to beat a really nice aerobatic display in a modern glider. Yet there are still many airshows which do not include a glider to serve as a contrast to the high speed jets and other noisy machines. Even simple glider manoeuvres such as spins, loops and wing overs can make a worthwhile contribution and a lasting impression on the general public.

However, although these manoeuvres are simple to perform, it is important to realise that they can quite easily go wrong and therefore it is vital to have proper instruction. Even the experienced power pilot can get into serious trouble unless he has been shown the subtle differences between glider and powered aerobatics.

Whereas it is possible to teach yourself rolling in a modern powered machine by pulling up into a slight climb and applying full aileron, this just won't work in a Tiger Moth and may be fatal if you attempt it in a glider.

Even if you only intend to try a few loops and stall turns, it is most unwise to go up and do them without having had at least one session with an experienced gliding instructor. At best, you will stagger over the top of the loops and only frighten yourself; at worst, you will end up with a full-blooded tail slide instead of a neat reversal on your attempt at a stall turn.

The problems are caused by the lack of power during the looping manoeuvres and the very high inertia of the long, heavy wings which make the rudder ineffective at low speeds. The long wings also result in a much lower rate of roll than on the average aeroplane, together with far more adverse yaw caused by the aileron drag.

Flight limitations

Unfortunately, the placards in the cockpit do not list all of the limitations for which the glider has been designed. For example, the use of a full deflection on any control is only permitted for speeds up to a maximum of Va, the manoeuvring speed. At this speed the gliders are usually stressed for 5.3g, but at the Design Diving Speed, they are only stressed for 4g.

When the airbrakes are open, the design load goes down to only 3.5g. This is because of the redistribution of lift over the wing: the lift is spoilt round the airbrake area. The effect can be seen on many of the larger span high performance machines as they come into land. When the airbrakes are opened, the wing-tips bend up several feet as more of the lift is transferred to the outer portion of the wings. (Just imagine how far they would bend at 3g with the airbrakes open!)

Whereas most pilots are aware of the dangers of pulling back too rapidly and overstressing the wings with high 'g', it is far more likely that problems will arise through exceeding the maximum diving speed and developing flutter. Flutter is a serious hazard with a flexible, long wing span glass fibre glider.

In a modern glider, even a shallow dive is sufficient to pick up a lot of speed, and any steep dive held for a few seconds too long will result in over-speeding. For this reason it is necessary to keep a close eye on the speeds and loads during aerobatics, because gliders are so much 'cleaner' and accelerate so much faster than the average powered aircraft. It is also important to remember that in turbulent conditions a gust load could add to the stresses and result in extra g and possible damage. Therefore, glider aerobatics should only be carried out in reasonably smooth conditions.

With the light control forces, it is not difficult to overstress a glider at high speed and it is important to have an accelerometer (g meter) fitted, as it is impossible to judge how much load is being put on the aircraft.

Loops

Improvements in performance have helped to make loops a little easier. In the old days, even a loop required finesse. Having dived down to get the necessary speed, the pull up had to be just right. Too harsh a movement resulted in high 'g' and a vast increase in induced drag, and too slow a movement resulted in the form drag slowing the aircraft down too much as it pulled up and over the top. In both cases the glider would arrive at the inverted position with only a few knots, so that there was some doubt about the direction in which it would fall. To complete a good loop, a pilot soon learned the need for the steady progressive pull up into the climb, followed by the continuous backward movement until full up elevator was reached at the top.

The power pilot who is used to flying round the loops will get a rude awakening if he tries the same technique in a glider. He is bound to arrive at the top with insufficient speed and will hang in his straps, which is an unpleasant though not a dangerous situation.

How to do a loop
Most gliders will loop nicely with a maximum of 3-3.5g using about 80-90 knots for the entry speed.

After checking to see there are no other aircraft nearby, the glider is put into a 30° dive towards a definite landmark and is trimmed forward. As the speed reaches about 5 knots below the chosen speed for the manoeuvre (usually 90 or 100 knots in a glass two-seater), the stick is eased back smoothly. The pilot checks that the wings are level and moves the stick progressively further back as the glider nears the vertical climbing postion. It is normal to reach the back stop as it becomes inverted. A slight relaxation of the backward pressure is needed for a brief moment, as the glider is almost into a vertical dive, before continuing to ease back to recover to level flight, checking the original landmark to see if the loop has been straight. After each loop it is best to pull up into a climb to turn the excess speed into height.

Don't snatch back or jerk the stick back at the beginning of the loop when the speed is high. This could overstress and damage the glider. However, once it is down to less than about 80 knots,there is no risk of damage because it is impossible to pull high 'g' at low speeds.

If the stick is kept right back as the glider recovers from the inverted position, it will usually buffet as the wing stalls. This is a good example of a high speed stall occurring in a steep diving position. A slight relaxation of the backward movement prevents this.

It is important to realise that although the backward pressure must be relaxed just after the top of the loop, if this relaxation is even slightly overdone, the glider will inevitably exceed the Vne during the recovery to level flight. For this reason it is prudent to practise individual loops instead of a series of consecutive ones to avoid over-speeding in the dives and to get exactly the required speed for the next loop.

Stall turns

With the stall turn, the power expert is also liable to make bad errors if he attempts the usual power type of manoeuvre. On no account must the glider be pulled up into a vertical climb, otherwise it will end up in a violent tail slide, perhaps with serious damage. Pulling up steeply and then applying the full rudder, as in a powered machine, usually leaves the glider pointing skywards and refusing to respond to the rudder. If you must attempt this kind of manoeuvre, try it first at about forty five degrees instead of the vertical.

It is not recommended that pilots attempt true stall turns; instead, they should be shown a 'lazy eight' or a 'wing over' type of manoeuvre which does not depend on the power of the rudder to yaw the glider. In gliding circles these manoeuvres are known as chandelles, although the name really refers to a precision climbing turn which ends up at very low speed heading in the opposite direction to the entry.

In a true stall turn the change in direction is made at very low speed by yawing round with the rudder, aided by the propeller slipstream. On gliders, which have no slipstream to help, the rudder is almost totally ineffective at low speeds and a tail slide is probable. This can be dangerous, because gliders are not normally designed for flying backwards!

The Chandelle

This is basically a cross between a steep turn and a loop on its side. It is mainly a looping, and not a yawing, manoeuvre.

The glider dives down to gain speed and is then pulled up progressively, the pilot applying bank as it reaches a gentle climbing attitude. The rolling movement is stopped as the the bank reaches about 45°, and then a backward movement is made to pull the glider over the top of the turn and back into the dive. As it dives out, the backward movement is relaxed and the bank is taken off using the stick and rudder together, before pulling out to level flight again.

It should be noted that hardly any rudder is needed during the initial banking movement, because at the higher speed there is little or no adverse yaw. During the second half of the manoeuvre, the speeds are lower and therefore more rudder is needed as the ailerons are used to level the wings.

Normally, very little rudder should be required once the bank has been applied. However, if the glider is obviously very slow and is not going round the turn easily, extra backward movement is needed to tighten it and extra rudder should be applied to prevent a slipping movement.

In essence, the chandelle is made by pulling back and looping over the top and not by a yawing movement. There are many variations on this pleasant and good-looking manoeuvre. The formal manoeuvre requires the entry and exit to be in opposite directions and at the same angles and height to make it look symmetrical. This is surprisingly difficult to accomplish.

If the banking movement is not checked, the rolling continues and the recovery will be 270° or more to the entry; this is actually part of a barrel roll. Caution is needed in this case to maintain full aileron as the speed increases above manoeuvring speed (usually about 85 knots).

If the speed gets rather low at the top, the secret is to pull back to tighten the looping part of the Chandelle. In a looping manoeuvre the speed can fall to a few knots, but gravity is still doing the work of changing the direction of flight and, with very little load on the aircraft, the stalling speed is close to zero.

Rolling and inverted manoeuvres

I have already cautioned against attempting aerobatics in gliders without having at least an introductory dual flight with an experienced instructor or pilot. This is vital if you are thinking about trying the more advanced manoeuvres which become 'critical' very rapidly. I knew two expert RAF aerobatic pilots who were killed attempting rolls in gliders, and I cannot stress too carefully the need for extreme caution. Moreover, you must make sure that the glider is cleared for these manoeuvres – many are not.

Although most gliders are stressed for up to −2.65g, this does not mean that they are safe for inverted flying. In many cases there is insufficient control to allow such manoeuvres to be carried out safely, and the inevitable side-slipping and falling out of a roll, for instance, will almost certainly take the glider well beyond Va, the Manoeuvring Speed, which is the limit for using full aileron or for side-slipping.

Rolling gliders

There are additional difficulties in rolling a glider. The rate of roll is very slow, a maximum of about 25° per second, compared with 100° a second for a normal light aircraft. There is no thrust or slipstream effect to help maintain the speed or enhance the rudder power, and the elevator power is usually limited at low speeds, but sensitive with very low stick forces at high speeds. Even more significant, gliders are much more 'slippery' and pick up speed far more quickly than other aircraft, making it easy to exceed the maximum diving speed, which is most dangerous.

During tests that I made some years ago in a Skylark 2, which is a relatively

A Grob Acro flying upside down over Lasham airfield, England

light and low performance glider, I found that at any speed above 50 knots, a half roll and loop out (split S) took me very close to Vne. Since the minimum speed for steady inverted gliding was about 55 knots, this meant that unless the speed could be reduced by pushing forwards and getting the glider's nose up, any slight loss of control such as letting the nose drop while upside down and then having to loop out, could be fatal. Having discovered this during the tests, I have always been careful to make quite sure that I never pull through if things go a little astray, which they often do, particularly when students are flying.

The situation can be saved by opening the airbrakes in order to limit the speed, but unfortunately they only limit it in a dive of up to 45° or so in most modern gliders. And remember that with the airbrakes opened, most gliders

(photograph courtesy of T. Joint)

are only stressed for 3.5g, which is easy to exceed. So, a simple half roll and pull through from level flight is an almost suicidal manoeuvre in many gliders, and loss of control upside down and having to pull through is fraught with danger. It must not be allowed to happen.

Of course, we all believe that in a case like this we would remember to open the airbrakes. However any aerobatic instructor who has experience teaching slow rolls in a Tiger Moth (which in many ways is similar to a glider for rolling) will tell you that students never complete their first attempts at a slow roll and, in spite of careful briefing, they never remember to close the throttle when things go wrong. They all seem to get stuck upside down and, after an attempt to raise the nose to stabilise the situation, pull back to loop out to normal flight,

179

usually at a cost of several thousand feet. This is not particularly dangerous in an old biplane, but it would be fatal in most gliders.

After these experiences, I consider it suicidal to attempt rolling gliders without proper training. Furthermore, experience in a modern powered machine with a high rate of roll is not of much value, except to become acquainted with the sensations of inverted flying.

Why are there difficulties?

Why is it so easy to become 'stuck' half way round a roll in a glider? Well, quite apart from the awful sensations of hanging in your straps for the first time and feeling as though you are going to fall out at any moment, as the aircraft gets upside down the rate of roll suddenly slows down. This is partly because you are unable, while hanging in the straps, to reach far enough forwards and to keep on full aileron, but also because, undetected, the glider has started to yaw and any yawing affects the rate of roll.

Almost all normal aircraft have differential ailerons. In other words, the gearing is arranged so that the up-going aileron moves one and a half, or even twice, the amount of the down-going one. This is done to reduce the drag caused as the aileron is deflected down to increase the lift to roll the aircraft into the turn. This makes the handling more pleasant and reduces the amount of rudder required during a turn entry. The long wing span of the glider accentuates the effect of this extra drag, making rudder essential whenever a glider is rolled into or out of a turn.

During inverted flight this differential is a serious disadvantage, since it results in much more adverse yaw. What is a large upward movement in normal flight becomes, in effect, a large downward movement. This creates large amounts of extra drag which the rudder will not be able to overpower. If a yawing movement does occur, it will reduce the rolling power, as it is yawing the glider against the direction of the roll. Even full rudder will be insufficient to prevent some yawing. First attempts at rolling in these machines usually result in getting stuck and having difficulty in completing the manoeuvre.

Control movements for a roll

If you work out the rudder movements needed to overcome this effect, you will see what is required for a complete roll. Because of the extra speed, starting the roll involves little rudder. Then, as the glider is moving over towards a vertically banked position, the rudder must be gradually applied to stop the nose from dropping. This must be kept on as the roll continues in order to counteract that very pronounced adverse yaw which occurs as the loads are reversed. At the same time, the nose must be prevented from dropping by pushing forwards. This is a much larger movement than you might expect, and it is advisable to sit much further forward than usual, to make quite sure that you can reach easily. Full left rudder in a roll to the right is needed almost all the way around the roll until the negative loads are reduced. During the final 90°, the rudder is reversed to stop the nose dropping.

Of course, the exact timing of each movement affects the accuracy of the roll and to most pilots it presents a real challenge to perform it neatly and accurately. It is a great help to have rolling experience in powered machines, but this is no substitute for instruction in a two-seater glider.

Teaching rolls

The best way to teach the manoeuvre is to start by making a half roll, and to try flying steadily upside down. Only when this has been mastered should the second half of the roll be attempted. An easier alternative to rolling out from the inverted position is to push forwards to reduce the speed and then to pull through in a half loop to normal flight. On no account must it be pulled through without slowing down first. However, if anything does go wrong, the airbrakes must be opened fully to restrict the speed.

First attempts, whether dual or solo, should be made above 3000 feet, as the height loss in a pull through is far more than in a normal loop unless the speed is reduced close to the stall before starting to loop out.

If you have already tried to fly in an inverted position steadily, you will have discovered the need for your safety harness to be really tight and for extra cushions to enable you to reach fully forward. Tighten those bottom straps until they hurt, and then re-tighten them just before you start the aerobatics. Surprisingly, you will probably find that your feet stay on the rudder pedals even if there are no toe straps fitted.

How to execute a slow roll

Let me explain a roll to the right. It helps to trim nose heavy (forward) before starting to dive. Your left hand should be on the airbrake lever to pull it if things go wrong.

Note: it is dangerous to attempt this solo without having some proper dual instruction.

After gaining speed to 80-90 knots, the nose must be brought well above the horizon before beginning to roll. At this position a small check forward is required to stop the nose rising further, otherwise the roll will be pulled off to the side as the bank steepens.

The roll is started by applying the aileron firmly. Because of the high speed there will be very little aileron drag and so the rudder need not be used until the bank begins to steepen. Then full left rudder is gradually applied to prevent the nose from dropping. As the glider goes past the vertically banked position, the stick must start a movement forward to stop the nose from dropping. If it is an early attempt, the roll should be stopped upside down when the wings are level. In this case, adjust the attitude to settle at about 70 knots and then reduce the speed by pushing forward into a steep climb. As all goes quiet, it is time to pull right back for a tight loop out to normal flight. Only when you can do this consistently should you try a complete roll.

Whatever you do when upside down, do not pull back!

Complete the roll in the following way. As the roll is continued past the inverted position, the full left rudder must be kept on to limit the adverse yaw. Maintaining full aileron, the forward movement on the stick is reduced and, as the bank is near vertical, the rudder position is reversed to stop the nose from dropping. Finally, some backward pressure is needed to stop the nose dropping as level flight is resumed.

It is seldom possible in a glider to roll out if things go wrong while upside down and the speed gets very high. The rate of roll becomes so slow that the glider exceeds all the limitations for the use of full aileron and full side-slipping, besides going far past Vne and the 3.5g limit when the airbrakes are opened. This is why you must have an instructor with you on your first attempts to ensure that you don't allow the nose to drop while you are inverted. Incidentally, I have never known a glider pilot who, after his first attempts at rolling, wanted to go up and try solo without more dual instruction. Once you have tried it, it is quite obvious that it would be dangerous.

Flicking out and other problems

If, during the push-up to slow down, the wing happens to stall, the result will be a neat flick roll back into a normal dive. Most onlookers will probably congratulate you on your roll out. When inverted, one or other wing-tip is almost certain to stall first, because the normal 'wash-out' is acting as 'wash-in' while the glider is upside down.

Flicking out when the glider is slowing down ready to loop out can be avoided: as it gets up into the inverted climb, the stick should be moved back a little from the forward position to reduce the negative loading and to prevent a stall. This enables a lower speed to be obtained so that the pull through takes a minimum of height loss.

Even if you are very experienced at inverted flying in gliders, occasionally you will be surprised. During a practice flight one day, I got the glider flying a little too slowly and into a high drag situation, losing height rapidly and semi-stalled at about 50 knots. I found that it was impossible to raise the nose to slow down for a loop out and the glider was flying too fast to loop out in the height available. However, I was able to roll out with a horrible slipping movement while the speed built up to over Va, the maximum for full aileron and full side-slip. I was lucky. There was no damage, but I had the glider checked over very carefully just in case.

There are two solutions to this predicament: either the nose must be lowered to regain normal flying speeds so that it can then be pushed right up ready for a pull through; or, the half roll can be made deliberately using bottom rudder to prevent any slipping, rather than 'top' rudder to keep the nose up for the last part of the roll. This eliminates the dangerous full side-slip which might otherwise damage the fin or rear fuselage through overstressing. When the glider is on its side during a roll it is often easier to think of 'top' or 'bottom' instead of left or right rudder.

Displays and air shows

Statistics show that many airshow fatalities with powered aircraft occur during looping out manoeuvres at low level. The height loss is seldom predictable: a slight misjudgement, or increase in entry speed, can so easily result in a greater loss of height than anticipated and a tragic accident. Normal loops at low level can be made safer by ensuring that the entry speed is well above normal. This ensures that energy is available to gain height in the manoeuvre. If the correct speed is not attainable, the loop must be changed into a wing over or Chandelle in preference to taking the risk of running out of air space during the pull out.

The effects of any strong wind can be very serious, particularly with glider displays. Usually, the problems result from being misplaced for a high speed low run downwind before pulling up into the final turn for the landing. After rehearsing in light wind conditions, the effect of pulling up through a strong wind gradient is a considerable extra loss of speed. This reduces the height gained, leaving the glider flying slower than normal. Then, on the final descent, the wind gradient causes a further loss, resulting in more reduction of height and speed, with the risk of an undershoot or at least a heavy landing.

In a strong wind it may be impossible to start the initial dive from the ideal position so that the speed obtained is less than is required for safety. In this case a quick change of plan is vital while there is sufficient height to make a more normal low circuit and approach.

Even slight drizzle can also have a disastrous effect. I will never forget my 1984 Tiger Club display when my display slot was in continuous light rain. Loops required an extra 10 to 15 knots just to get round without stalling and I was forced to leave the wheel up to conserve speed until the very last few seconds, because of the loss of performance.

Tape recordings for gliding instruction

There is nothing new about using tape recordings as an aid to instruction, but I am surprised that they have not been adopted more widely for gliding. They can offer an attractive alternative, or supplement, to reading and they are relatively inexpensive to make.

Because of the individual nature of gliding instruction, it is impractical for the instructor to cover every detail with each student. Usually, the instructor has a number of students, all at varying stages. Inevitably some are left to read, or to discover for themselves, information which the instructor would have wanted to cover if only he had had the time.

Many people don't have the inclination to read and absorb a lengthy book, but welcome listening to a tape as they drive to work or to the airfield for their next flying session.

A plain audio cassette has the advantage of being cheap and requires only a cassette player. This is ideal for a short subject. Ideally, it should be accompanied by a booklet of illustrations, or an automatic slide projector and slide transparencies, to give the listener visual information at the same time. But this, of course, is both impractical and undesirable in a car.

An actual talk by a competent instructor is always better, but a tape has the advantage that it can be played over again and perhaps used as a refresher at the start of each session.

I always use tapes for 15- 20-minute briefings on launching emergencies and for a briefing on field landing technique. They form a good basis for air instruction and seem to be very effective.

There are a number of exercises in the training of a glider pilot that really do need more than just the air instruction. But how many students receive these briefings at the gliding club? A lack of basic knowledge is bound to cause difficulties in learning and understanding the instruction, and may even cause accidents. Bad weather lecture programmes are one way of tackling this problem, but there will always be a number of students who miss some or all of the sessions.

Stalling, incipient and full spins, the effects and use of airbrakes, aerotow and wire launch procedures and emergencies, and circuit planning, including situations such as running out of height, are all subjects which must be covered by a careful briefing and can be done with tapes.

I have produced notes for instructors to help them give comprehensive lecture briefings, and these have to be signed off on a progress sheet before going solo. Where this proves impractical, the tapes can be used. These lecture briefings are important, because they help to extend the knowledge of the student. The pilot who only thinks and learns about gliding on his training flights at the gliding site seldom acquires much background knowledge.

For a beginner, it saves time and money to read books and to listen to and discuss other people's experiences; it is for this reason that I have produced a number of tapes for the gliding movement.

During the Motor Glider Study in Texas, the instructor's time was paid for by the student and there was seldom time to de-brief at length. After a flight and a short explanation, I would put on the tape briefing for that stage, or refer the student to an appropriate chapter in a book. Students also had access to the tape again when they arrived for their next flying session, to remind them of their last lesson. It proved very popular with them.

This kind of briefing also provides the instructors with a useful guide and review if they are going to give a similar talk themselves. In addition, they help to maintain standards in general instruction.

Recording talks

There are several ways of making these recordings. I prefer just to record an actual briefing, or to imagine that I am talking to a group of students. The alternative is to write out the whole thing and to get a good reader to record it. This is a very lengthy business and, unless it is done well, it often lacks the enthusiasm and spontaneity of a live recording. In any case, the recordings don't have to be perfect, because they are only listened to by each person once or twice.

A few sketches or photocopies of drawings help the explanations and keep the students' attention. However, even without these visual aids, the students seem so highly motivated that they listen intently and often insist on playing the tape through a second time at one sitting.

For courses and larger groups, the synchronised tape/slide presentation is very effective, but it does need a special projector, and it takes an incredible amount of time and effort to put together. Moreover, such presentations soon begin to date as new types of glider and new techniques are adopted.

Recording in the air
A number of my American students always brought their own pocket recorders and every word I uttered in the air was carefully preserved to be listened to again and analysed at home. Students quite often forget exactly what their instructor has said, and misunderstandings arise from time to time. Being able to play back and relive the flights must be a very valuable aid for learning quickly. (Knowing that every word is being recorded can also have a salutary effect on the instructors and, hopefully, makes them think more about their instruction.)

This is, of course, the normal technique on instructors' courses where it is particularly important for the trainee to be able to hear his own instruction and to recognise how he can make it more pertinent.

Chief instructors might like to try recording their instructors at work with students on training flights. They would be surprised how ineffective many instructors are, and would be able to help them improve their techniques.

Video

Videos offer even better possibilities for training. Once again, they are time-consuming to make, and only certain aspects of flying training lend themselves to useful programmes.

Unfortunately, unless the original recording is made on film, or with a professional standard video camera, copies are poor. The original 'take' must be edited to produce a master copy, and then the prints are third generation and are not really saleable. However, clubs can make use of the master copy. A number of clubs run a video programme as an introduction for visitors to explain about the club and safety rules for the airfield.

If you decide to make tapes for your club, don't expect all instructors and pilots to agree with everything you say. This is one of the slight disadvantages you have to live with if you make the tapes for club briefings.

SECTION 4

Converting to gliders

There are large numbers of glider pilots who are professional pilots or who fly powered aircraft. They enjoy the skills of flying other aircraft and find great interest and fun in gliding.

This section is intended to help pilots with power experience decide whether to take up the sport of gliding. Once the choice has been made, it will help them to make rapid progress through their basic training.

DG500M soaring

Coming into gliding

Perhaps you have made a start at learning to fly and have found it too expensive to continue. Maybe you have been flying powered aircraft for many years and are simply getting a little bored.

So, you have various possibilities if you want to try something new. Today there are microlights, hang gliders, soaring parachutes and, of course, gliding.

Gliding is certainly one of the best introductions to flying, because of the way it teaches airmanship and good handling as well as providing information about climate. In reasonable conditions it is quite easy to soar and stay up for several hours and, with modern training methods, it is not unusual to make a soaring flight on a first solo.

Competition cross-country flying in gliders is, to my mind, the supreme thrill in flying. There is the excitement of racing towards a good looking cumulus in the distance, hoping to get a reasonable climb and beat the other competitors; and then there is the feeling of depression on arriving just a few minutes too late and finding only weak lift and having a struggle just to stay up. Cross-country soaring has this incredible way of changing from minute to minute: down to five hundred feet, struggling to get back up again and avoid a possible landing in a farmer's field at one moment, and then up five thousand feet without a care in the world less than ten minutes later.

Even the apparently never ending circling to gain height becomes a challenge when there are several other gliders nearby. You watch them to see if any are out-climbing you and then you have the decision to stay safe or to leave the weak lift to go and join the other glider climbing faster some distance away.

These are only some of the decisions you have to make to get the best out of the conditions and it takes some years of experience before you can hope to compete with the experts.

In the majority of European countries, glider flying and gliding instruction is organised by non-commercial clubs. In other countries, such as the USA, most of the training is done by commercial gliding schools and these operate in a similar way to the non-commercial ones elsewhere. As a result, gliding is far cheaper than power flying in the UK, whereas in the USA it is more expensive. This is because gliding is a very labour-intensive sport which requires several people just to do the ground handling and to launch the glider, all of whom have to be paid in a commercial school. In gliding clubs, the members have to be prepared to do this work free of charge.

The following notes apply mainly to gliding clubs and not necessarily to commercial gliding schools.

Making a start

Flying gliders is one of the most rewarding ways of flying for fun, but is it for you?

Certainly, the best way to find out is to give it a try. Go along to your nearest club and have an introductory flight to get some idea about whether you are going to like gliding, but don't join the club there and then. Visit all the clubs within a reasonable travelling distance to compare their facilities.

You should consider whether a weekend or a full-time club is best for you. If you have time off during the week or you have long holidays, it will be worth travelling to join one of the larger clubs which have flying on every day. The location is also very important, because airspace restrictions, such as controlled airspace over the site, can make it difficult for early cross-country flying. But perhaps of most importance to you, especially if you are a power pilot, is what types of single-seaters are available to fly once you are solo, and how long it is likely to be before you are able to fly a modern single-seater for cross-country flying.

In the early days of gliding, you would have been wise not to mention any previous flying experience because 'power' used to be a 'dirty word' in gliding clubs. This stemmed from the fact that most of the training used to be by the solo method; in other words, the pilot was put on a simple glider and briefed about how to fly it.

Power pilots, with all their flying experience, were expected to be able to fly gliders and were often put onto them without even a proper briefing. The early gliders had poor handling and flew very slowly, making them particularly vulnerable to wind gradients and other hazards. Power pilots were frequently launched in, what was for them, a completely strange device, only to crash it if the cable broke or they were not able to adapt their flying quickly enough to the strange handling. This gave rise to the fallacy that all power pilots were a menace and broke gliders.

However experienced you are, you will receive proper dual instruction in two-seaters and the instructors will be well trained and competent so that you are sure of proper instruction at least up to the stage at which you fly solo. Nowadays, make sure that your instructors know about your previous experience.

If you have already undertaken a fair amount of training towards your PPL or you are an experienced pilot, you are over half-way in the training towards going solo in a glider. You just need to learn about the handling of the aircraft and about the effects of lift, sink and wind gradients on the circuits and landings.

If you are an absolute beginner, it generally takes at least two weeks of full-time courses to reach solo standard. For a power pilot of good average ability, a one-week gliding course in good weather should get you solo.

However, gliding is greatly affected by the weather and it is normal to make daily dual flights before further solos for a period after a first solo in order to get experience of different conditions. This will mean further courses, or joining in the fray with other club members.

The main point to remember is to arrange your introduction to gliding in such a way that you don't become frustrated before you have made any real progress. For this reason, I would strongly advise you to go on a course of some kind, so that you don't get involved in the weekend queues of members waiting all day for a flight. On most residential courses, you will be sharing the glider and instructor with three or four other people, and you will be flying as much as is possible each day.

If you are serious about getting solo quickly and being well trained, I would suggest avoiding a difficult hill site. Hills seem to attract low cloud and windy weather, and for training you don't need long soaring flights in hill lift. That kind of experience is of more value to you after you have gone solo.

Although on first arriving at a glider club you may be welcomed by an enthusiastic member extolling the virtues of the sport, you are just as likely to be ignored completely. You may be lucky and get some priority for your first flight in a glider, but after that you will be expected to become one of many trainees taking your turn in the queue for training flights.

This is particularly hard go bear if you have been used to ringing up and booking your Cessna for an hour's flying and arriving to see it waiting on the tarmac all ready to go. Many experienced pilots find being reduced to 'the new boy' and having to start learning all over again particularly difficult to accept.

It is a great help to understand a little about the psychology of a gliding club. A fair proportion of members genuinely believe that it is essential to keep the club spirit by making the training a testing time for the new member. They expect every member to spend the whole day at the launch point helping to push gliders and keeping the flying going, even though simple arithmetic often shows that it is quite impossible for everyone on the flying list to get a flight within the daylight hours.

However, it is not unusual to find a totally different attitude with the more experienced members and private owners. They generally treat the club as a means to get them launched and as a provider of helpers. No one really minds this, as it is fun to help rigging new types of glider. It also helps to pass the time.

There seems to be a feeling amongst private owners that, once they have gone through the learning stages, they have the right to do their own thing: do more flying and less of the hard work on the ground. It is true that many private owners drive the towplanes and, of course, many become instructors. Both of these activities involve more flying and fun for them.

Clearly, if you are already a pilot and can afford to buy a share in a glider, you will want to progress to this stage quickly so that when the weather allows you can be sitting happily at 4000 feet, instead of pushing gliders about on the ground. This may mean investing in a quarter share in a modern machine, but your investment is safe, as they do not depreciate or wear out.

If you are a beginner, you will use the club gliders for training and early solo flying, so you don't need to concern yourself about having a share in a glider until after you have gone solo.

It is important to realise that even when you are competent to fly gliders, you will always have to spend at least a half day at the club whenever you go flying. It is never possible to book, have an hour's flying and then leave the gliding site. This will still be true even if you buy your own glider.

Unless you can do most of your training on a motor glider, the best you can hope for is sharing a club two-seater glider with four or five other people and, since it needs an instructor and crew to operate, there can be no question of leaving as soon as you have flown. To be fair to the others you must be prepared to help out and to play your part to earn your right to fly.

Buying your own two-seater is seldom a satisfactory solution, because you still have to have help to get you into the air. There is unlikely to be room for another two-seater in the hangar, so that yours would need rigging and derigging each day. It would still be necessary to share the flying, as the other club members would become tired and would give up rigging your machine if they couldn't see any hope of flying in return for their work.

Also another two-seater does not necessarily help you materially to get more flying unless the conditions are very good and there are launches waiting for the gliders instead of gliders held up waiting for the launches.

Certainly, during the initial stages you will find the training rather tedious and time-consuming, although as you will soon discover the future gets easier and gliding has much to offer as you become more skilful.

Power pilots learning to glide

The first point to realise about gliding is that you won't miss the apparent security of having an engine. After one or two flights, you will soon forget your anxieties about being unsure of your judgement on the (forced) landings. With your previous experience of flying, the airbrakes make spot landings extremely simple, and learning to use more judgement will be of infinite help if you are still continuing with your power flying.

Unfortunately, not all gliding instructors have power experience, and some of them still tend to think that glider flying is totally different from power. In reality, there are only minor differences in the flying part. If you can fly one, you can fly the other.

However, don't expect moving onto gliders to be like converting from one type of powered machine to another. You will have to develop some new habits, and habits take time to become established.

The long wings and low speeds of gliders make the rate of roll poor and the adverse yaw much more obvious. This means that you must learn to use the rudder correctly going into and coming out of turns. Like any other aircraft, very little rudder is needed in a steady turn.

The landing is identical, except that the whole procedure has to be much closer to the ground because of the lack of a long undercarriage. Also, it is very like a flapless landing in the sense that the power of the elevator does not decrease rapidly during the final hold off. Many power pilots have the bad habit of pumping the elevator during the hold off and this causes overcontrolling and ballooning in modern gliders which have light control forces. Every power pilot starts by rounding out and holding off much too high, but you will soon learn to get it right.

In gliders, the airbrakes replace the normal flaps on a powered aircraft for steepening the approach path and cutting down the float on landings. However, they have the great advantage that, if necessary, they can be closed to reduce their effect during the final stages of the approach or landing. Unlike flaps, which cannot be raised safely near the ground, airbrakes can be closed at any time to extend the glide. Once you have learned what you can and cannot do, they provide a very easy and effective means of adjusting the glide path and of controlling exactly how far the glider will float before touch down.

With the normal cruising speed at only 10 knots above the stall, stalling, incipient spins and spin recoveries become important. If you are apprehensive about spinning, extra training will be particularly valuable. You will find that spinning in a glider is not as worrying as in a light aircraft. Once you have overcome your initial worries, you will feel more comfortable in all your flying. Being apprehensive about stalling and spinning is a sure sign that you have not had adequate instruction and experience, or that you have not kept in good practice since your early training.

In gliders, shallow-banked turns are the dangerous ones, from the stalling and spinning point of view. In a gently banked turn there is always a greater tendency to over-rudder than in a steeper one. Also, in a gentle turn the stalling speed is so low that the handling and control response is poor. When the glider stalls, a considerable amount of height is lost while picking up normal flying speed and regaining good control. In contrast, in a well-banked, steeper turn, the stalling speed is much higher, giving crisp control right up to the moment of stalling. Furthermore, with only a small movement forwards on the stick, the wing unstalls and there is plenty of flying speed and control response immediately. It is also a fact that most gliders run out of elevator power before a complete stall occurs in steeper turns, making it quite difficult to spin off a steep turn unless the stick is pulled back violently.

It is normal to circle in steeply banked turns at speeds as close as 3-5 knots above the speed at which the pre-stall buffet begins. This is often essential to make the best use of narrow thermals where a small radius of turn is needed.

The actual rates of turn are, of course, much higher than are possible in light aircraft, and the turns have the appearance of being made on a wing-tip. A complete circle takes from fifteen to twenty seconds, instead of two minutes in a normal rate 1-turn. At first you will almost certainly have a tendency to turn in gentle banks without realising it, because even then there is a rate of turn which seems higher than is usual in a powered aircraft. You will also notice that on the base leg you will tend to start the turn onto finals far too early, because your normal turn for a powered aircraft is so much larger in radius.

If you are learning on a site which uses winch or car tows, it is quite natural to be a little alarmed on the first few launches. They look terribly steep, but like most things in flying you soon get used to them. In fact, these 'wire' launches are much easier than aerotowing. The glider is relatively stable on the climb and almost flies itself, except for the initial climb away. This must be kept under control, so that there is plenty of speed to recover to normal flight in the event of a launch failure or cable break.

At most gliding clubs you will see practice cable breaks and realise that they are not so much an emergency as a nuisance because of having to retrieve the glider from the far end of the field.

Many quite experienced power pilots find keeping in position on aerotow difficult at first. Don't see this or any other problem you experience as a reflection on your flying ability. Aerotowing is difficult until you have learned to use the stick and rudder together.

Flying speeds

Whereas in most powered aircraft the aim is to keep well away from the stall at all times, in a glider using a thermal to climb it is desirable to be turning tightly close to the pre-stall buffet speed. This is in order to keep inside limited areas of strong lift. Extra speed simply means a larger radius of turn and a slightly higher rate of sink.

At other times, and particularly at low altitude while preparing for the approach and landing, it becomes vital to maintain extra speed, as the airspeed can so easily be eroded by gusts and wind gradients. At height, this speed control must be largely a matter of flying by attitude, with little or no reference to the ASI, whereas at low altitudes, it must be done as in a powered machine, by continuous reference to the ASI. This is because the attitude will be difficult to judge in poor visibility or when landing in hilly country or on sloping ground.

Most training two-seaters have a best gliding ratio of between 25 and 35:1 at about 50 knots. Above that speed the gliding angle becomes steeper, but you will be surprised how well they glide at 60 or 70 knots.

The handling

At first you will find a glider almost uncontrollable and unresponsive; it is not at all like flying a Cessna or a Cherokee. The glider just doesn't seem to want to fly straight and the rate of roll is poor, as though the aircraft is semi-stalled all the time. If you bank it one way, it swings off the other, and in rough air it seems to respond more to the bumps than to the controls.

However, once the necessary stick and rudder co-ordination is established, the handling will be reasonable and quite adequate for flying in very turbulent conditions.

The relatively large wing spans and slow flying speeds of gliders make the adverse yaw the predominant feature of handling and it is a waste of time attempting to teach straight flight as is so often done in a powered machine. Instead, pilots should concentrate on turning at various angles of bank and changing the direction of the turn in order to establish the co-ordination of the aileron and rudder.

Straight flight is not possible without this automatic movement of the rudder. This is because any correction for a wing dropping as a result of a gust or bump will produce a yawing movement unless both the stick and rudder are used together. Even experienced power pilots will find that this takes quite a lot of practice, because the rudder is employed in a different manner in a powered machine; i.e. in a powered aircraft it is used as a correction for any yaw caused by a change in power setting, and a few seconds' delay is of little importance. But in a glider it has to be used automatically during the entry and exit from a turn and at any time the glider is being rolled into or out of a banked position.

Very little rudder is needed during a turn (in any type of aircraft or glider) and this makes it necessary to reduce the amount of rudder once the turn is established.

Incidentally, it is necessary to leave a small amount of rudder on, but to 'hold off' the bank slightly during turns, and a slightly 'crossed' control position is normal. This is because of the large span and low flying speed which causes the tendency to over bank in turns.

Circuit planning and judgements

It is in the circuit planning that there are really significant differences between power and glider flying. The glider cannot be driven round the circuit with the

195

expectation of losing a standard amount of height flying from A to B. Sometimes it will fly through rising air and lose little or no height on the downwind leg, and on other occasions it will meet sink and lose a phenomenal amount of height. The pilot may have to change his plan and perhaps even turn in to make a landing on an alternative landing area. Failure to do this may result in a dangerously low final turn or even in colliding with the ground during that turn. This makes a rigid circuit pattern unsatisfactory. To be safe, the glider pilot must learn to spot what is happening in terms of abnormal lift and sink, and must vary his circuit accordingly.

Both angular and height judgements need to be cultivated rather than relying on the instruments. Away from the airfield, the heights indicated by the altimeter will be far from accurate because of the variations in ground level, and this could cause serious problems for the pilot who is depending on it for landing. With little or no vibration the altimeter inevitably sticks and exaggerates the height during a descent. This can influence the instrument-conscious pilot into believing he has more height than he really has.

With no option to go around again, the pilot must also learn to fit in with the other power and glider traffic without putting himself into a dangerous position. Thus a different kind of judgement and decision-making ability has to be developed to fly a glider safely.

All of these reasons make it desirable to teach planning and judgements in a slightly different way from the conventional method of instructing power pilots. Instead of practising perfect or near perfect circuits, glider pilots are taught circuits which require decision making and judgements. For example, it is not unusual to put the student in a position where a normal circuit is difficult or even impossible, to see if he recognises the situation and takes a decisive action either to remedy it or to choose a totally different landing area if that is necessary.

There are no 'good marks' for a nice square circuit; pilots are encouraged to cut the corner and have a continuous 180° turn if that solves the problem of too little height. Obviously, whenever possible, it is desirable to keep a margin of height in hand during the circuit to guard against the possibility of an unexpected loss due to turbulence or sinking air. It is easy to get rid of height by opening the powerful airbrakes. In fact, on the approach they can be used in a similar way to a limited amount of throttle. An impending undershoot can be prevented by closing the airbrakes and getting back the normal gliding angle which in a modern machine is incredibly flat. In practice, it only takes a few approaches and landings to become accustomed to the idea of not having an engine up front.

Glider pilots are always amazed that so many power pilots are literally scared to go in a glider. In reality the risks of an accident are far smaller than in a light aircraft, because there is no engine to fail, the landing speeds are much slower and there is no potential fire hazard. Often their reluctance even to try flying a glider stems from a fear of making a wrong judgement or making a fool of themselves. They need not be so concerned: instructors all know that very few pilots can step into a new kind of aircraft and fly it really well on their first attempt. Everyone has a natural reluctance to become a beginner again, with something new to master. As a result, they miss much of the fun in flying, which is trying out new types of aircraft and adapting one's skills.

But learning to fly the glider is only a small part of becoming a competent soaring pilot. It opens the way to soaring cross-country and exploring all the interesting phenomena involved in keeping the glider from a premature landing.

What gliding offers the power pilot

Although gliding is so weather-dependent, you are unlikely to receive any formal instruction about meteorology. However, you will be surprised by how much more you will know about the subject after a year or so of flying gliders. It is no exaggeration to say that your whole attitude to weather will change. No longer will you walk down the street looking in shop windows. Your attention will largely be on the sky, particularly on a fine sunny day, and it will soon become very trying to have to work on an excellent soaring day.

You will become far more observant in the air. Every little bit of smoke will mean an update on the wind direction and you will begin to notice the subtler changes in the sky, such as a thin veil of upper cloud moving in to obscure the sun.

Driving in the country or travelling by train, you will find yourself looking at the state of the fields and crops, and looking for electric fences and other hazards to landing an aircraft.

But the real attractions of it all are the fascinating flying, the subtleties in interpreting the conditions, and making the most of them. No two days are ever the same and, at first, flying is a constant struggle just to stay airborne. Later, when you are better acquainted with gliding, it is a matter of using only the strongest lift and of making progress cross-country. With no radio aids, you have the additional challenge of map reading and navigating. On a good day in a modern machine, it is quite normal to make flights of 3-400 km at average speeds of 60 m.p.h., and only using a launch to 1500 feet or so to get you started. In some conditions the experts can travel faster than many light aircraft, but that depends on your skill, and it takes most people years to develop their flying to that level. Gliding is a game of observation and deduction as well as a way of satisfying that yearning to be in the air.

Landing out has almost become almost a thing of the past in a modern machine once you have reached a certain level of experience. Many pilots fly thousands of miles cross-country and virtually never land away from their home base, except in competition flying and record attempts.

Motor gliders

Quite naturally most power pilots would like the best of both worlds, which at first sight appears to be a motor glider. However, it must be realised that these aircraft are very expensive, when compared with normal light aircraft, and that some require a considerable knowledge and experience of gliding to operate safely. Looking ahead only a matter of a few years, it seems likely that every new glider will be fitted with an engine to avoid the nuisance of landing out.

There are two main classes of motorised gliders:

1 High performance gliders fitted with an engine which retracts into the fuselage just behind the wing. These include the PIK20e, PIK30, DG400, DG500M, Janus CM, Nimbus 3DM, ASH25M, ASW22M and Discus CM. They are all standard production gliders modified to use a two stroke engine. These are Self-Launching Motor Gliders and pilots of all of them need a Self-Launching Motor Glider Private Pilot's Licence (SLMGPPL) to fly them as Pl in the UK or an FAA Private (Glider) Rating in the USA.

There are also Self-Sustaining Gliders which look identical, but which require a normal winch or aerotow launch to get airborne. These use their small engine mainly as a means of avoiding a field landing and to fly home if the weather deteriorates. Known as Turbos, they include the Ventus CT, Discus T and Nimbus 3T. Because they cannot take-off unaided, they are treated as normal gliders and pilots do not require a licence in the UK.

Both these types of gliders are scarcely affected by the engine installation and have almost the same performance as the normal glider versions. The additional weight of the engine and fuel is very small and has little affect on the performance. It just reduces the amount of water ballast that they can fly with on a good day.

DG400, a self-launching motor glider

DG500M climbing under power

DG500M engine installation

a

b

c

*Ventus 'get you home' turbo. The
sequence shows the retraction of the
engine*

d

2 The other class of motor glider usually have the engine in the nose and are nearer to a high efficiency light aircraft with a soaring capability. They include the Scheibe Falke series, Grob 109, Dimona, Valentine Stemme S10 and HB23.

Most of them are powered by VW or similar 4-stroke engines and have variable pitch and feathering propellors. Being a compromise, they tend to have a reasonable power performance, with cruising speeds of up to 100 knots at just over 3 gallons per hour, but not a very good soaring performance when compared with the average 'pure' glider.

Although their glide ratio is perhaps 25-30:1, the gliding speeds are higher than most gliders so that their circling radius is rather too large for using small thermals.

They are all suitable for instruction, although not many gliding clubs use them for regular basic training. The older Scheibe Falke series are still favoured by the gliding movement for training, because they have a lower stalling speed and are more comparable with normal gliders.

Ideally, every power pilot coming into gliding should have at least an hour of handling and circuit planning flights in a motor glider to become thoroughly acqainted with glider flying. It would save them time and money and would speed up their conversion to gliders.

Whereas it is a relatively quick conversion for a power pilot to move onto a conventional SLMG, such as the Grob 109, the high performance tuck away engine machines need considerable glider experience to fly safely. In addition to being competent to fly the equivalent glider version, the pilot must be prepared to handle a forced landing with the engine extended should it fail to restart.

Many gliding clubs restrict the use of motor gliders to gliding instruction and

Grob 109B motor glider

HK36 Dimona, a two-seater motor glider

AMF Chevron ultra-light, a microlight aircraft with soaring capabilities

for private ownership to pilots who have a considerable amount of gliding experience. This ensures that the pilots understand the normal glider traffic and have the basic knowledge to operate these machines safely. For example, at the Lasham Gliding Centre all motor glider pilots must have a Silver C gliding badge as well as a Motor Glider Licence.

Incidentally, in the UK even if your PPL has an endorsement for Group A and SLMG, you are not covered legally to fly an SLMG without a Certificate of Test in your log book. This is a matter of having a conversion and a General Flying Test on a motor glider.

Index

Other books by Derek Piggott

BEGINNING GLIDING
This is a useful book written for beginners, power pilots and instructors. It covers many of the problem areas which can prove difficult, such as the landing, making judgements and circuit planning. Although simple, the explanations are detailed and will solve many of the beginner's problems. It will also be especially useful for the less experienced gliding instructor in furthering his understanding and in helping with his explanations to students.

DEREK PIGGOTT ON GLIDING
This is based on the most useful magazine articles that Derek has written over the past 30 years. It includes the popular series 'Which Glider', giving advice for the first time buyer, as well as the 'Back to Basics' articles for beginners and instructors.

GLIDING (6th Edition): A handbook on Soaring Flight
The complete re-write of his original book *GLIDING*, which was first published in 1958, is recognised all over the world as the foremost reference book on gliding.
It covers a wide spectrum of topics, ranging from learning to glide to helping the cross-country pilot. It includes Derek's latest ideas on instruction for beginners and, for the more experienced pilot, it offers help with hill and wave soaring, thermalling techniques, field landings, instruments and advanced cross-country techniques. It is also particularly useful for power pilots converting to gliders and wanting to progress rapidly to soaring.

GOING SOLO
Going Solo is a helpful book covering all the aspects of glider flying that a pilot needs to know to reach solo standard. It is laid out as a syllabus, with the lessons placed in a logical order. This is an essential book for all beginners and is often used as a course book. More detailed explanations can be looked up in *Beginning* and *Understanding Gliding*. It will go in any jacket pocket and can be used for last-minute briefings or for reference out on the flying field.

UNDERSTANDING FLYING WEATHER
This is an introduction to flying weather and was intended for pilots preparing for their Bronze C meteorology test. It includes over 70 questions and answers of the type used for the Bronze C test paper. It is particularly orientated towards soaring conditions and includes hints and tips on using them in both gliders and light aircraft.

UNDERSTANDING GLIDING
This book is a continuation of *Beginning Gliding*. Like its counterpart, it is written in Derek's characteristic clear and simple style. It is easy to understand, yet embraces topics of immense complexity. Some of the areas covered are spinning, stability and control, aerobatics and converting from glider flying to powered aircraft. It aims to improve a pilot's understanding of the handling of a glider and so make for safer flying.